TRANSFORMING AMERICA THROUGH PROVERBIAL COACHING

*"How actualizing the knowledge of Proverbs will
overcome personal dysfunction,
correct societal wrongdoing,
and bring excellence to the American experience."*

HOWARD A. TRYON JR.

Volume II

"Actualizing Biblical Wisdom"

(Draft)

Unless otherwise indicated, Scripture quotations are from the New American Standard Bible, © the Lockman Foundation 1960, 1962, 1963, 1968, 1971, 1972, 1973, 1975, 1977.

Cover design: Jason May
Book design: Create Space

Library of Congress Cataloging-in-Publication Data

Tryon, Howard A.
    Transforming America through proverbial coaching.

ISBN-13 978-1537379173

Printed in the United States of America

Contents

Transforming America through Proverbial Coaching

Volume II: Actualizing Biblical Wisdom

Preface

Throughout this twelve volume series titled: Transforming America through Proverbial Wisdom the author seeks Biblical accuracy, historical authenticity, relevant communication and practical application. Concerning the style of writing I chose to embed the documentation within the manuscript and not foot note or end note the sources. In this manner the reader will view the documentation immediately within the context of the argument thereby encountering the evidence at the moment of its appearance. Also, in accord with Solomon's writing of Ecclesiastes, I inserted extensive, everyday experiences from my own life, family and ministry. Please don't get hung up on the personableness and number of these stories for they are written to be enjoyed and establish a human connection with you the reader. So too, following Solomon's genre of Proverbs I sought out customary events and familiar situations in this case from our national experience, providing an American historical template to enhance and engage personal, social, ecclesiastical, political, and community dialogue on the many difficult and unresolved issues we face as a nation.

Based upon this personable and relevant style of writing this author challenges you the reader to add your personal and familial illustrative insights and anecdotes, historical documentation and events, reflections even revisions, resulting from your own pilgrimage, profession and plight to add greater understanding and impact to this enterprise. In so doing this author aims to launch a living commentary on Proverbs, adding multiple stories from the varied and diverse experiences of our American citizenry to illumine the practical principles and practices of the Lord's wisdom.

Moving beyond style to significance it is important to note that "Transforming America Through Proverbial Coaching" seeks not to be defined within the existing boxes of American conservative, liberal, or moderate ideology and implementation. If one looks to justify or substantiate these existing intellectual, social, ecclesiastical, and political templates by means of this endeavor one will encounter not only dissatisfaction but miss essential insight into how God's wise and benevolent will for mankind may be actualized. Instead this work introduces the paradigm of Christian Actualism. Christian Actualism (CA) is defined in Volume I of the series. It is the hope of this author that Christian Actualism (CA) sets forth a sound Biblical hermeneutic to understand the meaning and application of Scripture while engaging a most Christ honoring movement to bring goodness for man and glory to God.

CA's initial work focuses on the Old Testament book of Proverbs. In this enterprise the author aims to define and apply the wisdom (hokmah) and moral teachings (musar) of Proverbs to actualize personal, family, and societal improvement. As the twelve volumes are released to the public the principles and practices of Proverbial wisdom and goodness will be directed to specific American issues, dysfunctions and evils. However, with that stated other cultures and country's can take Proverb's universal guidance, do the rigor of their own nation's history, and then implement the precepts to advance the living condition of their particular people. In this manner the work extends beyond national to global.

Upon perusal of the book's cover one encounters the word draft. Why draft status for this manuscript? Two reasons: one because of the flawed writing style of the author.

While I find satisfaction in the verbal communication of each of the twelve conferences on "Transforming America through Proverbial Coaching" this author remains unsatisfied with the written form of the messages. However, since there are no Actualists to edit the endeavor at the time of this original publication I felt it best to present the information without adjustments presented by conservative, liberal, or moderate thinkers who knowingly or unknowingly tend to bend the writing to more comfortably align with the past, status quo or progressive thought and action of their position. In this regard this author possesses no desire to tweak CA positions to align with the convictions, conscience or constituency of those paradigms of American thought and practice. This determination stems from the desire of this author to present an alternative to present paradigms of Christian Theology and practice.

However, please realize this does not mean the work should remain unedited. Certainly the manuscript contains flaws. It needs to be tightened up. However, after twelve years of work and turning sixty-four next month it was time to bring this endeavor before the American people even in its lesser state. Therefore in this volume the reader possesses a pure but flawed document for analysis and refinement. In this project your feedback is desired to improve the accuracy and impact of the manuscript. Each reader, each institution, each community, each country can tell its own story of how it followed the wisdom of the Lord and benefited from its template, but also how it violated the wisdom and moral teachings of God and suffered the negative consequences. For the furtherance of Christ's kingdom let us now proceed.

Acknowledgements

Over the last twelve years of developing this twelve volume series titled: "Transforming America through Proverbial Coaching" I have been blessed with the interaction of six consultants in this project. They have provided much mental, cultural, and spiritual exchange on the material. These men are:

Mr. Burt Ellison, BA in Governmental Studies, University of Texas at Austin; former Director of State wide Re-integration Program for Ex-offenders
Dr. Earl Field, Doctorate of Educational Philosophy, Grace Graduate School
Dr. Ray Husband, Ph.D., Psychology, University of Michigan
Dr. Willie Peterson, D. Min., Western Seminary
Dr. Terrance Woodson, D. Min., Dallas Theological Seminary
Dr. Dave Wyrtzen, Ph.D., Old Testament Theology, Dallas Theological Seminary

Many others have invested time, effort, and money to help me accomplish this work. Special thanks go to Jason May who developed the Art Work and always provided the encouragement of a friend and fellow minister of the gospel. Mary Wyrtzen made multiple recordings of the initial live trainings on CD and DVD's. Sam Wells edited the now retired DVD series titled "Proverbs Now," and Krystal Williams, transcribed the original recordings into the first written manuscript. Also, thanks to David Neal who functioned as the NFL historian in this project.

Key financial investors in this work included: Dan and Jeannie Baucum, Dan and Dawn Boss, Jim and Cathey Bradley, Scott and Amy Gillesby, Dick and Marty Griffin, Scott and Susie Griffin, Tim and Julie Griffin, Bob and Judy Husband, Ray and Carol Husband, Cindy and Sid Leedham, Kim Lewis, Kevin and Paula Martin, Phil and Marlene Mead, Eric and Rachel Mitchell, Brian and Taryn Mitchell, Craig and Kathy Nash, Tobi Neal, Wayne and Brenda Pirmann, Curtis and Carol Pope, Bill and Nancy Prikryl, Ken and Sara Pritchett, Doug and Donna Queland, Richard and Tammy Reno, Keenan and Lauren Robinson, Bob and Julie Scandalaris, Frank and Cathy Tanana, Jeff and Sheila Saunders, Mike and Laura Thomas, Gatlan and Denise Turk, John and Claire Tryon, Pamela Clark Tryon, Steve and Julie Vanker, Rick and Sara Warren, Randy and Anita Welty, Dave and Nancy White, the White Foundation, Richard and Barbara Widstrom, Paul and Michele Zipp, and others...

Also thanks to Midlothian Bible Church and the Lighthouse Church who provided much communicative practice in developing the instruction. At MBC the initial training on Proverbs began in 2004 with the teaching of 10 men on Thursday mornings, Church seminars and preaching at the fellowship followed through the years. From 2010-2014 Lighthouse Church provided avenues for multiple seminars, preaching, and other communication of proverbial principles for the benefit of their members. So many other Churches brought me in during the developmental period of this work to preach and minister from the study such as: Bethel Bible, Bibleway, Cornerstone Baptist, Harmony, Mt. Olive, New Life Community, Northwest, Spring Arbor Free Methodist, Waxahachie Bible. A special thanks goes to Woodside Bible Church in Troy Michigan, with pastor

Doug Schmidt. Woodside filmed the conference which coincides with this book on April 4-5th, 2016. One can view the video training at Proverbial Coaching.org.

Trust me when I say that only a few people hung with me through the twelve years of this work and never gave up on the project. In this regard I want to particularly thank my brother John and sisters Cindy and Pam. Your love and confidence never wavered. For those who went down the road and drifted off your investment of time, thought, prayer and financial support were used by the Lord to get this work to where it is today. I cannot thank you all enough. I wouldn't have gotten to this level of development without your participation. Today, as the endeavor progresses throughout the American community virtually all of the people of the past have once again joined with me in this work. Praise God for this encouragement.

The entire twelve volume series titled:
Transforming America through Proverbial Coaching
stands as follows:

Volume I: The Paradigm of Christian Actualism
Volume II: Actualizing Biblical Wisdom
Volume III: Moral Coaching and Race Relations
Volume IV: Understanding Scripture Proverbs Style
Volume V: Producing a Good Land
Volume VI: Actualizing America's Greatest Difference Maker
Volume VII: Excelling American Education
Volume VIII: Stopping the Slaughter of the Innocent
Volume IX: The Biblical Fool and Error in the Court
Volume X: Enjoying Sexual Freedom
Volume XI: Proverbial Coaching and Disciple Making
Volume XII: Engaging a Spiritual Movement

Whatever God does with this series I want to thank my Lord and Savior Jesus Christ for coming into my life on March 14, 1970, when as a seventeen year old senior in High School I got down on my knees and trusted my life and eternal destiny to Him. As it was then and remains true today my life's passion is to know and serve Him. May the Savior receive the praise to the glory of His saving grace and matchless wisdom.

This work is dedicated to my loving wife Betty
without whom this series never would have been completed.

May our children: Stephen, Philip and Lauren
discover much blessing, love, and guidance in their dad's work.

Volume II:
Actualizing Biblical Wisdom

Chapter 1: Proverbs, the Biblical Book for Today

Volume two of "Transforming America through Proverbial Coaching" seeks to establish that the wisdom of Proverbs provides humanity with practical and proven principles to actualize personal and societal betterment in the here and now. In this writing one will discover Scriptural wisdom is not legalism, it is not law; instead, it is fully applicable in the age of grace, capable of emancipating, empowering, and excelling human living. Its truths and goodness offer man liberation that if actualized will dramatically improve the human condition for individuals, families, communities, even countries.

Furthermore, proverbial knowledge is not restricted by conservatism; it does not need to be expanded by liberalism; it is not neutered by moderation. As a result, the book is capable of uniting Bible honoring people whether African American, Arab, Asian, Caucasian, Hebrew, Hispanic, Native American, not only to walk hand in hand as brothers, but shoulder to shoulder as neighbors to overcome the challenges we face today as a nation.

Let us begin this quest by asking and answering the question:
What makes a great golfer?

What distinguishes the greats of the game of golf from the rest of us common folk? What sets apart Hall of Fame golfers such as: Walter Hagan, Bobby Jones, Gene Sarazen, Ben Hogan, Sam Snead, Arnold Palmer, Gary Player, Jack Nicklaus, Lee Trevino, Tom Watson, Phil Mickelson, Tiger Woods; and the latest golfing phenoms such as: Rory McIlroy, Jordan Spieth, Jason Day, and Dustin Johnson from weekend warriors such as you or me? What makes the legends of the links whether: Betsy King, Babe Saharias, Kathy Whitworth, Nancy Lopez, Annika Sorenstam, Lorena Ochoa, Inbee Parks so magnificent? What makes the greats of the game of golf so great?

First, great golfers know their set of clubs.

Professional golfers know that their clubs are crafted at the highest level of human perfection. Manufactured by Ping, Calloway, Hogan, Nike, Taylor Made, and Titleist the clubs of the professionals are constructed with precision. They are made from the most expensive materials combined with proven technology for the highest level of golfing performance. Furthermore each club in a professional bag is personally formed to that golfer's particular size, strength, weight, posture, and swing plain. In the creation of a pro's set of clubs the manufacturers invest millions upon millions of dollars in research and thousands upon thousands of production hours to provide the game's elite with the finest set of hand-made clubs specifically designed for maximum effect. As a result, when the greats of the game step onto that first tee, they enter tournament competition with full confidence in their equipment. They know they possess the finest set of clubs man can produce and money can buy.

Now, each professional bag contains fourteen clubs. If a pro enters tournament play with fifteen or more they incur a penalty and possible disqualification. If they go with less they are at a disadvantage, for each of their clubs is tailor made for a specific shot during their course of play, and the tougher the course the more a competitive golfer will need each and every club in their bag.

For instance, in a round of eighteen holes a golfer will need the driver. When a golfer stands on the tee of a long par four or par five with a wide open fairway it is time to select from their fourteen clubs the driver. The driver is crafted for the long shot off the tee. When a pro golfer finds oneself two hundred forty yards or less from the green, it is time to pull out one of the irons from their bag to hit the shot. Finally when they reach the green it is time to choose the putter and sink the ball into the hole. This is what the putter is designed to do it is the golfer's tool to put the ball into the cup.

While it is the responsibility of the manufacturer to equip the golfer with the finest set of fourteen clubs, the responsibility of the player is to select the right club for each and every shot in their round. As a result, a golfer must analyze the present shot facing him/her on any particular hole. They must accurately judge the wind, the terrain, the distance, the adrenaline flow, the type of roll or wetness of the ground. Each and every component must be figured in before they select their club. In this respect championship golf involves the cerebral before the physical. Pros must accurately discern the appropriate club for each shot in their course of play. Then they pull out of their bag the proper club for that particular shot.

What makes a great golfer? The greats of the game whether Jones, Hogan, Saharias, Palmer, Whitworth, Player, Nicklaus, Sorenstam, Tiger know the precise purpose of each and every club in their bag. They know precisely why each club was been crafted. As a result, from their expertise and experience at the necessary moment they reach into their bag and select the proper club for every shot they face in a round of golf. Yes, the greats know their set of clubs.

Second, great golfers know how to swing each club with precision and power.

The legends of the game not only know the proper club to pull out of their bag for every shot they encounter in their round, but they also know how to swing that particular club precisely as it was manufactured to be swung. It is possible to possess the finest set of clubs money can buy with each club perfectly crafted to one's particular set of specs. However, the possessor of such clubs does not determine greatness. You see there is a world of difference between the greats of the game and the customary golfing hack in the way the clubs are swung. To envision this reality imagine the difference of swings between the Big Easy - Ernie Els - compared to Mr. Hitch - Charles Barkley (Suggestion: view their swings on youtube).

The premier golfers like four time major winner Els master each and every one of the 14 clubs in their bag precisely as the club was crafted to be swung. As a result, the professionals know how to swing each and every club in order to hit the ball with the exact amount of spin, elevation, distance and direction. This unveils the finer nuance of the game for under scrutiny the swings of the greats are not repetitive, mindless motor memory. Why? Pros execute minor adjustments made in their swings to move the ball according to the wind, distance, curvature of land, obstacles that face them at any given moment of play. It is this refined performance skill to hit each and every club with accuracy and power that distinguishes the best players from the rest of us common folk. For instance,

The greatest golfers know how to hit the driver.

Picture Jack Nicklaus in his prime hitting the driver. I remember my dad taking me to Oakland Hills Country Club in Birmingham, Michigan to watch the Carling World Open in 1964. As a youngster I made it down to the practice range and observed some of the golfing legends warming up, honing their swings before their scheduled tee off time. I watched professional greats such as Julius Boros, Billy Casper, Ben Hogan, Arnold Palmer, Gary Player, Chi Chi Rodrigues, and Sam Snead prepare for their round.

Now, in 1964 the practice range at Oakland Hills measured only two hundred eighty yards long with a twenty foot fence separating the end of the range from a subdivision of homes. Why was the range less than 300 yards in length? Realize that back in the sixties armed with the equipment of that era an average pro hit his drive about two hundred forty yards. The range successfully contained the drives of the pros in the tournament, but then Jack Nicklaus entered the range to practice before his round. All of us heard of this young upstart from Ohio and his reputation for booming monstrously high and long drives. We watched with anticipation as he loosened up with the lofted clubs and longer irons, but then as we all so longed to see he pulled out his driver. First shot, WHACK, we hear the crack of the wood (yes, drivers were made out of wood at that time), and he flies the ball over the fencing, hitting the top of the roof on a house on the other side of the barrier. Wow! Drive after drive Nicklaus kept launching the golf ball over that barrier punishing that defenseless home. Yes, Jack could overpower courses with the driver. The greatest golfers know how to hit their driver.

The greatest golfers know how to hit the Irons.

3

While the driver demonstrates power, the greats of the game also must master the irons in a golfer's bag. The irons require the precision of a ball striker. Greg Norman, known as the Great White Shark, stood number one on the pro tour for over three years. He once explained he could adjust his swing in hitting a two hundred yard iron shot to land the ball two feet further or two feet shorter. Talk about precision.

Six-time major winner Lee Trevino epitomized precise iron play. Lee was one of the superlative iron players in golfing lore. Trevino was a masterful ball striker. He could fade his iron shots, draw them, hook them, slice them, hit them low, hit them straight. However, when it came to hitting the one iron Trevino mused,

> "If you are in a thunderstorm surrounded by lightning, just lift up a one iron high into the air, for even God can't hit a one iron!"

Now the Lord must have a sense of humor, because after Lee's jest, He proceeded to hit him twice with lightning on a golf course.

Yes, to excel in the game a golfer must learn not only to master the driver but also how to become precise in the iron play as well. Historically, before the advent of the hybrids it was the mastery of the long irons that separated the greatest of the pros from one another. In this regard, picture Nicklaus, once again, but this time taking out his one iron, on the par three 200 yard 17th hole of Pebble Beach during the last round of the 1974 U. S. Open. Facing a strong wind in his face Jack needed a precise shot to secure victory. With other golfers using a wood off the tee Nicklaus selected his one iron. In his back swing he instantly realized he took the club slightly to the inside. Using his ability to immediately correct the misalignment he adjusted his powerful swing and struck that ball with precise accuracy, launching it high into the air, cutting through the wind two hundred plus yards and landing it two feet in front of the pin. The ball took one bounce, hit the bottom of the flagstick and stopped six inches from the cup. Even today, hall of fame golfers such as Tom Watson and Johnny Miller still consider that one iron shot by Nicklaus performed at the crucial moment of the U. S. Open as the greatest shot in the history of the game. Yes, the greats of the game hit their irons with precision. Forbid the hybrids on the PGA tour and the greats among the greats rise to the forefront. The greatest hit the one iron.

The greatest golfers know how to sink their putts.

Once the ball is on the green, it is time to select the putter. The art of mastering the putter involves reading the undulations and grain of the green in order to discern the correct length and break of the putt. The golfer must properly line up the putter, take one's stance, engage a few practice strokes, and then with steady nerves and unflinching technique, strike the ball with perfect line and speed. When a person pictures putting one can visualize the romantic vision of a youthful Arnold Palmer, knees locked, head over ball, and with a quick thrust of his wrist, striking the orb straight and true. With the minds eye one can see Arnie's contorted look of anguish if the ball lipped out of the cup or his exultant facial joy after sinking the winning putt of a major. Arnie won many a tournament with his putting.

The old adage is that one drives for show but putts for dough. Golfers know that the one who sinks the pressure putt receives the highest glory the game offers. Imagine the celebratory white man's six inch vertical jump of a Phil Mickelson when his twenty foot putt on the eighteenth hole of Augusta circled the cup before falling in for his first major. Picture Justin Leonard sinking a fifty footer to win the Ryder Cup for the United States and sealing the victory against the Brit's. Yes, the greats of golf know their equipment and how to swing each and every club precisely as it was crafted to be hit from the driver to the irons to the putter.

My half brother Bill, who recently passed away, won the New York State Amateur three times in 1962, 1965, and 1968. In the 1965 NY Amateur Bill faced a thirty-five foot put on the deciding hole to win the match play championship. As he stroked that putt and the ball began to roll his caddie began to yell: "It's in! It's in! It's in!" Please realize I wouldn't tell this story if the putt didn't drop. Way to go Bill! What makes a great golfer? First, a great golfer knows his/her set of clubs. Second, a great golfer knows how to swing each club with power and precision precisely as it was crafted to be swung.

Third, the greatest golfers excel during the most crucial moments of championship competition.

Those of us golfers from the baby boomer generation who played the game as juniors regularly practiced our putting by imagining putts under major championship pressure. We envisioned ourselves on the final hole of a golfing major having to sink a twelve foot putt to beat Gary Player, Arnold, or Jack to win the Masters, PGA, British, or U.S. Open. Of course if we missed the putt we would quickly reset the scenario and continue to do so until we sank the putt to win the tournament. However, creative our imaginations one does not get a second chance under real pressure of tournament golf. In the heat of competition a golfer has one shot at greatness. No mulligans. When the putt must be made the greats sink the putt. Lesser players miss.

One shot ahead of Jack Nicklaus, Doug Sanders faced a two and a half foot putt on the eighteenth hole to win the British Open. Golf glory lay just thirty inches away. As he stood over the putt he froze. An exorbitant length of time passed. He could not pull the trigger. Suddenly he mysteriously reached down and brushed away an imaginary object from his line. The British commentator on the airwaves remarked: "Oh dear." Then Sanders once again adjusted his stance and faced his two and a half foot putt to secure his place in golfing lore. Finally he pulled back the putter and pushed the ball to the right of the hole. As the ball left the putter's clubface Sanders agonizingly reached out with his club to redirect the wayward orb into the cup, but stopped himself before incurring a penalty. With victory in his grasp, with the pressure on he failed to execute the shot. The next day on that same final 18th hole he was tied with Jack. However, Nicklaus drove over the green, hitting his drive over 360 yards. He then chipped to eight feet of the pin and sank the birdie putt to win by one. He beat the striken Sanders. In 2005 Sanders said this about his miss:

> "'If I had made that putt, all the endorsements, the clothing lines, the golf-course designs,'" Sanders said, almost wistfully. 'It's like buying a lottery ticket worth $200 million and then dropping it in the can and watching the numbers wash away.' Sanders shrugged, "I'm delighted to have had the opportunity to get that close, but I felt like I cheated myself,' he said."

Missed Putt Changed His Life in 1970, Doug Sanders vists British Open again
http: // articles.philly.com/2005-07-13/spirts/25434051

Yes, the greatest of the golfing greats make their shots under the most intense, stressful, crucial moments of championship play. To better understand this let us compare the two finest golfers in the history of the game:

Jack Nicklaus and Tiger Woods

Is there an element of golf that distinguishes one from the other as the greatest player in the history of the game? Certainly it is not in the way they hit the driver for both Jack and Tiger overpowered golf courses in their prime with their tremendous length. Nor is there a difference in the way they hit their irons. Both were superlative ball strikers. Under the pressure of the moment they sank their putts.

I once asked Andy DiMatteo, an old friend, if there was a five foot putt and the entire survival of the universe depended upon successfully sinking that putt who would he select to make the putt? "Andy, would you choose Tiger or Jack?" He replied, "Personally, I'd pick Jesus, but if I couldn't get Him I'd choose Jack." Personally, I'd choose Tiger. Keep in mind Tiger never missed a putt three feet or less for over three straight years on the pro tour. That statistic is unhuman. It is unbelievable. However, with that said putting does not separate the two.

The same can be said about the intimidation factor. It was said of Nicklaus that when he first entered into the locker room before a major tournament the other professional golfers became instantly silent. They became aware that golfing greatness stood in their midst. The man who possessed the "steely blue eyes" was now in their presence. The game was on. Opponents of Nicklaus said:

"He knew he would beat you. You knew he would beat you. Worse still, He knew that you knew he would beat you."

Only few greats such as Palmer, Player, Trevino, and Watson could stand up to Jack during the final round of a major. In Tiger's prime what other golfer withstood his competitive fire? Once Tiger possessed the lead competitors melted away under his presence during the final round of major play. The intimidation factor fails to separate Woods and Nicklaus from one another.

So who is the greatest golfer in the history of the game - is it Jack or Tiger? Let's review: both punished the ball with the driver, both excelled in precise iron play, both could sink that pressure putt, and both could beat their competitors through intimidation and concentration during the most intense moments of championship play. So what separates Jack from Tiger and Tiger from Jack?

For Nicklaus the most obvious is that he owns eighteen majors to Tiger's fourteen. Add to that Jack's nineteen second place finishes in the majors and no one will ever surpass his dominance in championship play. He stands alone. Woods through coaching changes, personal issues, multiple injuries and operations will never surpass the Golden Bear's major victories. It lies beyond Tiger now.

However if we dismiss the player who has won the most majors, is there an element of the game that separates Tiger from Jack? I submit from 2000 to 2009 golf never saw a player like Woods. During those years what set Tiger apart from Jack as the greatest golfer in the history of the game? It was Tiger's mastery of the wedges.

What are the wedges?

In today's modern game of power golf most professionals carry four wedges in their bag of fourteen. Mickelson sometimes carries five. The four wedges include a chipping wedge, gap wedge, sand wedge, and lob wedge which can be 54, 60, even 64 degrees.

The wedges are purposely crafted by the manufacturer to be used in times of **recovery**; i.e., they are designed to be hit when a golfer finds his/her ball in thick, unyielding rough. When a golfer is knee deep in the thicket, and has to get out of that mess and back onto the fairway the wedge is selected. When one finds their ball sunk deep, embedded in a sand trap the golfer chooses the wedge to hit that ball out of that trouble and onto the green or back onto the fairway. Yes, the wedges in a golfer's bag are specifically made to be used to get a golfer out of difficulty and back onto the course. In times of such trouble one needs to select the wedge.

The wedges are also designed to be used in times of **refinement**. The wedges are made for when a golfer is within 140 yards of the green and must get the ball close to the pin. They are crafted for the most dangerous and most delicate of shots. In today's power game of golf with dense rough and deep bunkers it is essential for the modern pro to master the wedges to excel whether in times of recovery or refinement. The wedges are crafted for such shots. In times of exactness one needs the wedges.

Tiger was masterful in his use of the wedges. He knew exactly why the wedge was crafted. He hit the wedge with masterful precision. He exercised the club under the most crucial moments of championship play. In this, avid golf fans can picture Tiger with his golf ball resting forty feet away from the hole on the far back side of the fringe on the sixteenth green at Augusta in the 2005 Masters tournament. He pulled out his wedge and skillfully chipped his ball twenty feet to the far side of the green letting it take a ninety degree turn down an embankment toward the hole. The ball rolled and rolled stopping right on the lip of the cup. Everything for a moment stopped except the ball slightly teetering on the lip. Finally it gave way to gravity and fell in. Vern Lundquist, the magnificent sports announcer, exuberantly yelled over the airways, "In your life have you ever seen anything like that?!"

Great golfers in the modern era must master the wedge. Just ask one of the latest golfing phenoms – Jordan Spieth. In the 2016 Masters Tournament it was Jordan Spieth's failure to precisely execute the wedge shot on the 12th hole that cost him his second Masters jacket. Twice he put his wedge shot into the water, misfiring and leading to his defeat preventing him from back to back victories in the Masters.

It is in wedge play that sets Tiger apart from Jack as the greatest golfer in the history of the game. However, keep in mind in Nicklaus's era golfers possessed only two wedges: the chipping and sand wedge. Wouldn't it be fascinating to have Jack and Tiger go at it in their prime with both using the same equipment and playing the modern golf course? Add Bobby Jones to that pairing and I say let the games begin.

So what makes a great golfer?

Whether it be Jones, Jack, Tiger, Rory, Spieth, Day, or Dustin every professional golfer goes to the course with the finest set of clubs that man can make and money can buy. Each of the fourteen clubs - from the driver - to the irons - to the putter – to the wedges -- are exquisitely crafted to be hit for any shot occurring during a round of golf. The greatest golfers know the exact club to select for each particular shot and through perfected performance hit that chosen club with power and precision. The geniuses of the game do this time and time again especially during the most intense, crucial moments of competitive play. The pro's know that the tougher the course, the more intense the competition, the more essential it is to master every single one of those fourteen clubs in the bag. In so doing, they perfect the use of their clubs. This is what distinguishes the greats of the game from us common folk.

Now, let us apply what we have learned about the greats of golf and answer the question: what makes a man or woman of the Word of God?

First, a person of the Word knows his/her set of Books.

The Bible is not fashioned by Callaway, Hogan, Nike, Ping, Titleist, or Taylor Made, well maybe Tailor Made. The Scriptures are not manufactured by the mind and might of man. Instead the Bible is crafted by the very mind and might of God. The Bible discloses itself to be the **revelation** of the Creator God to man. Over 3,000 times in the Old Testament is the equivalent saying, "Thus saith the Lord." The Scriptures declare from Genesis to Revelation that they are God's unveiling of Himself and His will to man. As a result, the Bible asserts itself to be the revealed Word of God.

In its divine disclosure the Scriptures proclaim to be **inspired**; i.e., God-breathed, meaning what is true of the Almighty has been breathed by Him into the written Word. The Scriptures declare themselves to be **infallible**, meaning that whatever God's Word proclaims it will come to pass; i.e., the principles, practices, and prophecies of its writings will never fail; they will never be broken; properly interpreted and implemented they will not let you down. The Bible also defines itself as **inerrant** in the original manuscripts; i.e., the Word presents itself to be without error from cover to cover. The claim of Scripture's inerrancy is consistently affirmed by the teachings of Jesus, the writings from Moses to David to Jeremiah, the New Testament accounts authored by John to Paul to Peter, all affirm the Bible errorless. As a result, the Old and New Testaments uniformly declare its declarations to be trustworthy, authoritative for faith and practice. You can trust it for eternity and you can trust it in the present.

Like a pro golfer who knows his set of clubs a person of the Word knows what it is he/she holds in his/her hands – the revealed, inspired, infallible, inerrant, authoritative Word of the living God. Upon literary and historical analysis there is no other book in humanity's possession that can compare with it. The Bible stands alone. However, across America today too many of our citizens have lost sight of what a Divine wonder we have in our possession with the Scriptures.

Years ago I read a book by Brother Andrew titled: <u>God's Smuggler</u>. Brother Andrew would smuggle Bibles into communist countries. The penalty for such behavior was imprisonment and possible execution. Upon arriving at an entrée into the country Andrew, with his little Volkswagon filled with Bibles in the back seat, would pray, "Lord, once you made blind eyes see. Now, make seeing eyes blind." Time after time the guards would thoroughly check over his car looking for "illegal" hidden contraband, but they never recognized the hundreds of Bibles in clear unobstructed view lying open in the back seat.

On one such journey deep into a communist country, Andrew met a Russian pastor. When the Russian pastor saw his Dutch Bible he held it ever so carefully in his hands. He caressed the book ever so caringly as he ran his fingers down one side of the Bible and then down the other. The Russian pastor then said, "You know, Brother Andrew, I have no Bible."

Here was a minister of a Church who did not own a Bible. Why? The Scriptures were forbidden in that communist country and the actual practice of following Christ under the tenants of atheism and anti-theism was "religiously" cleansed. Please realize in the twentieth century over seventy-five million Christians were executed for practicing their faith in communist countries. Today, so many of us take the Bible for granted. We forget the Word of God was penned by the blood of the saints. It is God's Word crafted especially for you. This is what you hold in your hands. The very Word of God divinely revealed from the Creator to you and to me.

Consider the Books of the Bible

As fourteen clubs are designed for every shot and situation a golfer faces on a course; so God crafted sixty-six books and each writing contributes to the guidance the Lord gives to man to successfully walk the course of life. In this regard, 2 Timothy 3:16-17 addresses how the Bible puts on board what is necessary for a person to live well when it states:

> "All Scripture is inspired by God, and profitable for teaching for reproof, for training in righteousness, that the man of God may be adequate, equipped for every good work."

In these two verses the Apostle Paul tells us the Word is **inspired** (God breathed; i.e., what is true of the Lord He has breathed into the Scriptures), and **profitable** (beneficial) for **teaching** (lessons in living) **reproof** (correction, change), for **training** (coaching) in **righteousness** (the best life offers), in order that a person may be **adequate** (up for the task), **equipped** (fully furnished), for **every** (not some, but all), **good** (wholesome, positive) **work** (the will of God for your life). What a set of books!

So as a golfer needs each and every one of his fourteen clubs to successfully play a round of golf, so too a person needs each and every one of the Lord's sixty-six books to productively live out his/her pilgrimage of life. So also as a golfer must know why and for what a club was crafted for in order to select the proper club for the right shot, so too one must discover the precise reason, the what fore, the why for each and every Book of the Bible. Understand the purpose and one will know which book to select for each and every shot in the course of living.

For example take the Gospels. More specifically the Gospel of John. John's Gospel clearly identifies its purpose in chapter 20:30-31, where he writes,

"Many other signs therefore Jesus also performed in the presence of the disciples, which are not written in this book; but these have been written that you may believe that Jesus is the Christ, the Son of God; and that believing you may have life in His name."

When one understands the purpose of John's Gospel one realizes that every term, every verse, every passage, every illustration within its writing is penned to bring people to Christ. With this in mind one can readily grasp why this book includes the most widely known verse in all of Scripture – John 3:16:

"For God so loved the world that He gave His only begotten Son, that whosoever believes in Him shall not perish but have everlasting life."

In keeping with our golfing analogy consider the Gospel of John as God's Driver

As American golfers love to hit their driver, so too, evangelicals and their movements are passionate in their communication of God's driver of salvation. On any given Sunday people throughout our nation can enter into a Bible believing Church and hear preachers proclaim the Scriptural driver of salvation, heralding the good news of forgiveness in Christ, His death and resurrection, and calling people to trust in the Lord and receive eternal life. Recently I spoke at an African American church in North Dallas. The youth had just come back from summer camp. The camp's theme was: "Once I was lost, but now I'm found". What club did they select from their Biblical bag? Clearly the driver, the entire camp experience was geared for the young people to come to Christ, and during the service twenty teens shared how they had placed their faith in the Savior.

From the great evangelists such as George Whitfield, D.L. Moody, and Billy Graham American Christianity loves to swing the driver of salvation, and rightfully so for one does not want to miss out on eternity with God. If you know Jesus Christ as your personal Savior you can thank the Lord right now for the book of John. However, mastering only a single club in a golfers bag, such as the driver leaves a golfer at a disadvantage during his or her round.

There is an old story of a gorilla who sauntered up to a practice range, dressed in his golfing best, he pulled out a driver and began hitting 500 plus yard drives straight as an arrow time after time after time. He then arrived for his tee time foursome and was confronted with the first hole measuring 586 yards, par five. The gorilla with intense focus lined up his drive, adjusted his hat, set his stance, and with a massive swing powered that ball 585 yards, two feet, eleven inches with the ball stopping on just twelve inches from the rim of the cup on that 1st hole. Unbelievable! The foursome including players and caddies let out shouts of praise as they paraded down the fairway to the green. Finally, it was the gorilla's turn to tap in his putt. Curiously he once again pulled out the driver from his bag - walked up to the ball adjusted his hat, aligned his stance, and boomed another drive 585 yards back onto the first tee. Regardless of how exhilarating it is to hit the driver, mastering that club alone is insufficient to get oneself successfully around a golf course.

Following the same vein, mastering the message of salvation is inadequate to fully equip a believer to properly live out the Christian life. Once a person receives eternal life, they now need instruction in how to live. In this regard, the Bible includes books crafted to help one walk in a manner worthy of their Savior. In this respect, one needs the Epistles.

Consider the Epistles to be God's Irons

The Epistles, like the Gospels, are books in the New Testament. The Epistles are letters written by the apostles to newly planted Churches and young leaders of the expanding Christian movement. While the Gospels show one the way to life, the Epistles show a person the way to live. The Epistles give instruction in how to grow in one's personal relationship with God, how to walk as a new person in Christ, how to live in the power and presence of the Spirit, how to relate with others who know the Savior, and how to impact the world for the glory of God. Therefore, if one wants to become the man or woman God desires them to be, a person needs the Epistles because these books flesh out the principles and practices of how to live out their new life in Christ.

When Philip, our second son was born he came out a bluish color. His vital signs on the APGAR score out of a possible healthy ten scale measured a life threatening one or two. Our son entered the world with the umbilical cord wrapped around his neck. The doctor used forceps to get him out of the womb immediately. Once he popped out, Doctors and nurses filled the room in number and took our baby from us. In concentrated, coordinated effort they began administering emergency aid to our son. Thanks to the expert knowledge and skill of the medical personnel his life was sparred. Our son Philip had life but then, he needed to live. This is what the Epistles are crafted to accomplish. While the Gospels show us the way to eternal life, the Epistles teach us how to live out our new faith right now. This is the over-riding purpose of the Epistles whether Ephesians, Romans, 1 & 2 Corinthians, Galatians, Philippians, Titus, Hebrews, 1 and 2 Peter, James, 1 - 3 John, Philemon.

I thank God as a new believer I was privileged to be discipled by Dr. Ray Husband, the man who led me to Christ. Looking back upon Ray's insightful teaching, he focused heavily upon the driver John, and the irons of the Pauline Epistles, especially Romans and Galatians. He knew how to swing those Biblical clubs really well. As a result, I was grounded in the sacrificial love, forgiveness, and saving grace of God. He taught me to see myself as a new person in Christ. He embedded into my awareness that my sins were removed as far as east is from west. I was now justified, declared righteous before a holy God. Why? Not because of my goodness but because I had been given the gift of Christ's righteousness – I was clothed in His righteousness. I now was a new person, set free from the enslavement of sin to live as God created me. Free to live in the power of the Spirit. Free to live according to His Word. Ray equipped me in God's iron play of the Epistles. Thank you, Ray.

As believers, we need the transforming truths written in the Epistles. Take for example Paul's Epistle to the Ephesians. The book of Ephesians fleshes out the wonders of the grace of God in a believer's life. In the initial three chapters, Paul spells out one's wealth in Christ, explaining the wonders of grace that come with salvation. He writes of how God poured out spiritual blessings upon the believer in Christ as Ephesians 1:3 states:

> "Blessed be the God and Father of our Lord Jesus Christ, who has blessed us with every spiritual blessing in the heavenly places in Christ."

However, once Paul establishes a believer's position in Christ in chapters 1-3 of Ephesians he then moves in chapter's four to six, identifying a believers practice in Christ. He shifts from establishing one's wealth to declaring how a person is to walk. He moves from belief to behavior. This transition from who a person is to how a person should live begins in chapter 4:1:

> "I, therefore, the prisoner of the Lord, entreat you to walk in a manner worthy of the calling with which you have been called..."

While a Christian is to grasp and rest in the gracious, loving work of God on his/her behalf (Ephesians 1-3), they are called to live out their new life in Christ in a God honoring way (Ephesians 4-6). The outworking of one's faith is based upon what God has done for them first. In this manner, behavior is directly connected to the actions of God on behalf of the believing person.

Yes, people need to come to Christ for life and then grow in the Lord to live. Today we live in an age of stunted spiritual growth. In this Christians must master their iron play and learn to walk in a manner worthy of the God who has saved them.

In this regard I consider the Epistles to be the irons of the Bible. When one hits the driver of salvation and gets onto the course to live for the glory of God, it is essential to know how to hit those irons. However, there is more to God's Biblical bag of clubs than the driver and the irons. One needs to learn to putt.

Consider the book of Revelation as the Putter

When a golfer gets to the green it is time to select the putter. Golfers know that the one who sinks the pressure putt receives the highest glory the game offers. In this analogy consider the Book of Revelation as the putter in the Biblical bag. It describes the ultimate award for sinking the eternal championship putt. It is the disclosure of Scripture detailing the glory to come. Yes, the book of Revelation was written to show you, the way things were, the way things are, and the way things are going to be. Revelation declares the final destination of a believer with the celebration and glory to come – the culmination of the good news.

Many people fail to realize that twenty percent of Biblical information deals with things to come. In the canon eleven Old Testament books deal specifically with identifying what is coming next in the nation of Israel. Furthermore, the Old Testament prophets foretold of the coming of the Messiah hundreds of years before the literal fulfillment of its prophecies; so too, the New Testament Book of Revelation discloses events that will happen, culminating in the glorious return of Christ.

With respect to the promised Messiah, the entire counsel of Scripture can be broken into three great prophetic pronouncements:

1. Someone's coming
2. He came
3. He's coming again.

When I was a little boy, I had a custom in greeting my dad when he returned home in North Olmsted, Ohio from his business trips in Elmira New York, where he was President of Trayer Products or from Detroit in meeting with the car company executives. As dad drew close to home he would call mom and give her his estimated time of arrival. As the time drew near, I would place myself between the couch and the window in our family room. I would take with me some crackers, a drink, and some comic magazines. There I would stay awaiting his return. When I saw his car, I would immediately yell out "Dad's home! Dad's home!" I would run outside to meet him as he exited the vehicle. I followed this faithfully, however there was an exception. If for some reason I was in trouble with mom and awaiting the coming punishment from dad my enthusiasm for his homecoming significantly diminished. For a believer who understands the forgiveness of God the expectant return of Christ has us longing for His return.

One must keep in mind that Christianity is an historical religion. The Bible's propositions are grounded in actual human events. While other religious writings extol philosophical propositions lacking historical affirmation the Scriptures of the Old and New Testament center their message in verifiable human events. From Genesis to Revelation, from the prophets to the apostles the writings of Scripture posit themselves as the recordings of the Lord's actual intervention in human experience. The Word of God therefore provides man with recorded historical documentation of God's empirical actions with created people. As a result just as the literal fulfillment of Christ's first coming declared in over three hundred Messianic prophecies written hundreds even thousands of years before His entrance, actually came to pass in human history, so too in the same manner the prophecies concerning His second coming will come to completion also.

I remember talking to a young college atheist who asserted that he saw no difference between a crazed individual who proclaimed that he went to the Gulf of Mexico, stood on the shoreline, and parted the waters as compared to the Bible saying that Moses parted the Red sea. He asserted that believing either is equally absurd. He spoke that anyone can say they did the miraculous. He proclaimed that both stories are unbelievable and foolish. Anyone can make a miraculous declaration. I responded the difference is that over a million and a half Hebrew people saw the parting of the Red Sea and then walked across the dry land for themselves. Furthermore, the Egyptian army seeking to destroy the people of Israel then suffered annihilation by the waters when they remerged.

The miracle of the parting of the Red Sea is historical. The nation of Israel can only be explained by the miraculous. Such miracles of the Bible, whether the deliverance of Israel out of slavery in Egypt or the resurrection of Jesus from the tomb are empirical proofs actualized in time space history. God's revelation of Himself to man did not happen in a vacuum void of witnesses. They are a part of man's recorded history.

Furthermore, Scripture does not present itself as an academic exercise without consequence. For instance, Revelation discloses the tragic destination of people who refuse God's gift of salvation. For those who deny forgiveness in Christ the Scriptures declare eternal damnation. Talk about the seriousness of the charge. In this regard, consider another conversation with a young female college atheist who stated she simply did not believe in God or His eternal judgment and therefore was unconcerned about the Scriptures declaration of an after-life. I responded that if the Bible is true then whether she believes in the Lord and His judgment or not there will come a day when she will see God and absent of His forgiveness will face judgment.

Dear reader, if the Word of God is actually the revelation of the Almighty to man then there is coming a day when all of us will see Christ. At that moment there will be undeniable empirical evidence verifying the validity of the Savior. However, the consequences between believers and unbelievers will be dramatically and eternally different. For the Christian, at the moment of death he/she will enter into the fullness of their salvation as a completed child of God. In Romans 8:18-25, Scripture declares that even the angels long to look at what a redeemed person is going to be like when they appear in the fullness of their redeemed glorified, resurrected bodies.

In the same manner a golfer sinks the winning putt and glories in victory so too the resurrected saint will enter into the glories of an eternity with God. Revelation tells us that believers sink the winning putt. However, for the non-Christian there is coming an eternity of judgment. If you the reader do not know the Savior you have an eternity of reasons to fear your Creator God. Man must take His Maker seriously concerning free will.

What wondrous books the Lord has given to us in our Biblical bag, disclosing the way to life, the way to live, and the glory to come. The Bible declares the beginning, the parade, and the eternal destiny of man. As Christians, we need the whole counsel of the Word of God - from the driver of John's gospel to the irons of the Epistles to the putter of Revelation. For a person to grasp the fullness of the Bible and experience its full benefits in the course of life one needs each and every one of the sixty-six books. Just as a manufacturer crafts a set of clubs for a golfer to successfully maneuver oneself around the golf course; so too God gives to man the entirety of the Bible to provide the necessary guidance for humans to successfully navigate the course of life. Yes, the whole counsel of God is given to man and the tougher a person's life the more that individual will need the entire counsel of God.

However, besides the Gospels, Epistles, and the book of Revelation the Scriptures are made up of additional sets of books. For instance one discovers in the Bible the Pentateuch (Genesis, Exodus, Leviticus, Numbers, Deuteronomy); one finds the historical books (Joshua, Judges, 1 and 2 Samuel, 1 and 2 Kings, 1 and 2 Chronicles); one encounters the Prophetic books such as the major prophets: Isaiah, Ezekiel, Jeremiah, Lamentations; and the minor prophets such as Daniel, Jonah, and Habbakuk. All these books along with the poetry of Psalms make up the collection of writings placed within our Biblical bag. Yet, even with all these books the Biblical bag is not complete. Why? There remains another set of clubs that need to be mastered.

Consider the Wedges of the Bible

In the whole council of God Scripture also offers us another set of books among the sixty-six. These books were not written for salvation – such as the gospel of John. They were not directed toward sanctification – such as the Epistles. They were not written for glorification – such as Revelation. They are not written for history or poetical worship. Instead they are crafted to guide human living in the practical day by day expressions of mankind. They are revealed to guide the ways of humanity in the how to's of the now.

In this regard these Biblical books function like the wedges in a golfer's bag. Like the wedges they are crafted to be used when people find themselves in need of recovery; i.e., when they are knee deep in the rough or caught in the traps of life. These books are also crafted for refinement; i.e., they are written to show people how to exercise the finer aspects of life; i.e., when one must get the ball close to the hole in the here and now.

Now, the books of the Bible that function like the wedges in a golfer's bag are the wisdom books of Scripture. There are five wisdom books revealed in the Bible:

> Ecclesiastes
> Song of Solomon
> Job
> Proverbs
> James

Beyond the five wisdom books in the Word of God one also discovers wisdom writings contained within the sixty-six books such as "Psalm 90" and "The Sermon on the Mount." The wisdom books and writings are disclosed by God to provide you necessary knowledge to live life well, giving pertinent information to get you out of life's trouble and back onto the course of better living. The wisdom books disclose relevant data to guide you in the finer details of living better. It is in the wisdom writings that people encounter God given principles to lead them to healthier, more wholesome living in the present. It is in Scripture's wisdom books and writings that we discover God's vehicle not only for personal and family improvement but also for positive societal advancement. Biblical wisdom provides the necessary principles and practices to equip mankind to live out the faith person to person, neighbor to neighbor, community to community, country to country.

So when does a believer need to pull out the wedges during their course of life? What shots require the wisdom books? To grasp this one needs to understand how God's wedges of wisdom are crafted. To accomplish this let us now focus upon…

The Wisdom Book of Proverbs

What is the purpose for which the Lord put the wisdom book of Proverbs in His Biblical bag? In Proverbs, you don't have to read all the way to the end of the book like the Gospel of John to discover the precise purpose it plays among the sixty-six Biblical clubs; instead, God identifies His exact aim for the writing in the initial six verses.

In Proverbs 1:1-6 one discovers five Hebrew infinitives. Each of the five infinitives unlocks a specific purpose delineating why Proverbs is to be used in the course of human living. These purposeful infinitives, clearly identified in the New American Standard Bible (NASB), disclose the reason and intention of the Lord in including this book into the Scriptural canon. The infinitives specify what this book intends to do for you and for us.

Now an infinitive, for the non-grammar student out there is when you have a "to" connected in front of a it's word of meaning. Here is the Proverbial passage containing its five purpose statements:

> 1:1 "The proverbs of Solomon the son of David, king of Israel:
> 2 to know wisdom and instruction,
>   to discern the sayings of understanding,
> 3 to receive instruction in wise behavior, righteousness, justice, and equity,
> 4 to give prudence to the naïve, to the youth knowledge and discretion
> 5 a wise man will hear and increase in learning and a man of understanding will acquire wise counsel,
> 6 to understand a proverb and a figure, the words of the wise and their riddles."

TO KNOW (1:2a)
TO DISCERN (1:2b)
TO RECEIVE (1:3)
TO GIVE (1:4-5)
TO UNDERSTAND (1:6)

Even a cursory reading of these five purpose statements reveals that Proverbs was crafted to take people to a fuller, better place to be. It is in the principles and practices of these purposes that we discover God's relevant guidance for people to actualize positive change both personally and socially in the here and now. The first purpose of Proverbs "to know wisdom and instruction" aims to equip people in the essential knowledge of wisdom (hokmah- performance skill) and instruction (musar- moral coaching). The second purpose "to discern the sayings of understanding" seeks to impart to mankind the ability to gain the ah-hah of grasping what is true and the nuances of implementation. The third purpose "to receive instruction in wise behavior (haskel), righteousness (sedek), justice (mispat), and equity (mesharim)" seeks to coach up humanity in ethical living, knowing and embracing what leads to success (haskel), righteousness (sedek); i.e., the best life offers according to the judgment of God, justice (mispat) the correction of life when righteousness is broken, and (mesharim) that necessity of fairness.

Oh, if our nation applied the principles of God's moral coaching wisely, rightly, justly, and fairly to Native and African Americans at the onset of our Republic how different things would be today. Proverbs then is written to lead people to wellness of living in their temporal pilgrimage, providing practical application to improve the human condition at all stages and situations of existence.

Therefore, wherever you are as a person whether you are in your human pilgrimage whether you are ten, thirty, or ninety this book has something essential for you. At each step of your personal and professional development, wherever you are, in whatever you are going through, whatever your immediate concern Proverbs is designed to better your life. If nothing else the book is worthy of your perusal, but even more your most persistent study.

In addition to individuals the wisdom of Proverbs is discernable and reachable for us as a people. The principles in this book are applicable for the improvement of citizens, families, neighborhoods, schools, businesses, commerce, government, courts, communities, country, even the global network. As a result, Proverbs offers human transformation not only for individuals but also for our American life and liberty as well.

Why did the Lord include the book of Proverbs in your Biblical bag? The answer is discovered in these five purposes. Throughout the entire twelve volume series titled: Transforming America through Proverbial Coaching this author will analyze each of the purposes, but for now, let us peruse just one part of purpose four of Proverbs:

"To give... a man of understanding wise counsel."

The Hebrew term for wise counsel is Tahbulot. Tahbulot carries the idea of steering. The word was used to define how sailors expertly adjusted the ropes on their sails to successfully maneuver their vessel during their nautical journey. In this manner they were able to steer their ship out of the dock, or turn their vessel to face the waves of a storm, through their expert knowledge of steering they navigated their ship across the body of water to successfully arrive at their destination. In the same manner the book of Proverbs was written to provide people the ability to steer their lives, families, businesses, communities through life's hazards, challenges, and joys throughout their journey of living.

In our pilgrimage through life we all have need to learn to steer. To drive this home when I moved our family after seventeen years of ministering in the Phoenix area to a small country community called Midlothian, Texas, located forty miles south of Dallas. We drove into town about nine P.M. at night on the fourth of July, 2002. We so appreciated that this small city of less than 8,000 people celebrated our arrival by shooting off impressive fire work displays launched from the back yards of their properties. We were impressed.

Before leaving Phoenix I made a promise to my older son Stephen, then fifteen years of age, that I would sign him up for driver's education at the first possible opportunity. So the next morning we went down to enroll him in the course. His lessons began in a week.

When the moment arrived, the first day of class, I told him to get behind the wheel and he would drive both of us to the destination. It was my intent to take the easiest, safest route to his driver's class. Keep in mind, however, the roads of Midlothian were still a mystery to me. With my limited knowledge of the roads, Steve pulled out of the driveway and we began our excursion to his Drivers Education class. As envisioned I kept him on back roads absent of complicated turns and dangerous traffic. Everything went wonderfully well until we came to a T in the road that connected our little used country road of Ashford to FM 663 a major two lane highway with cars screaming by at 55 plus. I hadn't counted on the difficulty that now faced my son. Where Ashford dead ended there was no light, only a stop sign. The main thoroughfare of 663 into town had only two lanes. To our right there was a hill with cars coming and to our left was another hill with traffic flying by. We were in a small valley. Adding to this danger is that immediately to our right was a fifteen foot drop off protected by a guard rail to keep wayward cars from cascading down into this small ravine. Steve respectfully and appropriately inquired, "Dad what should I do?"

Well, I could have gotten behind the wheel to drive the rest of the way, but I wanted him to gain experience. I thought with some guidance he could successfully steer the car through this challenge and in so doing build his confidence. I responded, "Wait son, until I tell you to go." We sat at this intersection for about a minute while traffic kept coming from left and from right. Finally, when traffic cleared I said, "Go."

As soon as he started his right turn onto 663, at that very second a truck came over the hill from the right and a car appeared screaming over the hill from the left. Stephen, then under steered the vehicle partially entering the lane with the truck coming at us head on. Confronted with the incoming truck he immediately took evasive action and began to spin the steering wheel to get back into our lane. With this he made a second mistake and overcompensated his steering by sending the car toward the railing with the fifteen foot drop off. At that moment I thought, "It is time for some intervention." I reached over to help straighten out the wheel. My little finger hit into the steering wheel in the place where the horn was connected to the rim. The torque of Steve's turning split the bone in my hand and we could hear it pop. The bone snapped!

Well, I can't say we made it successfully to the driver's education location, but we did make it. After Steve went inside I got behind the wheel and drove directly to the emergency room at Baylor Medical Hospital in Waxahachie. After the x-rays were taken a physician appeared in the room, threw the pictures onto the light and pronounced, "Well you just "blanked up" your hand! You just "blanked it up!" Trust me, it didn't take sentence enhancers to realize from the x-rays that I had split the bone down the middle like a chicken wing – all the way from top to bottom.

As I was writing this story I called Stephen and reminding him of how he broke my hand. He responded, "Dad, you put your hand there. It was unnecessary. I had control of the car." Is this a matter of interpretation or what? Whether my son actually needed some help may be arguable, but the Lord's guidance to help man steer is not.

Far too many of us today are steering our lives into the ditch. We are steering into the oncoming traffic. Trying to make corrections we overcompensate into accidents leaving us scarred and causing injury to ourselves. Worse still, as we get older more and more people enter into our vehicle. We now have the responsibility of passengers such as spouses, sons, daughters, relatives, friends, work associates we transport from location to location. In our chosen profession we enter into business, politics, schools judicial benches with people riding in our vehicle of thought and action.

Think of this, just one part of one purpose of the book of Proverbs is guidance from your Heavenly Father to equip you to steer your life properly. How we need to learn to steer through life properly. Learning to steer is a purpose of Proverbs. The book is designed to tahbulot you; i.e., to teach you to steer your life successfully, whether around or through the challenges and hurdles you face in life. Like driving a car the book instructs you how to navigate successfully the driveways, the back roads, the dirt roads filled with holes, mud, and bumps, it seeks to teach you to travel on the main thoroughfares with abundant lighting and markings, to speed down the four lane interstates, it will instruct you in the congestions of city driving even the intricacies of parallel parking. The book of Proverbs is penned for you to become equipped in how to successfully steer your life, marriage, family, business, profession for your benefit and their well-being. Throughout its pages the book offers divine guidance to steer your life, friends, constituents, neighbors, schools, communities, even country to better living.

All this is disclosed in just one part of one purpose for why the Lord included this book in the Bible. How we need to know this Biblical club and when it is essential to select this book for the proper shots we face in life today.

Throughout this writing you will discover the purposes why God has blessed humanity with such wonderful wisdom. You will learn how Proverbs works and how it will work for you - for your benefit and for the sake of others. You will come to know what it is you hold in your hands and understand accurately the blessings of its insights for living. You will know the preciseness for which this book of the Bible was crafted by God and disclosed to you.

Yes, as the great golfers know their set of clubs and the purpose for each and every club in their bag, as they know how to select the right club to match the present shot they face on the course so too a man or woman of the Word knows how Scripture works and precisely why the Lord crafted each of his sixty-six books. The wisdom book of Proverbs is clear in its purpose for how you are to use its principles and practices in your course for living. This author asserts across America it is time to select the book of Proverbs out of our Biblical bag to address, overcome and defeat the dysfunction and evils we face today as individuals and as a people.

So what makes a man or woman of Scripture? A person of the Word knows his/her set of clubs.

Second, a person of the Word knows how to use each book with precision and power precisely as it was purposed to be understood and applied.

As those who flail their way around the golf course because they do not know how to swing their clubs properly; so too, mishandling the Word of God leads to distortion of Biblical meaning and the loss of human potential whether eternally or in the now. Therefore, as golf shots go awry due to faulty, undeveloped swings so human living becomes disjointed because of misinterpretations and misapplications of Scripture.

It is in the realm of figuring out the meaning and application of data that the second purpose of Proverbs focuses when it states that the book was written "to discern the sayings of understanding." In other words Proverbs was crafted to help people gain the ah-hah's of life; i.e., the moment of enlightenment when an individual grasps what is true over falsehood, what is wise over foolishness, what is good over wickedness, what is right over wrong, and the nuances which underlie and advance the principle or practice. Therefore Proverbs brings to the human enterprise training in recognizing, analyzing and carrying out veracity and benevolence whether in thought or action.

Now, let's apply "to discern the sayings of understanding" directly to Scripture. Please realize if the Bible is actually the revealed, inspired, infallible, inerrant, authoritative Word of God then mankind can discover no greater knowledge of meaning and action than those of Scripture. In this regard, Proverbs offers specific coaching in how to properly interpret and implement the Words sayings to reach their intended destination of human transformation. In so doing Solomon addresses the way a person must understand not only Proverbs but also the entirety of Scripture to obtain the true sense and consequence of the Lord's communication.

In fact, I submit there is not a finer more cogent unveiling in how to become a person of the Word than Proverbs 2:1-4. In this passage one discovers three conditions in becoming a man or woman of the Word. If these three conditions are satisfactorily met the benefits of the book will be actualized. Here are the conditions:

> 2:1 "My son, **if you will** receive My sayings, and treasure My commandments within you, 2 make your ear attentive to wisdom, incline your heart to understanding, 3 for **if you** cry out for discernment, lift your voice for understanding, 4 **if you** seek her as silver and search for her as for hidden treasures; 5 then you will…

> Please note that each condition requires your volition:

> > If you (2:1-2)
> > If you (2:3)
> > If you (2:4)

In each condition the responsibility is placed upon you as an individual. Therefore, the opportunity of actualizing the benefits of God's knowledge for practical living lies within your reach. Simply put no one can stop you from becoming a man or woman of the wisdom of God - not your family, not the government, not others – only you.

In Volume IV of Transforming America through Proverbial Coaching titled: Understanding Scripture Proverbs Style, this author presents eight lessons from Proverbs 2:1-4 to equip you to become a man or woman of the wisdom of God. For now, let us take one such personalized instruction from Proverbs 2:2b:

"Incline your heart to understanding…"

The Hebrew term "heart" (leb: lebe) in the Old Testament refers not to the physical organ but to the very core of one's character, decision making, and conduct. Biblically the heart defines who a person truly is. Scripture presents the heart as the determiner of how one thinks, feels, and behaves. As a result, the heart capsules the totality of who you really are as a person. This is why when God looks at you, He looks at your heart as 1 Samuel 16:7 insightfully uncovers:

> "But the Lord said to Samuel, 'Do not look at his appearance or at the height of his stature, because I have rejected him; for God sees not as man sees, for man looks at the outward appearance, but the Lord looks at the heart."

Now, Proverbs declares that to become a man or woman of the wisdom of God one must "incline their heart to understanding". The word "incline" means to make a commitment; i.e., to set your personhood to accomplish something. Therefore, when an individual makes the decision to incline their heart they make a conscious decision to take who they are at the deepest level of their being, and focus their mind, their emotions, their will to the subject or task at hand.

Please realize dedication to a task is not new for people incline their hearts to many things. For instance, my Dad during my junior year of high school football would go up and down the field with the yard markers. I went up to him after a game and said, "Dad, why are you doing this when you know it may be bad for your heart?" He responded, "Son, the reason why I do this is because I love you and I want to be as close to the game when you play as I can." Wow, what do you do for a father like that?

Six months later dad died of an aortic aneurism embolism. After his death, I made a personal decision to incline my heart. I dedicated my senior year of high school football in memory of my father. I told no one. All the summer workouts, all the weightlifting, all the running, I did for one purpose - that when I stepped onto that field, I would play at the highest level of my ability in honor of my dad.

Now, in this pursuit the workouts of our team proved insufficient for me. Many times I stayed on the practice field after everyone left for the showers and ran additional sprints and jogged extra laps. As the year progressed I did this more and more.

Before every night game, I would open my Dad's scrapbook detailing his golfing exploits. I read over and over again that my father was considered a golfing-prodigy when he won the Rhode Island State Junior Golf Amateur Championship at the age of sixteen. Each time I would read all the articles through, detailing his success in tournaments across the country. As I did this I increased my motivation, by listening to the song "The Impossible Dream." Over and over again I would play this song. Now, I couldn't just hit a button on the CD or the replay curve on You Tube I would have to manually put that needle back to the beginning of the recording each and every time. Finally, when I got to the point, where I felt mentally and emotionally prepared to play the game I would leave to join the team. In this manner, I set my heart to play the game in memory of dad.

This is precisely the idea of incline your heart in Proverbs 2:2b, but in this directive Solomon challenges you "to incline your heart to understanding." As I dedicated my senior year of football in memory of my dad, this condition calls you to take all that you are as a person, and dedicate your mind, emotions, will, and effort to understand what the Word says and how the Word works.

Throughout Proverbs there are two Hebrew words translated by the English term understanding. The first term is discovered in Proverbs 1:2B, "To discern the sayings of understanding". The Hebrew word used here for understanding is "Bina". "Bina", is concerned with meaning; i.e., the grasping of proper identity, correctness of thought, preciseness of definition. Bina is what people should strive for in communication. One must gain the precise meaning of what a person is saying or writing. Only when the hearer or reader crystallizes in their mind the exact meaning intended by the speaker or writer does one properly understand bina. Proverbs challenges you to incline yourself to grasp the meaning of its truths.

The second Hebrew term in Proverbs for understanding is tebuna. Tebuna is the word used in Proverbs 2:2b "incline your heart to understanding [tebuna]." While bina focuses upon definition, tebuna aims at comprehending application. Therefore to understand the Word of God properly, Solomon reveals that one must come to discern what the Word actually says (that's bina), and to grasp how the Word actually works (that's tebuna). Only when both are achieved does one arrive at the proper understanding of the text.

As a result, a person who "inclines their heart to understanding," a person of Biblical wisdom knows how to swing the club properly. One knows the meaning and the application and actualizes the potential of the book. Please realize "incline your heart to understanding" is just one of seven lessons by which Solomon discloses how a person becomes a man/woman of the wisdom of God.

How, does a man or woman become a person of the Word? First, they know their set of books. Second, they know how to understand the meaning and application of each book. This brings us to the third means by which a person becomes a man/woman of the Word.

Third, a person of the Word actualizes the Bible's full potential during life's most critical moments of decision making and deed.

As the final element in golfing greatness lies in the ability to hit crucial shots with precision and power during decisive moments of championship play; so too, the concluding ingredient in being a man or woman of the Word necessitates engaging Scripture's principles and practices at the most crucial moments of human living.

In this regard Proverbs chapter two asserts that if an individual learns to swing the wisdom and moral coaching of Proverbs properly as the three conditions of 2:1-4 spells out:

> If you will receive...
> If you cry out...
> If you search.

Once the person masters the proper handling of the book then they possess the necessary acumen to perform five crucial shots in the progression of human living. The five shots are revealed in Proverbs 2:5-22 and are as follows:

Crucial Shot #1 (2:5-8)

> 5 "Then you will discern the fear of the Lord, and discover the knowledge of God.
> 6 For the Lord gives wisdom; from His mouth come knowledge and understanding.
> 7 He stores up sound wisdom for the upright; He is a shield to those who walk in integrity, 8 guarding the paths of justice, and He preserves the way of His godly ones."

You will know God

Crucial Shot #2 (2:9-11)

> 9"Then you will discern righteousness and justice and equity and every good course.
> 10 For wisdom will enter your heart, and knowledge will be pleasant to your soul;
> 11 discretion will guard you, understanding will watch over you."

You will know goodness

Crucial Shot #3 (2:12-15)

> 12"To deliver you from the way of evil, from the man who speaks perverse things;
> 13 from those who leave the paths of uprightness, to walk in the ways of darkness;
> 14 who delight in doing evil, and rejoice in the perversity of evil;
> 15 whose paths are crooked, and who are devious in their ways;"

You will be delivered from evil

Crucial Shot #4 (2:16-19)

> 16 "To deliver you from the strange woman, from the adulterous who flatters with her words;
> 17 that leaves the companion of her youth, and forgets the covenant of her God;
> 18 for her house sinks down to death, and her tracks lead to the dead;
> 19 none who go to her return again, nor do they reach the paths of life."

You will be delivered from sexual harm

Crucial Shot #5 (2:20-22):

> 20 "So you will walk in the way of good men, and keep to the paths of the righteous.
> 21 For the upright will live in the land, and blameless will remain in it;
> 22 but the wicked will be cut off from the land, and the treacherous will be uprooted from it."

Together we will produce a good land

What a book! If we as believers actualized the potential of Proverbs we would hit the crucial, critical shots in the course of living that enable, equip, and empower us to…

> 1) discern God
> 2) discern goodness
> 3) be delivered from evil
> 4) be delivered from sexual harm
> 5) produce a good land

When I founded and functioned as Executive Director of "Praying For You," a para-church ministry to reach people for Christ through relational prayer witnessing, I participated in many a prayer meeting asking God to bring revival to our nation. Yet, year after year our country continued to stray from the Biblical God and suffer a downward slide toward dysfunction, immorality, and evil. When I began this intensive study of Proverbs in 2004, I discovered in my exegesis of the book that its wisdom and moral teachings spoke directly not only to individuals but to society as well. I arrived at the conviction that the Biblical correctives necessary to overcome social ills and evils lay in actualizing the principles and practices disclosed in the book. However, I also ascertained that this wisdom book which addresses societal betterment in the now was very much neglected.

You see, if you need salvation, pull out the Gospel of John. If you need sanctification, get into Romans. If you want to see how this all ends go to Revelation. But, if you are knee deep in the rough or you need refinement in your marriage, parenting, business, decision making, community, when you find yourself facing even the most complex issues in life then pull out the book of Proverbs. Proverbs is the book God intended for you to select from your sixty-six books for recovery and refinement. Furthermore, what is true of us as individuals is also true of us as a people. In this

Proverbs is crafted to overcome societal ills and evils in order to usher in human goodness across institutions, neighborhoods, communities, and countries. How we need this book to better American life today.

We need the book of Proverbs right now

Hal Sutton, in The Players Championship led Tiger Woods by one stroke going into the final hole of the tournament. After an excellent drive, Sutton faced a 176 yard approach shot on the eighteenth hole. He knew a birdie would clinch the match. Sutton selected his six iron and swung the club. Looking up he fixed his eyes upon the flight of the ball. He saw it going straight for the pin and with intense emotion uttered, "Be the right club. Be the right club today!" The ball struck two feet from the pin and stopped. Sutton cried out, "Yes!"

As Sutton chose the right club for the right shot at the right time and hit that club precisely with victorious results, so too believers need to pull the book of Proverbs out of the Biblical bag and hit the shots in the right way - right now. We are a people in need of the wisdom and goodness of Proverbs. If we would master this book and apply its principles to the issues and evils that confront us today there will be a resounding "Yes!" by the citizens of our nation.

Yes, Proverbs is the Biblical book for today. Proverbs is the Biblical book for societal transformation in the now. By actualizing its knowledge we will better humanity for God's glory and the good of man. You see, Proverbial wisdom is not law; it is not legalism; it is fully applicable in the age of grace. It's hokmah contains the potentiality of uniting Bible honoring people whether African American, Caucasian, Hispanic, Asian, Native American, Arab to walk not only hand in hand as brothers, but shoulder to shoulder as neighbors, to overcome the problems we face today as a nation.

Do we not need some recovery across our United States? Are we not knee deep in the rough? Are we not embedded in the traps of life? Beyond recovery, do we not need some refinement – refinement in our marriages, parenting, schools, businesses, leadership, neighborhoods, politics, justice system, security? I submit it is time to pull out God's wedge from our Biblical bag, learn to swing the club with precision and power and experience its wellbeing for the betterment of our people and our Republic. It is time to actualize the wisdom of Proverbial coaching.

Next Chapter

Chapter 2: The Wisdom of the Ages

Vince Lombardi, the legendary coach of the Green Bay Packers 1960's dynasty, the man whom the Super Bowl trophy is named (The Lombardi Trophy), started each new training camp by holding up a football and proclaiming to his team, "Gentlemen, this is a football!" He then proceeded to delineate the sacrifices each player must make for the Packers to be champions. Even his All-pro's had to re-orient themselves each year to the Lombardi style of professional football. His way worked for in Vince's nine years as head coach of Green Bay the Packers went to six NFL World Championships winning five, including the initial two Super Bowls.

In this chapter I hold up before you a proverb. As a result you will know what a Biblical Proverb is, how it works, and the difference it will make in your life, family, community and nation. Let us begin with Proverbs 1:1:

> **"The Proverbs of Solomon, son of David, king of Israel."**

There was a good King who determined to do something positive, wholesome, beneficial for his people. He called his wise men together, and challenged them saying, "I want you to write for our citizens the wisdom of the ages. Put your minds together, work on this, and bring it back in writing so we can give this gift of knowledge to our people. So they left. They began to work on it, work on it, work on it, and after a number of months sauntered back carrying an encyclopedia of fifteen volumes, twelve thousand eight hundred and forty-two pages long. The King gazing upon the mass of material exclaimed, "Men, this is too big! Our people will never be able to get through this stuff.

Shorten this up. Go work on it again. Our people need to know the wisdom of the ages." A couple of months passed and the wise men appeared before the King again, but this time they presented one book, three hundred and fifty-seven pages long. The King begins to read and then in frustration says, "Gentlemen, this is good. But, it is still too long. I want you to write the wisdom of the ages in five words!" Now, the wise men silently questioning the possibility of that command went back to their studies and they worked on it, worked on it, and worked on it some more. Finally they returned proclaiming "King we got it! We have the wisdom of the ages in five words!" Exuberantly the King responded, "Great, tell me! What is the wisdom of the ages?" A small, unassuming wise man stands up and utters, "There aint no free lunch".

The King desiring to do something wonderful for his people commissioned his cabinet of wise men to take the entirety of life's expressions, containing its philosophies, principles, and practices, and encapsulate it into a short, pithy, catchy statement in order to guide his people to live life better. The King was looking for a Proverb.

The Early American Proverb

Now, American's have always enjoyed a good Proverb. There is a dictionary that lists over 15,000 American proverbs. Some of these are quite familiar. In your mind say the second part of these proverbs as we progress through these examples.

"A dog is a man's _____   _____." 1
"Don't judge a book by ____ _____." 2
"Don't put all your eggs in   _____ _____." 3
"Don't throw out the baby with ____ _____ _____ 4
"Two' company- three's __ _____." 5
"Put up or _____ ____!" 6
"Put your money where ____ _____ ____." 7
"Practice what _____ _____." 8

(1- best friend; 2- its cover; 3- one basket; 4-the bath water; 5-a crowd;
6- shut up; 7- your mouth is; 8- you preach)

As the above demonstrates proverbial statements strive for delightful language, appealing to common reasoning with the added element of an identifiable outcome. It is in the delineation of a consequence that the genre of a proverb distinguishes itself from cleverness of speech. For instance, here are three clever statements:

> "I'd rather have people say there he goes than here he lies."
> "In politics, a man must learn to rise above principle."
> "If you think your boss is stupid, remember he hired you".

Now compare these catchy, funny, enjoyable statements to a proverb:

> "He that marries for money will earn it".

Please note: a proverb traditionally combines clever with consequence. It is by connecting a delightful, perceptive saying with an expectant outcome that the proverb presents a life truth. In this manner the early American proverb offered a vast treasure of wisdom disclosed in short, simple, catchy statements combined with identifiable outcomes thus providing a reservoir of guidance to our populace in how to live life well. In so doing the American Proverb addressed such subjects as: money, politics, work, war, friendship, manners, speech, religion, love, sex, etc.. As a result, in whatever expression of human living there arose an American proverb crafted for the goodness of our citizenry, speaking to issues from the smallest minutia of life to the most critical, most intimate areas of living.

While the volume of practical living contained in the scope of the American proverb came from insights of men such as: Washington, Lincoln, Douglass, Hemmingway, Edison, Emerson, Twain, one man must be specifically applauded for his work in crafting the American Proverb. His name was Benjamin Franklin. Ben Franklin, in his Poor Richards Almanac, penned, categorized, and put before the American people the mindset of a proverb.

Here are some of Franklin's proverbs:

"A penny saved is, a _____ _____." 1
"Early to bed, early to rise, makes a man, _____, _____, and _____." 2
"The early bird, _____ the _____." 3
"A stitch in time _____ _____." 4

(1- penny earned; 2- healthy, wealthy, and wise; 3- catches the worm; 4- saves nine)

You know these sayings because you are an American for the early American proverb is embedded in the cultural DNA of our populace. They bring to our people a treasure of wise and benevolent guidance, and our European ancestors expected the citizens of our nation to memorize these truth nuggets of practical and productive living and faithfully pass them down from generation to generation. Your recall proves the success of our founder's proverbial enterprise.

Using one of Franklin's examples, consider how the American proverb works; take for instance: "A stitch in time saves nine." Now what does this mean and what are its practical implications? If something is torn, if something comes apart, if something is broken, you fix it right away. You don't put it off, you don't procrastinate or it will get worse, and the time and effort that it's going to take now to fix it is far greater, far more difficult, and much more costly than if you sewed it right at the moment it was torn.

The early American proverb such as: "A stitch in time, saves nine", was crafted for the personal wellbeing of our citizens, serving as a guide to lead individuals into healthier and more effectual living. However, not only were these proverbs penned for personal progress they were also purposed to move the populace into a progressing social unit, providing mutually agreeable principles and practices.

In this regard the American proverb served as a societal play-call. Using another football analogy let's grasp the significance of the social emphasis of the American proverb. When you have a quarterback in a huddle, he calls a play. Inherent in the play are codes that instruct each and every player on the offense to move together in coordinated effort. After the play is called the quarterback concludes: "Ready, Break!" The team lines up, all of the players know exactly what the play is, what their part in the play requires, and each knows their proper place in that execution of the play that is called. This is what a proverb purposes to accomplish socially. The early American proverb was presented to us as a people to be our societal play call, putting forth principles to be practiced in the day to day living of our populace. As a result our nation moved in likeminded coordinated direction.

Yes, Americans have always enjoyed a good proverb. The rich heritage of our early proverbs is honorable, wise and good. Thus, the American proverb is the wisdom of the age's United States style – the communicative common denominator that guides our nation's way of life, laws, and liberty. As a result of this proverbial continuum we as a people are better off both individually and collectively.

The Biblical Proverb

When you come to the Old Testament Book of Proverbs, you have the wisdom of the ages not American style – but God's style. The wisdom writings of Scripture were crafted by the wise men of Israel. Who were these wise men of Israel? In Jeremiah 18:18 one discovers three primary religious leaders of Israel: the priest, the prophet, and the sage. The sages were the psychologists, the sociologists, the philosophers, the analysts of their day. They pondered life, seeking to identify beliefs and behaviors which ended in predictable human outcomes whether positive or negative.

However, the sages who crafted the wisdom writings and books of Scripture attributed their knowledge not as coming from men but from the mind and heart of God as Solomon asserted in Proverbs 2:6-8:

> 6 "For the Lord gives wisdom, from His mouth come knowledge and understanding. 7 He stores up sound wisdom for the upright, He is a shield to him who walks uprightly, 8 guarding the paths of justice, and He preserves the way of His godly ones."

Thus, the sages of Israel, and Solomon in particular, attributed the authority of Scriptural wisdom to the eternal character and creative activity of the Lord Himself. In this regard, wisdom is described as an attribute and action of the Biblical God as seen in Proverbs 8:22-31:

> 8:22: "The Lord possessed me [wisdom] at the beginning of His way, before His works of old. 23 From everlasting I [wisdom] was established, from the beginning, from the earliest of times of the earth. 24 When there were no depths I was brought forth, when there were no springs abounding with water. 25 Before the mountains were settled, before the hills I was brought forth; 26 While He had not yet made the earth and the fields, nor the first dust of the world. 27 When He established the heavens, I was there, when He inscribed a circle on the face of the deep, 28 when He made firm the skies above, when the springs of the deep became fixed, 29 When He set for the sea its boundary, so that the water should not transgress His command, when He marked out the foundations of the earth; 30 then I was beside Him, as a master workman; and I was daily His delight, rejoicing always before Him, 31 rejoicing in the world, His earth, and having my delight in the sons of men."

In this passage Proverbs reveals the wisdom of God preceded and participated in creation, bringing precise knowledge to initiate the magnificent structures and complexities of the universe. Just as wisdom delighted in the exercise of God's creative workmanship, so too wisdom rejoices in fulfilling its designed purpose to guide humans to better and bountiful living. This is the work of wisdom, and God rejoices in her compositional masterpiece.

Think of it in this manner. My step dad Ken was an architect. He told me how the construction company which successfully built the Silverdome, then one of the five finest domed football stadiums in the NFL, made a bid to construct the new headquarters for the company he worked for. Ken said in the presentation the salesman explained the intricacies and challenges of building that mammoth eighty plus thousand seat coliseum. At the close of the presentation he declared: "If our company can build the Silverdome, we can build your structure." With that proven performance Ken's company hired them.

If wisdom can build the universe, as that company can construct a building, so wisdom can fashion your life and make it better. Such is the work of God's wisdom, and He rejoices in its perfections. Thus, the source of wisdom heralded in Proverbs supersedes the American proverb in authority because Proverbs comes from and connects with the eternal character and creativity of the Lord Himself. Therefore, as our founder's were pleased when we as Americans engaged the wisdom of the ages United States style, so too the Lord is pleased when the people of our nation actualize the wisdom of the ages – God's style.

A Matter of Style

Along with this Divine distinction of source there is also a stylistic difference between an American proverb and a Biblical proverb. The American proverb communicates its assertions by means of an authoritative statement, focusing attention on one side of an issue with little or no contrast or comparison. For instance, "The early bird catches the worm." This short, pithy, catchy statement tells you one side of the story - it speaks directly to the bird; it doesn't say a thing to the worm. If it was designed to tell both sides of the story it would address the situation of the worm such as: "it might be better if you got up a little bit later" or "next time (if there is a next time) try digging a tad deeper." However, because the American proverb is crafted for acceptance and not comparison it speaks to one side of an issue.

A reason for this is that the European designers of the early American proverb assumed the practice of Biblical theism among the populace, and therefore did not see the necessity of comparing, contrasting and countering deviant life expressions. As a result, for over two-hundred years the American proverb articulated and advanced Christian principled living. It is only of recent history that secularism germinated and began to dominate America's public way of life, laws, and liberty.

The Biblical proverb on the other hand intends to persuade, and therefore carries a more complex communicative style. As a result, the basic Biblical proverb sites both sides of an issue, and identifies the expected outcomes of each principle or practice disclosed. Its guidance is presented not in authoritative statements, but authoritative comparisons combined with anticipated consequences. In so doing, the proverbial construct puts before the reader discernable, non-equivocated beliefs and behaviors declaring:

> "If you go this direction, you can expect this negative experience,
> but if you go in the opposite direction you can expect this positive outcome."

As a result, Biblical proverbs contain "Buyer Bewares" and "Buyer Buys." Both articulate behavioral practices that conclude with demonstrable results. The American proverb lacks such sophisticated communication. Now, to grasp the workings of a Biblical proverb let us…

First, begin with the "Buyer Bewares" of Proverbs

Over one half of proverbial content communicates by means of **"Buyer Bewares."** The "Buyer Bewares" present a negative description to the reader of what not to do, where not to go, how not to behave. They warn of life expressions that lessen even harm human existence. Here are a few "Buyer Bewares" identified in Chapter 11 of Proverbs:

> "A false balance is an abomination to the Lord…" Prov. 11:1a
> "When pride comes, then comes dishonor…" 11:2a
> "…the falseness of the treacherous will destroy them." 11:3b
> "Riches do not profit in the day of wrath…" 11:4
> "…the wicked will fall by his own wickedness." 11:5b
> "He who despises his neighbor lacks sense…" 11:12a
> "Where there is no guidance, the people fall…" 11:14
> "He who is surety for a stranger will surely suffer for it…" 11:15a
> "…the cruel man does himself harm." 11:17b
> "…he who pursues evil will bring about his own death." 11:19b
> "He who withholds grain, the people will curse him…" 11:26a
> "…he who searches after evil, it will come to him…" 11:27b
> "He who trusts in his riches will fall…" 11:28a
> "He who troubles his own house will inherit wind…" 11:29a

Here's How God's "Buyer Bewares" Work

Phil Mead, my college roommate and dear friend had the worst "luck" in buying used cars during our university days. He owned a couple of real beaters during those years. I mean if you bought any other kind of car besides what Phil purchased you would be in better shape. After all we were in college and we didn't have much money then (or now for that matter). He comes into the dorm room and says, "Hey! I got another car!", "Great Phil, lets go look at it"! It was 1950's Rambler, a matchbox of a car. He told us he bought it from a farmer who stored the vehicle in his barn for two years.

Five of us then squeeze into this tiny thing to travel down a country road to get something to eat at an all night truck stop. The first thing we noticed is that the Rambler smelled like horse manure. We were thinking, "How in the world is Phil going to go out on a date with this?" As we creak our way down that two lane highway the car is crying out with squeaks and groans expressing dissatisfaction with every bump, crack, crevice we ride over. Then, Phil hits a pot hole and the front hood flies straight up. Now we all are laughing uncontrollably as Phil gets out and secures the hood with a rope. Good deal on a car, eh?

Two days later, Phil is maneuvering his vehicle through the streets of Jackson, Michigan. He turns left at an intersection. Out of the corner of his eye, he sees a wheel going down the right side of the street. He gets out and runs after the tire. It costs him a couple hundred bucks to get it fixed. A few days later Phil again is driving in downtown

Jackson. This time he makes a right turn on a side of a hill, and out of the corner of his eye he sees the other wheel bouncing down the side of the street as Phil begins to yell for patrons to watch out! Now somewhere in that process, Phil probably thought, "Man, I should have looked at a Consumer Report on how to buy a good used car."

The book of Proverbs contains God's Consumer Reports for human existence, and the "Buyer Bewares" in Scriptural wisdom aim to keep people from purchasing the lemons of life. You see, while a person may buy many cars they only have one life to live as Hebrews 9:27 asserts:

"Inasmuch, as it is appointed for men to die once and after this comes judgment."

Therefore, during one's lifespan the "The Buyer Bewares" of Proverbs are crafted to protect man from messing up their one opportunity of earthly habitation. Therefore providing a sphere of protection the "Buyer Bewares" communicate warnings revealing to people harmful acts of impending danger.

Warning! Warning! Warning!

I used to do a lot of backpacking: five times my backpacking trips journeyed the Appalachian Trail in the expansive Smoky Mountains, numerous times I hiked and camped in the Grand Canyon National Park, three times my excursions took me to the White Mountains of New Hampshire. Now, the highest peak of the White Mountain range is Mount Washington at 6,288 feet with an altitude gain of over 4,000 feet from its base (2050') to the summit. While not exceedingly high Mt. Washington is extraordinarily deadly. It is listed number eight on GearJunkie's "World's 10 Most Dangerous Mountains" ranking between Everest in Nepal (7) and Denali in Alaska (9).

Mt. Washington's danger can be discerned when one understands why it is called "Home of the World's Worst Weather." Five different weather patterns cross the top of that mountain. Near the summit blinding fog occurs 300 days a year, freezing temperatures can fall to as low as -50 degrees farenheit, and when one adds wind chill temperatures plunged to -102 degrees farenheit as recorded on January 16, 2004. Sleet and snow may occur any day of the year with snow accumulating an average of 280 inches per year (over 23 feet deep). In one 24 hour period 49.3 inches of snow fell on February 1969. Hurricane force winds occur on the summit an average of 100 days per year. Staggeringly, the peak holds the world record for the highest straight wind speed known to man clocked at 231 mph on April 12, 1934. As a result, backpacking trails leading to the top of Mt. Washington are populated with warning signs stating:

"STOP! The area ahead has the worst weather in America. Turn back now at the first sign of bad weather, because many people have died above timberline."

With that stated, my initial excursion toward the summit of Mt. Washington began on June 23rd, 1973, when my younger brother and I drove all night from Detroit Michigan through Montreal to the White Mountains to start our week of backpacking adventure. At 5 A.M. on the 24th we arrived at Washington's Pinkham Notch Visitor Station. However, we discovered the establishment would not open till 9 A.M. This posed a problem for our intention was to buy a map of the trail system at the Visitor

Center. Now, we faced a four hour wait. However, with my experience of backpacking the Smoky's I was confident we could successfully navigate the Tuckerman Ravine Trail to the top of Mt. Washington and secure a map at the summit's Observatory Weather Discovery Center. In that manner we would possess the necessary map to guide us through our remaining three days of backpacking. So we started on the trail around 6 A.M. Within minutes we encountered the warning sign:

> "STOP! The area ahead has the worst weather in America. Turn back now at the first sign of bad weather, because many people have died above timberline."

As we climbed the signs kept reoccurring. This took me by surprise for I never saw these warnings on the trails of the Smoky Mountains. Furthermore, I did not possess the information on how deadly that mountain could be. Beyond that the trail itself lacked the definitions of the tree lined Appalachian paths of North Carolina and Tennessee. Then after an hour of climbing I got us lost. We backtracked searching for the trail. Through poor decision making I got my brother and I stranded on a ledge of a small waterfall with a fifteen foot drop off below. Praise God we got out of that. Finally we rediscovered the trail.

Once back on the path dark clouds appeared. We had a decision to make. Were we going to pay attention to those signs, or were we going to keep ascending to the top? I said to my brother. "Let's go back down, get a map, eat a good meal, stay in a motel, and try again tomorrow." He readily agreed. Heeding the warnings we turned around and went down. End of story right? Not yet.

After purchasing the map at the visitor's station, we secured our stay at a mom and pop type motel. That evening we ate dinner and went back to the motel. My brother after showering quickly fell asleep. However, troubled by my poor performance and contemplating the next day's hike, I lay awake. I turned on the TV and watched a Billy Graham crusade. Dr. Graham spoke of obeying God. After his message I opened my New American Standard Bible to Hebrews chapter 12. During our previous all night driving John and I listened to messages by Hal Lindsey of the Late Great Planet Earth fame. In one of his tapes he spoke on Hebrews 12 exegeting the statement that "Jesus was the author and perfector of faith." As I read the entire chapter I came across the following:

> **18 "For you have not come to a mountain that may be touched and to a blazing fire, and to darkness and gloom and whirlwind, 19 and to the blast of a trumpet and the sound of words which sound was such that those who heard begged that no further word should be spoken to them. 20 For they could not bear the command, 'If even a beast touches the mountain, it will be stoned.' 21 And so terrible was the sight, that Moses said, 'I am full of fear and trembling'…. 25 See to it that you do not refuse Him who is speaking. For if those did not escape when they refused him who warned them on earth, much less shall we escape who turn away from Him who warns from heaven."**

What would you do? After serious time in prayer I determined we could not climb that mountain the next day. Now, I needed to share this information with my brother. In the early morning we got up and got dressed for the day's backpacking climb. I said, "John let's go eat a good breakfast first." During breakfast I explained what transpired the night before with Dr. Graham speaking on obedience and how I opened my

Bible to Hebrews 12. I showed him the passage. I asked him, "What do you think?" He replied, "We can't go back up there."

Now, we knew there would be crow to eat. We didn't have to be prophets to foresee the ribbing we would receive from family and friends. Regardless, we started driving home but this time through upper New York in the Adirondacks heading toward Elmira to visit our half-brother Bill and his family. As we drove the weather, which had been brilliantly sunny in the early morning suddenly and dramatically worsened with severe thunderstorms, downpours, lightening, and strong winds. Finally, after hours of violent weather we exited the storms. When we arrived in Elmira the skies once again were sunny. We shared the story with Bill. He just looked at us. After spending the night at his home we turned my 1969 Mustang toward Detroit. Once home we told the story to our mom and step dad, Ken Beaser. They too just looked at us. So did our friends.

However, two days later Ken showed us an article in the Detroit paper stating that five people died from that storm which hit New York, Vermont and New Hampshire. It went over the Northwest White Mountain range – the area we would have been backpacking and pitching our tent on and around Mt. Washington.

Now, knowing about the actual danger of that mountain, judging from my inability to successfully navigate its trails the day before, considering how my survival skills got us trapped on a ledge of a waterfall, hearing about the message on the necessity of obedience by the incomparable evangelist Billy Graham, and then encountering the proscriptives of Hebrews 12 "to not even touch the border of the mountain lest you will die," how many of you would have joined me in ascending Mt. Washington if I pronounced: "Ah, let's not worry about those warnings! Let's climb!?"

Dear reader, just as the signs on the trail ascending that mountain spell out definitive and historically demonstrable reasons to turn back at the first indication of bad weather; so too, the Biblical proverbs of the "Buyer Bewares" declare the negative outcomes of contrarian human behavior. In its disclosure Scriptural wisdom delineates the uncomfortable endings, the tragedies that await an individual or nation that continues down deviant paths. As a result, each proverbial warning serves as a human preventive to keep a person or a people from lessening, lousing up, even losing their life.

Consider the Warning Signs of Proverbs 1:20-33

As you peruse this passage note how specific the "Buyer Bewares" of Proverbs are and recognize the seriousness of the proscriptives and severity of coming calamity. Note also the determined strategy and effort wisdom exerts to prevent human beings from suffering such senseless tragedy.

1:20 "Wisdom shouts in the streets, she lifts her voice in the square, 21 at the head of a noisy street she cries out, at the entrance of the gates in the city she utters her sayings, 22 'How long O naïve ones, will you love simplicity? And scoffers delight themselves in scoffing, and fools hate knowledge? 23 Turn to my reproof, behold, I will pour out my spirit on you; I will make my words known to you.

24 I called and you refused; I stretched out my hand and no one paid attention, 25 and you neglected all my counsel, and did not want my reproof. 26 I will even laugh at your calamity; I will mock when your dread comes. 27 When your dread comes like a storm, and your calamity

comes on you like a whirlwind, when distress and anguish come one you. 28 Then they will call on me, but I will not answer. They will seek me diligently, but they will not find me.

29 Because they hated my knowledge, and did not choose the fear of the Lord. They would not accept my counsel and spurned all my reproof. So they shall eat of the fruit of their own way and be satiated with their own devices. For the waywardness of the naïve shall kill them and the complacency of fools shall destroy them, but he who listens to me, shall live securely, and shall be at ease from the dread of evil.'"

Let us mull over five rationales derived from this passage.

First, notice the "Buyer Bewares" communicate their warnings right where people congregate, calling out to wisdom's rejectors to turn from their rebellion and receive reproof.

1:20 "Wisdom shouts in the streets, she lifts her voice in the square, 21 at the head of a noisy street she cries out, at the entrance of the gates in the city she utters her sayings, 22 'How long O naïve ones, will you love simplicity? And scoffers delight themselves in scoffing, and fools hate knowledge? 23 Turn to my reproof, behold, I will pour out my spirit on you; I will make my words known to you.'"

While wisdom challenges the multitudes to hear its guidance, the "Buyer Bewares" in this passage focus upon people who are naïve, mockers, and fools. This is quite a trio of individuals - a threefold cohort of rebels who resist the Biblical God and His ways. While mockers and fools reject the warnings of the Word, the naïve through their lack of Scriptural conviction and human awareness enable their wayward comrades to advance non-God, even anti-God agendas. It is to this trio of deviators wisdom calls for repentance of mind and behavior:

"Listen to my reproofs! Hear my corrections! Heed my warnings! Follow my paths! There is a way out! Turn, you are going the wrong way!"

One does not need to be entrenched in anarchistic rebellion to realize humanity carries a history of resistance rather than reception concerning reproof. Push back to correction manifests itself even among the "best" of us. For instance, Dr. Henry Brandt, one of my all time favorite Christian communicators, spoke how he took a wrong turn traveling to Detroit and began speeding down the interstate in the opposite direction toward Chicago. His wife pronounced. "Henry, you are going the wrong way." He responded, "Eve, would you just let me drive? I know where I am going!" As he passed the next exit he realized his wife was correct. Yes, they were heading at seventy plus miles an hour in the wrong direction toward the Windy city and not the Motor city. He needed to turn that car around.

So what was the initial reaction of this successful business man, Ph.D. in psychology, and now minister of the gospel? Dr. Brandt said, "Immediately, I began to think how I could turn that car around without revealing to my wife I was wrong." Think about that for a moment. Even though he knew his error, out of pride he drove past a few more exits searching to discover a way to correct his mistake without Eve knowing. However, unable to perform that resurrection he finally admitted to his wife the error and asked forgiveness. He then turned the vehicle around.

Like Dr. Brandt there are times when we make wrong turns and discover we are going in the opposite direction. Whether intentional or unintentional we find ourselves traveling speedily down ideological and implementational highways which run counter to the wisdom of God's guidance. However, the question arises, once we recognize our navigational error will we exercise our God given free will, heed the signs, and turn ourselves around or will we just keep on driving? Mockers and fools just keep on driving. Worse still they take the others riding in their vehicle with them.

Regardless of whether we need a minor directional adjustment or a complete turn around, God's wisdom provides man with the necessary guidance to get us back on track. As a result, wherever a person finds themselves in their life's journey, the wisdom of God longs to impart knowledge to improve their situation, heal their hurt, and overcome the injustice. So too whenever an institution, a community, a society finds itself awash with difficulty the wisdom of God presents its knowledge to correct the misdirection and improve the condition of mankind. Yes, on the highways of the human adventure people need to heed wisdom's warnings.

Second, realize God's reproofs come out of His goodness and love for mankind, seeking to prevent and protect the free agents of fallen humanity from harmful behavior and hurtful experiences. To understand human rebellion one does not need to look far to discover that people need directional and ethical correction. Besides looking at our own rebellious behavior parents know such defiance from their own children. As fathers and mothers we observe disobedience in our sons and daughters and discipline them for their own good and for the good of others. It is out of our love for our children we bring reproof to correct wrongful conduct.

As a young dad I would regularly take hikes up the South Mountain Preserves in Phoenix with my kids. On one exploration I had my two year old son Phil on my back, and Stephen, who was then closing in on five hiking with me up a trail. I warned Stephen to watch out for the jumping cactus. Jumping cactus are nasty spine filled cacti pieces that break off cactus plants and litter the trails. A person must be careful of these for if they step on one they penetrate the souls or sides of shoes with needle like spines sticking painfully into the skin. It is as if they really jumped on and implanted their needles in you.

I did my best to alert Stephen of the dangers of the jumping cactus. However, on this occasion he stepped too close to one and it stuck him. The spines punctured the side of his sneaker and reached his tiny foot. In pain he immediately stopped. We took the shoe off and removed those pins. From that moment Stephen was on a serious look out for any jumping cactus that might inflict further injury upon him.

Later that day Stephen broke an important rule in our house and was sent to his room. This was not a one-time episode for time after time he would go against our wishes and break that essential barrier. No matter what we did nothing worked. Over and over again we tried unsuccessfully to curb this improper behavior. Steve refused to get it. He failed to connect the discipline he received with the breaking of that rule. What's more, instead of learning the lesson he got angry at us for trying to correct his wrongdoing. However, I kept looking for a way to help him stop his misconduct and be spared from the resultant discipline.

Ok, what was the rule? Simply put: "Stop terrorizing your younger brother." There had to be a way to correct this misbehavior for his sake, for us, and especially for Phil.

The next day I journeyed to the mountain preserves with a jar and carefully put a sizable piece of a jumping cactus into it and secured the lid. I then went directly to Stephen's room, opened the jar and put that two by three inch cactus right in the middle of his bedroom floor. Then I went outside and got the attention of my son, saying, "Steve, there's a jumping cactus in your room!" Sheepishly he ventured into his bedroom cautiously viewing the needle pinned cactus. I put him on my lap and we sat in a chair looking at the "spiny monster" which invaded his room.

I asked him, "Steve, how did that jumping cactus get into your room?"
He answered "I don't know."
I asked, "Do you want to step on that cactus?"
He said, "No."
I asked, "Why?"
"Because it will hurt me," Steve replied.
"How do you know it will hurt you?" I inquired.
"Because, it stuck me in the foot." he said.
"Son, do you want to try and jump over that cactus?"
He said "No."
I asked, "Why?"
He responded, "It might jump on me."
"Steve," I asked, "Do you want to leave that cactus on the floor?"
"No," he replied.
"Would you like me to remove that cactus from your room so that you will not hurt yourself when you play in here?" I asked.
"Yes." He responded.

I then carefully put the cactus back into the jar and closed the lid. We sat down again but this time Stephen held the jar. As he looked intently at that cactus I made the following comment:

"Remember when dad told you how dangerous these jumping cactus were and how it could hurt you? I told you that to protect you. I didn't want you to get injured." I then said, "Son, mom and I tell you over and over again to treat Phil with kindness and respect. He is your brother. When you refuse to listen and continue to disobey us, when you treat your brother wrongly you will be disciplined. Your harmful behavior will also hurt you. Son, just as you know that stepping on that cactus will result in your foot being stuck with the pins, so too when you keep treating your brother wrongfully I will need to discipline you. However, I discipline you for your own good. Unlike that cactus mom and I are trying to help you realize there are consequences to your negative behavior. When you continue to disobey us it's just like you are wanting to step on that cactus not once but over and over again, refusing to learn that it is going to end up hurting you. Stop treating your brother unkindly. Treat him with respect and you will find your life will go much better."

Did it solve the problem? It helped. After all Phil just turned 27!

Now, if I as an imperfect dad so longed to help change a harmful behavior in my son, how much more does the Creator and Savior of mankind determine to guide humanity out of damaging misdeeds. Look at His effort in Proverbs 1:23-25:

1:23 "Turn to my reproof, behold, I will pour out my spirit on you; I will make my words known to you. 24 I called and you refused; I stretched out my hand and no one paid attention, 25 and you neglected all my counsel, and did not want my reproof."

Yes, the Lord's reproofs are given to prevent and protect man from senseless suffering. However, please note in this proverbial passage on the "Buyer Bewares," the Lord's passionate call of warning was willfully rejected.

> I called – you refused
> I stretched out my hand – no one paid attention
> I offered all my counsel – you neglected
> I gave you my remedies – you did not want it

Third, recognize the rejection of God's reproofs by mockers and fools enabled by the naïve reaches a point of no return. There arrives a time when there is no escape. The negative outcome of a "Buyer Beware" hits. The calamity comes.

1:26 "I [wisdom] will even laugh at your calamity; I will mock when your dread comes. 27 When your dread comes like a storm, and your calamity comes on you like a whirlwind, when distress and anguish come one you. 28 Then they will call on me, but I will not answer. They will seek me diligently, but they will not find me."

Teaching in Belle Glade, Florida I learned of the devastation of the tragic night-time Hurricane that emptied the waters of Lake Okeechobee down upon that community on September 16, 1928. This devastating category four came directly across this city, located on the southeastern shores of this large inland lake. The devastation of the 140 mph winds destroyed physical struct ures and injured hundreds of the residents. However, the destruction of the town occurred after the eye passed over Belle Glade and with the reversal of the winds emptied the waters of Lake Okeechobee onto that wind ravished city. Over 1,800 people died that night with some strapping themselves to trees attempting to preserve their lives and their children. Buildings, animals, people were swept away by the rampaging waters and hurricane winds that destroyed that community. No one who survived that storm was spared from devastation either from the loss of possessions or the tragic loss of loved ones. However, in 1928 the people of Belle Glade didn't know of the intensity of the coming storm. These dear people were unable to escape the horrific encounter with that hurricane which hit with full unobstructed force.

Today, intricate, precise weather equipment can identify the exact location and track the immediate direction of hurricanes. Brave military pilots fly into these monsters and measure with accuracy the intensity of their furry. Forecasters then herald the warnings throughout the media from radio, T.V. internet, crying "The monster is coming. Get out!" However, even with all the information, people must heed the warnings, for sometimes these hit with incredible destruction such as Camille, Andrew, Katrina, Ike. When these monstrous four and five category storms bear down on a population the only sensible thing is escape. Once the storm hits it is too late to get out.

The book of Proverbs provides man with God's sophisticated warning system, heralding the destructive outcomes resulting from harmful behaviors, even lifestyles. His warnings blare that the storms are coming. Therefore, stop, turn, get out now, for when the winds destroy and waters drown there will be no way out. There comes a point of no return. And at that moment it is too late to get away. As a result the warnings are no longer applicable. In fact wisdom now laughs at the calamity of the mocker.

Why? Please realize wisdom is not a Savior. Wisdom does not weep over the waywardness of man as Jesus did with the people of Jerusalem when He uttered: "O Jerusalem, Jerusalem how I longed to gather you together as a hen with her chicks but you would not." Wisdom does not cry out as Jesus did on the cross, "Father forgive them for they know not what they do." Wisdom does not promise a guilty but now forgiven man, who shared in the crucifixion, "Today, you will be with me in paradise." No, that is not the work of wisdom, but it is the redemptive work of the Savior.

Wisdom is not a Savior, but it is a revealer. It tells man how life actually works both positive and negative. It presents truth and goodness for all to hear and heed. It cries out its warnings. However, when the naive, mockers, and fools continue to refuse wisdom's warnings the storms will hit, the calamities will come, and when they arrive the rebellious resisters and rejecters become the poster children demonstrating the serious outcomes of God's "Buyer Bewares."

Fourth, the cause for the personal and societal tragedy lies in the unrepentant march of those who hate the Lord and His ways. The mockers and fools despising the counsel and reproof of their Maker resist, rebel, and reject God's warning signs. They lead the parade bringing themselves and those who enable them to a most disastrous end as Proverbs 1:29-32 asserts.

> 1:29 "Because they hated my knowledge, and did not choose the fear of the Lord. 30 They would not accept my counsel and spurned all my reproof. 31 So they shall eat of the fruit of their own way and be satiated with their own devices. 32 For the waywardness of the naïve shall kill them and the complacency of fools shall destroy them…"

Imagine going on a field trip to New York City with your Church congregation. As a speaker it was my responsibility to make sure everyone arrived safely. When we departed from the bus in front of the Empire State building you and I took a roll call to see if everyone was accounted for. As we went through the names everyone was present except for the youth pastor, Tim. I called out, "Has anyone seen Tim?" Upon that request we hear Tim yell out I'm up here!" We look up and at the top of the Empire State Building is the youth pastor. I yell, "Tim, what are you doing at the top of the Empire State Building, one of the tallest buildings in the world?" He enthusiastically responded, "Howard, I'm going to jump off, and when I hit the ground I'm going to bounce and have a great time!" I immediately countered, "Tim, haven't you heard of Howard's law? He or she who jumps off the top of the Empire State Building will just lie flat?" Tim defiantly cried out, "Howard, you are just trying to inhibit me. When I hit I will not lie flat I will bounce and have a wonderful time!" At that moment the choir director responds, "You know I think Tim has something here." He goes inside takes the elevator up to the highest point and joins Tim awaiting the jump off. In fact one half of the fellowship agrees with Tim and joins both that youth pastor and the choir director on the ledge awaiting their fall.

I then turn to you and say, "There's only one thing left the rest of us to do. We must stand against the side the building and watch them come down." Immediately Tim jumps, he's enjoying his fall, somersaults, twists, break dancing in the air - impressive, but then all of a sudden he hits, splat! All over our shirts, pants. Then the choir director hits, splat. One by one they come down, and every one ends the same tragic way. Now, you look at me and declare, "You know Howard, I think you have something here. Anyone who jumps off the top of the Empire State Building just lies flat."

Thank you Ken Poure, for this illustration

Laughter filled the auditoriums, that is, until 9/11. Then this story wasn't funny anymore. You see, originally I used the World Trade Centers as my buildings, but after 9/11 the story pictured the catastrophy of humans leaping to their deaths to keep from being burned alive by the flames, and then the total collapse of the building burying the innocent caused by the attack of radical Islamic terrorism. As a result, there was no humor only horror in the illustration.

Today, this story visualizes American society under attack both from without and from within. The consequences resulting from the rebellious refusing to heed the "Buyer Bewares" brings calamitous consequences upon our people and destruction upon our nation. Tragically our dads, sons, daughters, friends, neighbors, citizens are crashing down all around us from the willful violation of the Word's warnings. At every level of our national experience we increasingly enable those who resist, reject, demonize, and remove the public actualization of God's "Buyer Bewares." To such a degree Biblical warning signs are increasingly forbidden from public discourse. Even the communication of a Scriptural warning becomes defined today as a human wrongdoing. Secularized America flipped wisdom's directives presenting Biblical guidance as harmful to the well-being of humanity and its enterprises.

Following this reasoning people bypass or throw away God's guidance in His "Buyer Bewares," calling against its signs: "Don't restrict me!" "Set me free!" Holding to such deviant philosophies and practices our citizens, our institutions are jumping off in violation of clear Biblical warnings. Tragically, the historical account of this rebellion concludes in the tragic loss of human potential individually and collectively – what is presently called – the new norm.

While rejectors of God exercise volitional freedom in refusing His wise counsel the rebellious are not free from the calamitous outcomes. Instead, their wrongful behavior ushers in the damaging consequences. At that tragic moment **they** become the poster child for wisdom's "Buyer Bewares."

Worse still, when the number of the "they" becomes dominant, when the rejecters of God's wisdom gain social, political, commercial, ecclesiastical control, the entirety of a populace (them) becomes vulnerable to the storms. The negative outcomes hit us all. At that tragic moment **we** become the poster child for wisdom's "Buyer Bewares."

For example:
Consider the "Buyer Beware" of Proverbs 22:7b
"…the borrower becomes the lender's slave."

When the warning "the borrower becomes the lender's slave" is applied to the national debt of our United States is there not reason for our populace to be gravely concerned of an enslaved outcome? When I began the ministry of Praying For You in 1991 the national debt reached over three trillion dollars (3,665,303,351,697.03). In 2004 when I began this project intersecting proverbial wisdom and its moral coaching with an historical and existential analysis of our American enterprise our national debt had risen to over seven trillion dollars (7,379,052,696,330.32). As of Sept. 30, 2015 the debt of our United States reached over 18 trillion (18,150,604,277,750.63). Within the next year our governmental dependency will have heaped over twenty trillion dollars of dependency upon our young citizenry. Add to that the private accumulation of debt by our citizens reached over 13 trillion on January 26, 2016.

> National figures obtained by www. treasurydirect.gov/govt/reports/pd/hisdebt/hist
> Government – Historical Debt Outstanding – Annual
>
> Public figures obtained by wikipedia.org/.../History_of_the_U.S._public_debt
> History of the United States public debt

Just how much is a trillion dollars? A trillion George Washingtons stacked one by one would reach to the moon and back and half way there again – just a tad taller than Mount Washington- don't you think? At the moment of your reading our nation's debt reaches over twenty trillion dollars!

In the book David Copperfield by Charles Dickens, young David receives financial advice from Mr. Wilkins Micawber, recently released from Debtors' prison. In the 1935 movie of the same title, Mr. Micawber (played by W. C. Fields) speaks the following words of wisdom to the young boy David Copperfield (played by Freddie Bartholomew).

> Mr. Micawber, [Here's my words of advice to you Mr. Copperfield...]
>
> "Annual income twenty pounds, annual expenditure nineteen pounds, result happiness.
> Annual income twenty pounds, annual expenditure twenty-one pounds, result misery."
>
> Adapted from Chapter 12, David Copperfield.

Like Mr. Micawber's wise advice to young David Copperfield, the "Buyer Bewares" of Proverbs assert that such indebtedness ends in personal and public tragedy. Biblically the warning of indebtedness alerts us of coming individual, generational, and national enslavement. Personal and national debt leads to the servitude of our populace to the one's who hold the purse as Tennessee Ernie Ford once sang,

> "I owe my soul to the company store."

However, as America's most virtuous document "The Declaration of Independence" asserts: all people are created equal and possess God given inalienable rights of life, liberty, and the pursuit of happiness. The American pursuit of happiness included the opportunity to acquire and possess property and wealth free from the dictates of indebtedness and servitude. If our founders had extended the Declaration's actual meaning equally and fairly to Native and African Americans at the inception of our nation imagine how different our country would be today.

With that said, Proverbs 22:7b warns that whoever possesses the financial purse of those in debt directs the decision making and determinations of those under their economic thumb. What is the final outcome? The Biblical warning asserts: "the borrower becomes the lenders slave." Our government in violation of this "Buyer Beware" makes us all vulnerable to the consequence of financial collapse. When the economic storm hits it will reengage a form of slavery upon the American shore, stealing away the freedoms of our citizens and institutions into the hands of those who hold the certificate of debts. Sadly our nation and its populace will serve as the poster child demonstrating the tragedy of the outcome of the debtor's chains. Have we arrived at the point of no return when we cannot escape the storm?

The purpose of the "Buyer Bewares" prevents humans from lessoning their life potential. This is the intent of the warnings of Proverbs. They reveal the negative destination where the road ends. Some of the negative outcomes focus on the loss of marital happiness, others the loss of effective parenting, some disclose the harm in making unwise decisions. Still others address the damage of practicing evil and the injury inflicted from harmful sexual practices. Regardless of the proverbial subject each "Buyer Beware" spells out the dangers of impending loss and eventual harm resulting rebellious behavior.

Fifth, through its protections and preventions God's reproofs free people from harm as concluded in Proverbs 1:33b:

> "...but he who listens to me, shall live securely, and shall be at ease from the dread of evil."

At ten years of age I was an avid golfer. During the summer Mom and Dad would take me to Pine Lake Country Club several times a week to work on my game. Pine Lake offered three major sporting venues for its members: golf, swimming, and tennis. On this particular occasion, the day after hitting a tennis ball against our garage door with Andy DiMatteo, I decided to add tennis to my athletic repertoire. So, when my parents dropped me off at the club instead of making a bee line to the course I ran directly to the tennis courts. Two lessons and seven hours later, after hitting hundreds and hundreds of yellow balls against opponents and a green wall, my parents came to pick me up. I didn't want to go. I just wanted to keep on playing. After all I wasn't half bad. What's more I discovered the Junior Club Tennis Championship was only two weeks away! I actually thought I had a chance. Two weeks to learn the game, get in shape, and win that tournament – no problem. Sometimes we engage in delusional thinking do we not? Anyway, back to the story.

As we drove home my body began to weary. Entering through the garage door I told mom I was going to lay down before dinner. I fell asleep. When I awoke I couldn't move. I couldn't raise my arms, lift my legs, or raise my head. I couldn't even blow my nose. I tried to call out, "Mom!" I had no strength. Hardly any sound came out. Finally she appeared to tell me dinner was ready only to discover a completely immobilized son. I could move my eyes but that was about it.

Soon, Doctor Beck, our family physician, arrived at our house (yes, Doctors did that at one time) and examined me. He diagnosed my condition. I had exhausted all my upper body muscles. My body shut down. Dr. Beck then offered this piece of advice, "Howard, you can't do that." Lying flat on my back, what else could I do? I had to receive his words of medical wisdom. After all I was the poster child affirming his position. I nodded in agreement with my now moveable head.

In Biblical terminology Dr. Beck gave me reproof. Reproof identifies harmful behavior and calls the violator to turn from the wrongdoing and engage activities which are truly better. Like a good parent the reproofs; i.e., the "Buyer Bewares" of Proverbs tell it the way it is. However, it is the responsibility of the person to respond to the reproof and adjust their behaviors accordingly.

In the "Buyer Bewares" one discovers morality. To understand this better imagine Dr. Beck saying to me,

> "Howard, I bought you another tennis racket. Here it is! It's the newest model. It will dramatically improve your game. Now, I want you to take this racket, go out again this evening and play a few hours more. Anybody can just lie there. A real champion would get up and get back on that court! That extra few hours of practice will improve your mental state and physical conditioning. Let's go. In fact, I'll drive you back to the tennis courts at Pine Lake right now."

How moral would that directive be? Is there not an ethical component to reproof? There is goodness in the "Buyer Bewares." There is a moral necessity to tell a person the way life truly is. In this, Dr. Beck did it right. When the good doctor assessed my present condition he knew I had to stop that behavior. He then gave me a reproof. There was nothing in that directive that aimed to injure my best interest. However, it was up to me to recognize the truth of his correction, receive his reproof, and repent; i.e., to turn away from that behavior which proved injurious to my wellness. In the same manner Proverbs coaches up humanity to reduce and eliminate behaviors that will hinder success and harm one's progression in life.

Yes, God's warning signs tell you to stop, but then the reproof goes further for it gives you the reasons for the preventive and also the way out of the coming calamity. This proverbial act of deliverance attests God's intent in calling humanity out of harmful behavior into a life filled with prudence, nobility, rightness, and truth, bringing goodness and beneficent guidance to man as Proverbs 8:4-11 attests:

> 4 "To you, O men, I call, and my voice is to the sons of men, 5 O naïve ones, discern prudence and, O fools, discern wisdom. 6 Listen, for I speak noble things; and the opening of my lips will produce right things. 7 For my mouth will utter truth; and wickedness is an abomination to my lips. 8 All the utterances of my mouth are in righteousness; there is nothing crooked or perverted in them. 9 They are straightforward to him who understands, and right to those who find knowledge. 10 Take my instruction, and not silver, and knowledge rather than choicest gold. 11 for wisdom is better than jewels; and all desirable things can not compare with her."

Therefore, the reproofs of God's "Buyer Bewares" aim to free you from the coming storms. In this regard consider Proverbs 6:1-5 which heralds a principle of deliverance from financial ruin.

> "My son, if you have become surety for your neighbor, have given a pledge for a stranger, 2 If you have been snared with the words of your mouth, have been caught with the words of your mouth. 3 Do this then, my son, and deliver yourself; since you have come into the hand of your neighbor, go, humble yourself, and importune your neighbor. 4 Do not give sleep to your eyes, nor slumber to your eyelids; 5 Deliver yourself like a gazelle from the hunter's hand, and like a bird from the hand of the fowler."

Yes, the validity of the "Buyer Bewares" are demonstrated historically. Wisdom appeals to the human experience to authenticate its conclusions. You see, it is not the beginning of a rebellious excursion that authenticates the consequence of a proverb; it is the culmination of the journey. The empirical affirmation lies in the end result.

Think of it in this manner. While one may violate the warning signs on the paths up Mt. Washington with each continuous step the resister moves closer to possible injury even loss of life; as one can jump off the Empire State Building, refusing to believe in the consequences of gravity, the fool is not free from the eventual ending, every second of their "free" fall descends to their demise; so too, one can violate a warning sign of God's wisdom and as the rebellion continues the mocker locks in the coming tragedy. Yes, the warning signs of God's "Buyer Bewares" cry out:

> "Stop! Turn back now! Don't' be the poster child evidencing the consequence of violating the warning signs of the 'Buyer Bewares.' Hear the voice of God's wisdom. Be delivered from the storms to come, for 'he who listens to wisdom shall live securely and be freed from the dread of evil!'"

Dear reader, don't be naïve, don't be a mocker, and don't be a fool. Hear the voice of the "Buyer Bewares." Heed its warning. Follow its reproofs. Save yourself and others from damaging consequence. So how does a Biblical Proverb work?

First, a Biblical Proverb contains a "Buyer Beware."

Second, a Biblical Proverb Contains a "Buyer Buy"

The authoritative comparisons and anticipated consequences revealed in the book of Proverbs sets before a person not only "Buyer Bewares," but also serves up "Buyer Buys." The "Buyer Buys" present the good stuff; i.e., how to do things right, how to do things better, how to do things just and fair. They define positive expressions for human living, leading individuals and society to beliefs and behaviors that benefit life.

The Buyer Buys of Proverbs Refine You

The first time I saw my daughter Lauren run in an "official" sprint occurred in her elementary schools field day. Lauren, then a fourth grader ran against other fourth to sixth grade girls to determine the fastest girl in the school. The teachers divided the girls into four heats with about ten girls running per heat. If you finished in the top three of your heat you then qualified for the final race. In Lauren's heat she lined up with her head turned to the side watching the starter. He then yelled "Ready – Go!" Lauren started slow and trailed a gal who throughout the race stayed about one foot in front of her. As my daughter ran down the track she kept looking at the girl. After the race I watched closely the other three heats. I discovered that the starter first yelled "Go!" and then quickly lowered his arm, signaling the runners to sprint. However, his verbal command occurred about $1/10^{th}$ of a second before he physically lowered his arm. Girls that looked at him started just a tad slower than those who ran with his voice. I pulled my daughter aside and asked this question:

> "Lauren, do you want to win the race? She replied, "Yes". "Honey, here's how to beat those girls. First, when you line up to run do not look at the starter. I have watched him for four races and this is what he does. He yells "Go!" and then he lowers his arm. You watched him and began to run when he lowered his arm. This slowed you down. The girl that beat you ran when he yelled "Go!" Lauren, when you line up to start the race, look straight ahead and as soon as he

yells "go" explode out of the blocks. Second, when you run down the track do not look at the other girls. This too slows you down. Instead run the entire race with your eyes looking straight ahead. I am going to stand directly in your lane ten yards past the finish line – look and run to me. Don't slow down until you run way past the finish line. Do those two things and you will win the race."

Lauren lined up and got into her running position. "Go!" the starter yelled, and then as always he lowered his arm. This time Lauren took off at the sound. She was out in front. Keeping her eyes on me she easily won that race by a good couple of feet. As we celebrated her win I was so proud of her accomplishment and found delight that she trusted my advice. A couple of minutes later a high school football player, helping with the races on field day came over to me and asked, "Mr. Tryon, I saw you talking to Lauren before the race. I know she came in second in her heat. What did you tell her that helped her win the championship?"

This story displays what God desires to do for humanity in the "Buyer Buys" of wisdom. With Scriptural wisdom you have the creator God imparting His advice on how to improve the performance of His creatures and advance the society in which humanity dwells. In so doing the Lord brings to man His personal coaching on how to run life's race better. This is the design of His "Buyer Buys," and just as an athlete would do well to follow the refinements of a most excellent coach so too a person would do well to heed the directives of the "Buyer Buys" of God.

Think of what you have in your possession here – the coaching principles of the Lord to better mankind in the present. Look at the benefits one encounters with the "Buyer Buys" as expressed in Proverbs 3:13-18:

> 13 "How blessed is the man who finds wisdom and a man who gains understanding, 14 for its profit is better than the profit of silver, and its gain is better than gold. 15 She is more precious than jewels and nothing you desire compares with her. 16 Long life is in her right hand; in her left hand are riches and honor. 17 Her ways are pleasant ways, and all her paths are peace. 18 She is a tree of life to those who take hold of her, and happy are all who hold her fast."

Do you ever wish humans could go back to the Garden of Eden and start this whole thing again? Are there not times when you wish you could have a complete do-over? "Lord, one more time please?!" The book of Proverbs says the "Buyer Buys" are like a tree of life. They aim to produce a bountiful life that buds and blooms into blessing. I don't know about you but this sounds pretty good to me.

The "Buyer Buys" of this book will deepen your capacity to reach your God given potential. The "Buyer Buys" provide positive detailed instructions in how to speak, how to listen, how to build friendships, how to be fair with people, how to handle your money, how to gain solid marriages, improve your: love-making, parenting, teaching, decision making, justice, fairness, kindness, leadership, discipline, employment, success, all those principles you have in the Book of Proverbs. For instance, consider a few of wisdom's "Buyer Buys" concerning speech as revealed in Chapter 15:

1 "A gentle answer turns away wrath…"
2 "The tongue of the wise makes knowledge acceptable…"
4 "A soothing tongue is a tree of life…"
7 "The lips of the wise spread knowledge…"
23 "A man has joy in an apt answer, and how delightful is a timely word…"

26 "...pleasant words are pure."
28 "The heart of the righteous ponders how to answer..."

The details of these positive instructions on speech are fleshed out when a person grasps the meaning of the terms and their relationship with other proverbial directives concerning the topic being studied. If my two pieces of data directed to my daughter's race impacted her performance think of the wonderful advancement humans would gain if they learned and followed the advice of God's "Buyer Buys."

However, some people carry the misconception that God purposely hides Himself and His will from man. In this scenario, humans are left to futilely search for guidance destined only for uncertainty, even despair. In this view people see God's will like a man going through a forest in quest for the discovery of God, but only coming to the end of his exploration hearing God laughingly exclaim. "Ha-ha!! You never did find My will did you?" The book of Proverbs gives the lie to this sentiment for in its pages God reveals directives to improve man's lot in life; i.e., if you know how to unlock its gems of wisdom.

Unlock the Potential of the Proverbial Combination

When one combines the communicative package of the Biblical Proverb; i.e., the "Buyer Bewares" and the "Buyer Buys" there is marvelous truth and goodness afforded by the Creator to uplift the human experience. Such workings of proverbial instruction can be illustrated by the coaching style of John Wooden, winner of ten NCAA Basketball Championships in twelve years. John Wooden, considered the greatest coach in the history of college basketball exercised a certain method of teaching to correct improper play while infusing excellence on the court by his players. When Wooden observed something wrong during practice, he would stop the activity and demonstrate to his players how to do that particular right. After positively showing them the proper way to run the play he would demonstrate what they did wrong; finally he would once again show them precisely how to do it right. Then the players executed the play precisely as Wooden prescribed.

Wooden's approach to coaching mirrors the teaching style of Proverbs. In the book you have the negative articulations defining convictions and conduct that lessen even damage life as contained in the "Buyer Bewares." These are clearly identified and explained. Then you have the positive teachings and the benefits delineated in the "Buyer Buys." Both are presented together for comparison and contrast so that the recipient might make a knowledgeable, informed decision to lead humanity to better living.

For instance, consider how Scriptural wisdom speaks concerning the most public parts of societal living such as its directives in treating the poor and the needy. In this analysis realize the degree of recovery and refinement Proverbs offers to the disadvantaged among us. In Proverbs there are twenty-seven directives given from chapters ten to thirty-one concerning the poor. The following lists only the sayings designating a person's right and wrong behavior toward the downtrodden.

"...blessed is he who is kind to the needy." 14:21

"He who oppresses the poor shows contempt for their Maker, but whoever is kind to the needy honors God."   14:31

"A generous man will himself be blessed, for he shares his food with the poor." 22:9

"Do not exploit the poor because they are poor and do not crush the needy in court." 22:22

"A ruler who oppresses the poor is like a driving rain that leaves no crops." 28:3

"The righteous care about justice for the poor..." 29:7

"If a king judges the poor with fairness, his throne will always be secure." 29:14

"[There are those]...whose jaws are set with knives to devour the poor from the earth, the needy from among mankind."   30:14

"Speak up and judge fairly, defend the rights of the poor and needy." 31:9

"She extends her hand to the poor; and she stretches out her hands to the needy." 31:20

Just a simple reading of these sayings reveals that proverbial wisdom defines a righteous person as one who engages in respecting and helping the poor and afflicted in their need. Such moral coaching coincides with other teachings of Scripture establishing that the virtues in assisting disadvantaged people lie inherent in actual Biblical Theism. Thus, the Christian who engages such behaviors follows the way of their Master as Christ portrayed Himself, giving evidence to John the Baptist that He was the Messiah in Luke 7:20-23:

20"And when the men had come to Him [Jesus], they said, 'John the Baptist has sent us to You, saying, 'Are You the Expected One, or do we look for someone else?' 21 At that very time He cured many people of diseases and afflictions and evil spirits; and He granted sight to many who were blind.

22 And He answered and said to them, 'Go and report to John what you have seen and heard; the blind receive sight, the lame walk, the lepers are cleansed, and the dear hear, the dead are raised up, the poor have the gospel preached to them. 23 And blessed is he who keeps from stumbling over Me.'"

Throughout the Bible the God of creation, the God of eternity, the God of the here and now, the God who brought salvation to man through the death and resurrection of Christ, the Lord who carried out His ministry of caring for the needy, the afflicted, the poor, calls out to for people to actualize His wisdom. Imagine if we as a people engaged the Lord's revealed guidance afforded to mankind in proverbial knowledge. Imagine if we walked in His steps to carry out His ministry of saving grace and human care.

Such intersection between a "Buyer Beware" and a "Buyer Buy" is how Proverbs works. A Proverb discloses authoritative comparisons to be analyzed and deciphered to gain the precise meanings of the terms and the proper relationships between the terms. The anticipated consequences can be understood and historically affirmed by personal experience or social examples which verify the coming calamity or blessing. As a result wisdom provides the willing learner a set of historically demonstrable principles to guide one and society to better living.

Study Proverbs Topically

The development of Scriptural wisdom increases in clarity and completeness when the "Buyer Buys" and "Buyer Bewares" are categorized into specific topics. Through topical study each Proverb may be connected with their brothers and sisters of like meaning. Aligning the proverbs which address the same belief or behavior allows

"Buyer Bewares" and "Buyer Buys" to speak with collective force and nuance on a specific subject, providing a comprehensive understanding of that idea or implementation. In so doing gradations of definition and surety of conduct build into a comprehensive analysis for accurate interpretation and application.

In this topical study follow the book's proverbial progression of understanding. In chapters 10-15 Proverbs presents the "Buyer Bewares" and the "Buyer Buys" through simple comparison, combining the warnings with the blessings by means of the contrasting conjunction "but." In chapters 16-22:16 the development of a proverbial topic shifts from comparision to simili. Through simili proverbial knowledge focuses its attention upon building the understanding of a particular "Buyer Beware" or a "Buyer Buy," fleshing out its understanding and implementation by elaborating upon one or the other. Finally, from chapters 22:17-31:31 the book adds complexity to the proverbial topic by presenting nuanced analysis of the "Buyer Beware" or the "Buyer Buy." Therefore, to properly study a proverbial topic one must go through this natural development of thought and action. As a result, don't stop with elementary comparison (10-15), don't pitch your tent with intermediate simili (16-22:16); instead, study the topic all the way through to its graduate analysis (22:17-31:31).

Therefore, to gain a full understanding of a proverbial teaching on a particular subject such as: father-son; mother-son; wise-foolish; glad-grief; one should study each subject in its entirety as delineated in its natural progression in the book. Then, if a person desires further accuracy take the findings and relate this back to the other Old Testament teachings on the subject and then move forward to the New Testament teachings on the issue. In so doing one will gain a comprehensive theological understanding and unlock the benefits of how Scriptural Wisdom presents intense coaching in performance skills that lead to human excellence. As a result, from the very young, to the most gifted, to the very aged all persons can greatly benefit from such proverbial learning.

Realize the Potential of God's Proverbial Map

How specific is proverbial guidance? Think of the detail man has been blessed with in Proverbs. Personally, over the past twelve years, I have separated the various topics addressed in Proverbs into four hundred and eighty different subjects. As one proceeds in this study the multitude of subjects become well defined and their reproofs and refinements very, very specific.

Take for instance human speech. Previously I wrote of seven buyer buys from proverbs on the proper use of the tongue. Let us go further. When one combines the proverbial statements from chapter ten through thirty-one there are one hundred and thirty-eight directives concerning how to speak properly. Seventy-two of them are "Buyer Bewares," giving guidance in how not to verbalize and keep onself from the negative outcomes of those violations. Sixty-six of the principles are "Buyer Buys," expressing how to speak properly. Combined these proverbial directives concerning the tongue impart incredible guidance for recovery and refinement. This one example demonstrates the wealth and depth of knowledge Proverbs imparts to human living, even to the degree of 138 points of refinement in how to speak. How wondrously detailed this book becomes in clearing up mistaken paths and refining performance. This highlights the sophistication of Biblical wisdom.

Furthermore, Scriptural wisdom addresses the most private and intimate practices of human living such as in terms of marriage and sexual expression. In order to show how vivid, direct, and personal the moral coaching of Proverbs is let us look at Proverbs chapter five. In so doing let us arrange the "Buyer Buys" and the "Buyer Bewares" of sexual conduct separately and then compare them.

Let us begin with the "Buyer Buys" of Proverbs 5

"Drink water from your own cistern, and fresh water from your own well".

Where do you quench your sexual thirst? Where does your water of sexual satisfaction come from? My initial backpacking excursion was with Rich Olshock and Larry Appleby, together we climbed Mount Baldy in the Appalachian Trails of the Smoky Mountains. I knew I had to put purification tablets into the water for about an hour before I drank it. Before we ventured into this trail we explored a few of the sights. On one there was a small stream of water cascading down from a rocky ledge about fifty feet above the road. I immediately took my canteen out and began to fill it with it with water. Rich came over and asked me, "Howard, do you know what is up on that ledge where this water is coming down from?" I had no idea. Immediately I poured the water out and waited to fill my canteen with water from a source I knew was clean.

The "Buyer Buys" of Proverbs chapter five tell us the source of one's sexual enjoyment is to be replenished by their spouse. Biblically a person is to drink from this water source only. Please realize, whoever you have sex with carries a past history of drinkers which include each and every sexual partner and each and every sexual experience they brought to that well.

For protection, for purity, for pure enjoyment the "Buyer Buys" say drink deep of sexual satisfaction from your spouse. You know where they have been. Do you know where that water has been? The idea here is do you know where the woman you have sexual intimacy with has been? The "Buyer Buy" now moves from source to passion.

"Rejoice in the wife of your youth. Let her breasts satisfy you at all times. Be always exhilarated with her love."

Now, that's a "Buyer Buy!" Can all men reading this verse say "Amen?" Think of Adam and Eve. When Adam saw Eve his first comment was "this is now"; otherwise interpreted:

"Wow! Where have you been all my life? Wrap her up Lord, I'll take her! On second thought, don't wrap her up. I'll take her just the way she is!"

Tim Timmons, Tape Series: Maximum Manhood

One of the errors of American fundamental piety is that believers are ashamed to herald what God was not ashamed to create. The Book of Proverbs says," Love your wife, be committed to your wife, and be fully engaged in the joys of sexual expression with her and her alone." The will of God in terms of sexual relations with one's wife is to be fun, good, and thoroughly and continuously enjoyed.

In so doing the "Buyer Buys" of wisdom calls men to be totally, unreservedly enraptured with their wife. And the wives are to share their bodies wholly and completely with their husbands. That is the wisdom expressed in the Book of Proverbs concerning man's sexual practice - that's the "Buyer Buy."

Now, let us breakdown the **"Buyer Bewares"** concerning sexual expression disclosed in Proverbs 5.

> 3 "For the lips of a strange woman drip honey, and smoother than oil is her speech; 4 but in the end she is as bitter as wormwood, sharp as a two-edged sword. 5 Her feet go down death. Her steps lay hold of Sheol... 8 Keep your way far from her and do not go near the door of her house. 9 Lest you give your vigor to others, and your years to the cruel one... 11 and you groan at your latter end, when your flesh and your body are consumed."

Who is the strange woman in Proverbs? It is the woman who is not your wife.

The seduction of a woman's attractiveness, in this case exemplified by her lips, both in terms of visual beauty and verbal flattery entices a man, appealing to the tastes and hunger of his sexual nature. Although the initial temptation promises sweetness, the outcomes are altogether different. The negative consequences detail the damage of such encounters, even describing sexually transmitted disease and death. If you want to know how accurate this outcome of improper sexual expression proves to be imagine the health condition of American citizens today without antibiotics.

Realize that one out of every four teenage girls today has or has had a Sexually Transmitted Disease (STD). I expressed this statistic in a sermon where upon the moment of that disclosure sadly many of the young girls lowered their heads. Think of the tragic health condition of the American populace when gonorrhea, syphilis, AIDS, and other manifestations of violating clearly defined Biblical warnings were not offset by the wonders of modern drugs.

What is the problem? Proverbs tells us people are drinking from water that is not from their well. Where has this water come from? Is it contaminated? Realize that when one sleeps with a person one is having sexual expression with an individual possessing a sexual past.

> 20 "Why then be exhilarated with a strange woman, and embrace the bosom of a foreigner... 22b He [i.e., the man who violates this directive] will be held with the cords of his sin. 23 He will die for lack of instruction, and in the greatness of folly he will go astray".

Now, compare the warnings of Proverbs 5 to the modern American proverb –

"Just do it!"

"Just do it?" Ruminate on that for a moment. "Just do it?" Where are the "Buyer Bewares?" Where are the warnings? Where are the comparisons? Where are the outcomes? Do you see the incredible inadequacy and folly in that secular statement compared to the magnificence of Scriptural wisdom? Think how that one sound bite leads our teens astray! "Just do it?" To what extent has this lesser, harmful principle and others like it damaged American society and led to the harm of human living? It is as if one is climbing Mt. Washington with the skies darkening, the winds howling, the rain with ice pelts pummeling and the backpacker encounters signs stating: "Just Do It!" Such secular whim provides examples of the kind of diet the American people, especially our young are ingesting. Yes, there is a world of difference in the type of proverb heralded among us today.

For example: if one wants to see just how far modern American society has resisted, rejected and removed Proverbial "Buyer Bewares" and "Buyer Buys" from defining what is good and beneficial for our nation's personal and public expression of life and liberty consider the following scenarios.

Imagine Jesus when the Pharisees dragged before him the woman caught in adultery. The Pharisees determined to execute this woman by stoning her because of this infidelity. Remember the Lord's stunningly brilliant statement: "the one among you who is without sin let him be the one to cast the first stone." What happened? One by one beginning with the eldest the accusers departed. Once the people departed the encounter remained between Christ and the young adulteress. Jesus then asked her, "Does anyone condemn you?" She replied, "No one Lord." Jesus then responds, "Neither do I." After this wondrous act of forgiveness Christ goes further and confronts her sin: "Go, and sin no more." Otherwise translated – "Now, cut it out." Imagine the foolishness of the woman if she would have then responded, "But, Lord, if it feels good aren't I supposed to just do it?"

Here's another example: consider the Lord teaching the apostles about true discipleship saying, "If any man desires to come after me let him deny himself, take up his cross daily, and follow me." Consider the admonitions of the Lord to His men, "You are going to end up laying your life down for me and in behalf of your brother and then specifically to Peter that Peter is going to be hung upside down on a cross because of me." Think if Peter after all this instruction was to look at Jesus and ask, "But, Lord, aren't we supposed to do our own thing?" It's different, isn't it? There is an eternity of difference between Scriptural sacrifice and secular selfishness.

Think of Moses coming down from Mt. Sinai with the 10 Commandments and after disclosing the Decalogue to the nation an Israelite exclaims, "But Moses, you can't legislate morality!" Can't legislate morality? Where did that come from? It didn't come from the Lord. Scripture speaks clearly of private and public behaviors. It speaks to the believer, it speaks to the citizen, it speaks to society. Dr. Martin Luther King Jr. once said, "A law can't change a person's heart, but it can keep him from lynching me." A Biblical Proverb addresses the individual, gives directions to institutions, laws, and governing.

How about this one, consider Paul's Epistle to the Philippians when he writes in chapter two verses three through five:

"Do nothing from selfishness or empty conceit, but with humility of mind let each of you consider one another as more important than himself; do not merely look out for your own personal interests, but also for the interests of others. Have this attitude in yourselves which was also in Christ Jesus."

Think of this response by the Philippian believers:

"But Paul, aren't we supposed to look out for number one?"

Notice how all of these secular proverbs have drifted from clearly defined Biblical principles. None of these modern secular sound bites contain a defined comparison or detailed consequence. None of them stimulate evaluative thought and action. Compared to the Biblical Proverb the secular cleverness pales in comparison, offering rules and regulations for living that under scrutiny and actual outcomes prove to be inadequate, insufficient, impotent, even harmful.

Tragically our populace has bought into these lesser declarations and the American people and our way of living are suffering under its foolishness. The underlying premise of a secular Proverb is the absence of God and the removal of His identifiable mores for human advancement. Such is the line of secular thought:

"Sin lies in the restrictions!"

However, in stark contrast the "Buyer Bewares" and the "Buyer Buys" of Proverbs cry out,

"There is a God! He provides humanity with divine boundaries and blessings. His proscriptions bring wonderful protections and His prescriptions offer marvelous benefits. As a result, man is to hear and heed His wisdom and moral coaching. People are to follow the Lord's guidelines! They lead to human goodness and wellness of being."

Yes, the Biblical Proverb is very specific. In its disclosure the Scriptural Proverb offers analysis both from negative warnings and positive blessings presented from actual personal experience, historical examples, and social evidence. As a result, the Biblical Proverb stands unmistakable in its meaning, non-equivocal in its assertion, and open to honest investigation crafted for comparison to any other life expression. Therefore, each Proverb challenges the reader to contrast the principles and practices of any contrarian position with the revealed conviction and conduct presented by the sages of the Biblical God. As a result, the Biblical Proverb stands as the Scriptures primary guide to the practical outworkings of human experience.

Dear reader the wisdom book of Proverbs has blessed you with practical truth and goodness for your personal welbeing in the present. In its pages God declares:

"I have given my "Buyer Bewares" and "Buyer Buys" to help you, to keep you from hurting your life. Embrace what is right, just, fair, and good. Do not become snared by principles and practices that will harm you. Instead, turn from them and receive that which truly leads to goodness."

Accept the Divine challenge of Proverbs. Compare God's truths, analyze His principles, search out the His reasoning, and contrast the Scriptural outcomes to the failing set of modern assertions arising out of secularism buffeted by the naïve, the mocker, and the fool. As men and women who value the Scriptures we can do this as individuals and we can do this as a people. The book of Proverbs offers to our people a national reawakening of truth and goodness.

Remember, the early American proverb is still apart of our national DNA. Even in the midst of our present secular onslaught most Americans still know and respect the sayings and can verbalize their understandings even after two hundred plus years of passing. Yes, we as a people valued, treasured, and faithfully passed down our forefather's wisdom from generation to generation.

For over 200 years the vast array of American proverbs comingled its principles and practices with Biblical meaning and mores. Biblical guidance emanated out of the early American Proverb, but not today. Today, the modern American Proverb is secular. The modern American proverb finds its source and style in the mind and mode of the naïve, mockers, and fools, propagating its directives away from God, apart from God, even against God. Our populace and especially our young people are inundated with these secularized proverbs.

In so doing we preserved the Biblically based communicative continuum of our European founders. As a result we possess a national vault of wisdom. It is time we rediscover the wealth of our proverbial virtues. In this, the Old Testament book of Proverbs acts as a unifier and a purifier for our populace and our Republic.

Dear reader, for the sake of our personal lives, our families, our communities, our country it is time we actualize the wisdom and goodness of Proverbial knowledge. In so doing we discover that the God who saves us eternally is also...

The God who gives us hope in the here and now.

On May, 23rd, 1939 at approximately 8:45 A.M. the submarine USS SQUALUS (SS-192) sank on a test dive in the north Atlantic off the coast of New Hampshire. A catastrophic failure in one of its valves caused the sub to partially flood with water and it sunk killing 26 of their 59 men on board. The remaining thirty-three men came to rest in their sunken sub 243 feet at the bottom of the ocean. Completely entombed in the steel sub they immediately launched a buoy containing a device for the survivors to communicate with potential rescuers. Then they shot from the depths a rocket which penetrated through the ocean into the sky leaving a trail for ships in the location to discover their position. Soon another submarine the SCULPIN (SS-191) saw the rocket blast and discovered the buoy. They entered into communication with the thirty-three submariners. Now, other rescuers rushed to the scene. That afternoon, two additional ships arrived to join the SCULPIN in attempting to rescue the surviving crew of the buried SQUALIS, which had closed all the remaining water compartments in the sub. However, even by securing the hatches the water now had reached two feet deep. Then all communication lines between the rescuers and the entombed crew went dead. Throughout the long night there was no way of knowing whether the remaining thirty-three were still alive in that sub. Across America the news spread of the dire need to rescue those sailors.

The next morning, May 24th, divers were sent down who walked upon the hull of the sunken ship. As they checked the condition of the vessel they listened intently for any sounds of life within the sub. Then they heard a sound coming from inside the steel vessel. There was a tapping noise coming from within the hull. The divers came to recognize the tappings as Morse code. The message tapped out by the thirty-three sailors still alive in that sunken sub was: "Is there any hope?"

"Is there any hope?" That was the question that filled the minds of those trapped helpless men. "Is there any hope?" That was the question blazing across the radio waves throughout our nation "Is there any hope?" It was a perfectly legitimate question for never before in the history of man had a person ever been rescued from a submarine that had sunk to that depth of level.

However, now there was one crucial difference from the deaths of all the other failed attempts of submarine rescue. The difference was that now the navy possessed a newly designed Diving Bell, "the McCann Rescue Chamber – a revised version of a diving bell invented by Commander Charles B. Momsen." The McCann Rescue Chamber was specifically invented for this type of catastrophe. It was created to be lowered to incredible depths and then connected by divers to the sub's escape hatch. "It would then equalize pressure between the two vessels and allow the sailors to be taken to the surface in small groups." But, would it actually work?

USS Squalus (SS-192): "The Sinking, Rescue of Survivors, and Subsequent Salvage, 1939." http: ll www. history.navy.mil/faqs/faq99-1.htm,

When the navy vessel Falcon arrived at the scene they arrived with the McCann Rescue Chamber on deck. Now the process of rescue began in earnest and extended without stopping for thirteen straight hours. Up and down, up and down the McCann Rescue Chamber was used until all thirty-three men had been transported from their watery graves to safety on the deck of the Falcon.

"The Squalus Rescue", 1939, www. mevio. Com/episode/62320/mtih-343-the-squalus-rescue-1939/?mode=detail

Is there any hope? That question was gloriously answered in the saving of those men's lives who were entombed in that sunken sub. "Is there any hope?" That is the question so many people are crying out for today in their dire state of brokenness. I don't know what you are going through today. I don't know your circumstances or your heartbreaks. I don't know of your loss and suffering, but the Lord does, and Scripture tells us we have a Great Difference Maker who can reach down and bring you out of your darkness and into the light of life.

The Biblical God has always been a God of rescue for those who turn to Him. With respect to eternity He provided us with the Diving Bell, the rescue chamber of His Son. Through Christ we have the deliverance from our sins. This is the great eternal rescue of our God and Savior. He came down here to save man from his sin. The rescue chamber has been sent and His name is Jesus. He is there with His arms open to you. However, there is one requirement. Like the sailors in the sunken sub who had no way of survival but to get in that rescue vessel. So too you must get in the rescue chamber of Jesus Christ or die in your sins. However, if you embrace the deliverance of Christ, He will bring you safely into His presence in heaven. That is the great correction of eternal life. This is His rescue of salvation, but you must get in it for yourself. Then He will bring you safely to the top. Trust in Christ alone and live in glory forever.

The rescue chamber of Proverbs

Likewise, the book of Proverbs also serves as a great rescue chamber; not in terms of eternity, but in terms of the temporal, practical areas of living right now. It is in the book of Proverbs we discover the necessary principles and practices to rescue us, to straighten out our paths, to give us the wisdom and moral coaching to overcome the dysfunction and evils that afflict us today as persons and as a people and bring us to a better place to be. As we need to get in the rescue chamber of the Savior so too we need to get in the rescue chamber of Scriptural wisdom. He has revealed this wisdom of straightening out our areas of practical living in the book of Proverbs. How we need to pay attention to God's signs of the "Buyer Bewares" of warning and the "Buyer Buys" of His blessing. As Bible respecting Americans let us together get on the proverbial paths that lead us away from harm and into the goodness of better living. As persons and as a people let us embrace and engage the wisdom of the ages – God's style.

So what are the sayings and commandments disclosed in the wisdom writings of Scripture? Proverbs provides mankind with the wisdom of the ages God's style communicated in short, pithy, catchy, authoritative comparisons, with anticipating consequences. The Biblical Proverb gives man protections and preventions through its proscriptive "Buyer Bewares," and imparts to man practical principles, prescriptions of goodness through its "Buyer Buys." Combined they equip humanity to enjoy and experience fullness of living personally and publicly as Proverbs 3:13-18 asserts:

> 13 "How blessed is the man who finds wisdom and a man who gains understanding, 14 for its profit is better than the profit of silver, and its gain is better than gold. 15 She is more precious than jewels and nothing you desire compares with her. 16 Long life is in her right hand; in her left hand are riches and honor. 17 Her ways are pleasant ways, and all her paths are peace. 18 She is a tree of life to those who take hold of her, and happy are all who hold her fast."

Proverbs 3:13-18

Chapter 3: A Case of Missing Knowledge

Lining up for her first official 100 meter race, my then eighth grade daughter, Lauren, competed against five other young female athletes from middle schools in the Dallas area. I knew she possessed speed but I was not sure how she would fare in her first official sprint. I positioned myself expectantly at the finish line, readying the video camera to record the race. BANG! Off she went leading the pack, stretching out at the finish line she won the race! Good job Lauren! After congratulating her on the victory I contemplated the joy we would share as she ran in the meets to follow. Unfortunately, two days later during cheerleading try-outs she tore a hamstring and missed the rest of track season.

Fast forward a year later with Lauren now a ninth grader at Midlothian High School. Having made the varsity track team as a freshman she now entered the blocks to run her second official 100 meter sprint, but this time she competed against 15 High School teams. She would run against some of the finest varsity girl sprinters in the state of Texas. I mean some of those girls possessed the bodies of our nation's Olympic Sprinters. They owned some serious speed. Wondering what would happen I positioned myself about 50 yards down the track with my camera, ready to film every stride of the heat.

Lauren set herself in the blocks awaiting the gun. Ready, set, BANG! The starter gun goes off. Lauren, along with the other girls, exploded out of the blocks, but then… BANG! The gun goes off again. What does that mean? False start. The runners immediately stopped to go back into the blocks and start again. However, my daughter didn't know what a false start was. She kept right on running. Zoom, she flies down the track!

Immediately I stopped the camera not desiring to embarrass her on film. As she speedily passed by me I yelled out, "Lauren! STOP! It's a false start!" Zoom! She kept running with everything she had. Why? With no one in front of her, she thought she was winning the race. With about 30 yards to go, she finally saw the timers at the finish line waving for her to halt. She then came to a stop, embarrassingly turned and began to walk all the way back in front of 1,000 high school athletes and students who were now mocking and laughing at her misfiring.

Please realize while I am a Christian minister, I am also a caring dad. Seeing my daughter pass by me - head held down - hearing the jeers of her peers, I yelled out the following words of encouragement: "That's alright honey! It's not your fault! That's bad coaching!" Another father standing next to me responded, "That's right! You tell her!"

My daughter suffered a case of missing knowledge. She lacked a key informational component to successfully run that 100 meter sprint. She did not know the protocol of a false start. As a result, she entered the starting blocks disadvantaged. She failed to possess, contrary to her competitors, that specific piece of information. Then it happened, at the very moment when that particular piece of knowledge was needed, her data deficit cost her and a multitude of witnesses viewed the consequences.

Whatever you do in life you need accurate, appropriate, relevant information in order to do things right and do things well. Whether it be running a sprint, passing a test, acquiring a discipline, building a marriage, raising a family, solving a problem, living justly, organizing a business, being a good neighbor, teaching a class or leading a nation people need to master certain knowledge to be successful. Advantage goes to the one who possesses the necessary data. Disadvantage encumbers the person who lacks essential content. Yes, accurate, appropriate, relevant knowledge is fundamental to all aspects of living regardless of the enterprise.

Therefore, in a book crafted to lead people to better living, it is not surprising that the first purpose statement of Proverbs centers on knowledge:

> "The Proverbs of Solomon, son of David, king of Israel;
> **to know wisdom and instruction…"**
>
> Proverbs 1:1-2a

The Hebrew term for knowledge in this verse is da'at. The term da'at used here in its infinitive form lada'at means:

> "to become conscious of, to become aware of, to observe, to realize, to know."
>
> W. Schottroff, TLOT, 2:511, s.v. yd' Waltke, p. 175,
> The Book of Proverbs Chapters 1-15

Now, people can acquire knowledge through three primary sources.

First, an individual gains abundant information from personal experience - otherwise known as "live and learn" or "trial and error." I remember as a little boy venturing into our two-car garage on a rainy summer day. My mom had recently hung a clothesline across that entire twenty-two foot expanse. Looking at the clothesline I began to contemplate: "I wonder if I could crawl across this thing?" In my thoughts I picture the garage as a huge Canyon with a two-thousand foot drop, bone crushing boulders below, with the river populated by man eating crocodiles. Falling would bring instant death or something far worse. However, due to some earth saving double 007 necessity it is up to me to make it all the way across this chasm. With the fate of the world hanging in the balance I put my hands and legs around the rope, and started my death defying crawl. Immediately the rope sags to about two feet from the ground, however with the existence of the universe depending upon this feat I keep on going. Right in the middle of the garage, what happened? The rope snaps and bang! I fall not two-thousand feet but two feet to the concrete. With my breath knocked out, I'm laying there squirming, waiting for my lungs to clear (I knew this from previous unwise episodes) and thinking, "Oh man, that was kind of stupid." Did I gain some knowledge from my personal experience? Yes, and I contemplated my idiocy as I slowly journeyed back into the safe confines of my room and laid down on my bed for the next thirty minutes.

About a month later, I am swimming in Meadow Lake with Andy DiMatteo, one of my closest friends. In the middle of the lake, they had a raft, and we would row our boat out there to engage in raft fights against other hearty fifth and sixth grade boys. After the great battle subsided, Andy jumps off the raft and starts swimming to the shore. I'm watching him successfully swim all the way to the beach. I'm thinking. "I can run faster than Andy. I can throw a ball further... If he can do it – I can do it!" I jump off and start swimming, swimming, swimming, swimming. Exhausted, I look back to find myself half way between the raft and the shore. I had spent all my strength. I had given everything I had. I had nothing left. I knew I lacked the stamina to swim back to the raft or make it safely to the beach. I was going down. At that very moment, a sailboat came by, and a man grabbed me by the shorts and pulled me right onto that boat. I'm lying there coughing, sputtering, spitting, but living. Did I learn? Yes, Andy was a better swimmer. He had more endurance. I simply wasn't very good.

The first personal experience taught me the knowledge that cement floors are hard, but minus the intervention of the sail boat the second would have cost me my life. This reveals a pitfall of gaining knowledge from personal experience only. Some people go through life limiting the input of knowledge to live and learn. In fact the entire book of Ecclesiastes is written from Solomon's pursuit of wisdom through live and learn. He closes his writing in 12:13-14 with this:

> 13 "The conclusion, when all has been heard, is fear God and keep His commandments, because this applies to every person. 14 For God will bring every act to judgment, everything which is hidden whether it is good or evil."

However, why wait until the end of life's journey to discover this truth? Life is too short to obtain data through the component of live and learn only. I remember Muhammad Ali as a thirty-seven year old ex-champion, fighting newly crowned young heavyweight champion Larry Holmes. In my seminary room I was able to receive the broadcast on an Hispanic radio station. Not speaking Spanish, the only words I could readily understand were Ali and Holmes. However, throughout the fight I heard a heck of a lot more Holmes than Ali. Even in a totally different language I could discern that the great Muhammad Ali was taking a severe beating that night. Finally Ali failed to answer the bell for the twelfth round. After the fight Ali exclaimed, "I could see what I needed to do. I just couldn't do it any longer."

This reveals a glaring limitation of "live and learn", for just when you think you have life figured out it is time to check out. Life is too short and too precious to be limited to gaining knowledge through "live and learn" only. Fortunately the obtaining of knowledge is not limited to just trial and error. You don't have to bump your head to learn. There is another means to acquire knowledge.

Second, you can obtain abundant information from the experience of others - otherwise known as "look and learn." Look and learn involves observation. In observation one takes mental note of the positive or negative outcomes of peoples convictions and conduct and then adjusts one's thought or action accordingly.

For instance, as a pastor I came to realize that something always goes wrong at a wedding. I just prayed when I presided over a wedding ceremony it wouldn't be me. One pastor spoke of two weeping moms. The families were well off financially, the service formal, a traditional wedding. The Church had two sets of stairs on both sides of the stage where an unlit candle stood awaiting to be lit. The ceremony involved both moms coming out separately and ascending the stairs to light the candle on their side of the sanctuary. First, the groom's mom walked out and as she climbs up the steps she trips, falls, and knocks over the candle. Her husband helps her set the candle aright and light it properly. Embarrassed and weeping she is escorted to her seat. Now it is the bride's mother's turn. Unaware of the tragedy that afflicted her accomplice she appears and begins to ascend the stairs on her side of the sanctuary. Successfully she lights the candle, turns, smiles at the crowd, and begins her descent. Suddenly she trips, falls, rolls forward and moons the crowd. She too then is escorted to her chair, weeping. Did those two moms learn from their experience? Yes, but they will never get the chance to do it again. However, I guarantee that every other woman in that audience 'looked and learned' and arrived at the same resolve: "I will never do that!" They gained knowledge from the plight of those – shall I say acrobatic moms?

There is no question that a person can gain understanding by watching, reading, hearing about the frailties, faults, and failures of others. A fledgling upstart in the business world sought information from an older extremely wealthy, successful business owner. He asked, "How did you become so successful in business?" The older mentor replied, "Two words: good decisions." The younger man pried, "How do you learn to make good decisions? The older gentleman responded, "Two words: bad decisions."

Now, one can go through multitude experiences of making bad decisions, but this is unnecessary if one learns from the mistakes of others who preceded him/her on that failing process. In this scenario it is foolish to follow the paths of those who have stumbled and fallen. Look and learn provides a means to gain knowledge without the failing.

So too on the positive side of observation one can build off of the experiences of others who blazed the trail of success before them. Take the evolution of basketball. During the NCAA championships between 1959 and 1961 I would sneak down into the basement of our home in North Olmsted late at night, turn on the TV to watch the Ohio State Buckeyes with stars such as Jerry Lucas, John Havlicheck, Bobby Knight (yes, that Bobby Knight), and Larry Seigfried. They won it all in 1959 only to lose in the Championship finals in 1960 and 61. However, when one turns on to Classic Sports on

ESPN and watches these magnificent early players there is a noticeable difference in the manner basketball was played back then compared to today? The early players set a standard of play that later coaches and players built upon. In this manner centers such as Dwight Howard learned from Shaquille O'Neal who learned from Kareem Abdul Jabbar, who learned from Jerry Lucas, Wilt Chamberlain, and Bill Russell who learned from George Mikan. Yes, there is an undeniable progression in the evolution of the game.

This exemplifies the positive benefits of "look and learn" for one can take the proven principles and practices of predecessors through honest evaluation in order to make the expression better. One can improve upon the performances of those who went before. As a result, individuals should explore the experiences of others and society itself should learn from an honest evaluation of history. People should gain valuable insights from the past. This would hold true for an appraisal of philosophies, movements, institutions, and the origination, expansion and fall of nations. In this manner Christian Actualism analyzes the movements of Christian Abolitionism and Activism to discover what was right, just, fair and good to bring in Biblically Theistic societal correction for today.

However, as one can learn from the positive expression of others it is also possible to select the wrong persons and paradigms to learn from. In one such occurrence we were talking to a ten year old boy in a project area in Dallas. We asked him what do you want to be when you grow up? Without hesitation or shame he proudly pronounced, "I want to be a whore pimp." What? Why? In this boys experience the men he observed driving the "biggest and baddest" cars, the males who had the "finest" women on their arms and demonstrated "power" were the whore pimps. Does this not reveal a flaw in gaining knowledge from look and learn? Present appearances and superficial reasoning may prove deceptive in the long run once the foolishness of a decision or the wrongdoing of a behavior comes to its damaging and destructive conclusion. There is danger into buying into the newest, latest philosophy or way of behaving. The naïve among us have yet to learn that observation.

Yes, knowledge acquired from observation of negative behavior is beneficial to keep one from making the same mistake. One is to learn by seeing the eventual outcome of a path chosen or a behavior practiced to keep from making a false judgment from a momentary existential experience. In observation one must look for the end result – the eventual outcome. Proverbs speaks of this awareness in chapter 24:30-34.

> "I passed by the field of the sluggard, and by the vineyard of the man lacking sense; and behold, it was completely overgrown with thistles, its surface was covered with nettles, and its stone wall was broken down. When I saw this, I reflected upon it; I looked and received instruction. 'A little sleep, a little slumber, a little folding of the hands to rest.' Then your poverty will come as a robber, and your want like an armed man."

Observation or "look and learn" gains knowledge from the experiences and outcomes of others. However one must watch the ending and read the final chapter of the book. The principle of receiving knowledge from "look and learn" must include the historical outcomes to be expected from practicing a belief or a behavior. In this manner "look and learn" may also address the philosophies, principles, and practices being propagated by a person, a party, a community or a nation. Thorough historical analysis sheds light upon where the proposition, promise, or paradigm actually leads people in the end. In this a great error of American conservatism and liberalism lies in its resistance and refusal to evaluate the historical and present and future expressions and directions of our people. It is time for honest appraisal.

If there is an identifiable negative conclusion to the journey then does not the ignoring of such outcomes reveal the arrogance of man as he plunges himself and others down a stream that history affirms turns into a a river, then a torrent, and eventually a cascade plunging over a waterfall? What makes this new group of travelers any different from those who preceded them? If history records an inevitability of a negative end then what will make this "new" venture which plunges down the same faulty waterway any different? Honest historical evaluation is needed for if the ending is calamitous then would it not be wise to reject the paradigm or practice?

There is no question that people can gain knowledge from "live and learn' (trial and error) and 'look and learn' (observing others). Both of these means of acquiring knowledge are within the realm of human experience and exploration. However, there is a third means to acquire data.

Third, people can gain knowledge through the intentional teaching of another; i.e., you can obtain data by means of "learn and live." This approach to acquiring information comes from instructional authority. The one offering intentional teaching may be a parent, sibling, friend, professor, pastor, even a person on the corner. Whoever provides you with content for your intellectual or implementational ingestion fits this description.

However, keep in mind authoritative knowledge is only as good as its source. For instance, consider the following instruction this author presented in a recent conference on Biblical wisdom:

> "If you desire to learn how to play the game of golf you can acquire knowledge from men such as these. (The power point immediately shows a picture of the Three Stooges playing golf.) Now, you can learn to play golf by means of the Three Stooges instruction, but is this the source you desire to gain proficiency in playing the game of golf? In many ways this resembles the process of acquiring information on how to live from men on the corner. Men on the corner will share with you their knowledge about life, marriage, parenting, business, politics, religion, justice, fairness. They will philosophize with you about their data. However, think about this. If the knowledge coming from these men is so profound, so worthy then why are they still on the corner? What happened to their life, their spouse, their children, their business? Be ever so careful about gaining your knowledge from the men on the corner. However, if you want to learn about comedy, the Three Stooges supply you with an abundant authoritative source for slap stick humor – but golf? Why have these men be your authority base?

> With authoritative learning, you can gain knowledge in becoming a golfer. You can learn data from the Three Stooges or you can learn from a man such as this: (In the conference I put up a power point of Tiger Woods hitting a driver in his victorious record breaking 2001 Masters win.) The authenticity of this man's knowledge in golf would give you priceless lessons in the art of swinging your clubs. If you have the availability of gaining data from a man such as Tiger Woods it would be foolish not to garner all the information you can from his insights into the golf swing. However, you might want to consider another source to acquire advice on marital fidelity."

Now, Proverbs, as the entirety of the Biblical canon, discloses its authoritative teachings come not from the mind and heart of man but from the very mind and heart of the Creator God as Proverbs 2:6-8 states:

'For the Lord is the one who gives wisdom, from His mouth come knowledge and understanding, He stores up sound wisdom for the upright, He is a shield to those who walk in integrity.'"

Therefore, the data afforded in proverbial knowledge claims to be divinely inspired. As a result, the complete meaning of da'at in Proverbs 1:2a is to know life as God created and designed it to be specifically in the practical day in and day out expressions of living.

Therefore, when one comes to Scripture the acquisition of data through "learn and live" rises to the highest authority. Man can gain understanding through revelation. Revelation is God's unveiling of Himself, His will, and His ways of living to man, disclosing that which would otherwise by unknown or unsure into the realm of human reasoning, certainty, and behaving.

When I was sixteen years of age my father passed away. At the viewing, after everyone left for the night I stayed behind to be alone with my dad. I went up to the casket, looked down at his face and asked, "Dad. What should I do now?" Although I knew my dad could not answer, what I was calling out for was guidance. I needed direction in the practical outworking of daily life. "What now dad?" What I was calling out for although I did not know it at the time was to hear a word from God in the practical day in and day out aspects of life.

This is precisely the knowledge that our heavenly Father determines to communicate to man in the da'at of Proverbs; i.e., in the practical knowledge of living right now. The wisdom of the Lord revealed to you in the midst of your pilgrimage, joys, troubles, successes, failings, decision making, marriage, pain, parenting, business, leadership, ministry. In its authoritative instruction Proverbs brings to your awareness information not according to the whims of man but from God Himself.

Lauren's false start story provides a visual of a life truism. Pertinent knowledge underscores essential living. Failure to know relevant data proves costly for when crucial content is absent that piece of missing knowledge peaks at the precise point when it is needed the most, and when that absent information is not actualized people err, life goes awry and others take notice. It is necessary to the wellness of human living for people to grasp, to acquire, to gain, the vital information for any particular event of the human experience.

You know this from your own experience. Tell me how far along in your race did you go before you became aware that there were gaps in your knowledge base? When did you begin to discover flaws and failings in your personal understanding of how life works and how to live better? Is there not a data deficiency in your personal story? Did you not observe the lack in your own pilgrimage?

The problem of missing knowledge intensifies for you personally because you possess only one try at this thing called life. This is your moment on the track. As your seconds, minutes, years tick by you cannot reclaim it. Once your time is gone it is irretrievable. You cannot get back into the blocks and run it again. Furthermore the outcome of such data deficiency causes regret. You look back on certain episodes, paragraphs, chapters of your life and think: "If only I had known how to respond, how to love, how to care, how to parent, how to lead." Now, if that knowledge was actually available wouldn't you have wanted to obtain it?

All of us could have benefited from instruction in the practical, appropriate, relevant knowledge in how to run that particular part of our race better. However, while we understand that the past cannot be re-run, we can do something about the now. Therefore, if knowledge is available to us in our present situation would it not be good to gain it? Would it not be wise to get coached up in it? Why screw the next part up? However where do we go to gain the essential coaching?

Please realize the informational ocean presented in man's quest to acquire data appears inexhaustible. Dissemination of knowledge comes at us in volumes and volumes of never ending informational waves. Tidbits of fact and fiction never stop. In this cascade of encyclopedic content mankind becomes absorbed and overwhelmed. There is so much to know and far too much of the info appears unnecessary.

For instance, the term da'at is derived from the Hebrew root yada which carries the primary meaning of knowledge. When one considers the immensity of information afforded to humans today - from newspapers to libraries - from talk radio to twitter - from TV to wikipedia – from google to yahoo to Drudge one can readily understand the colloquialism "yada-yada-yada"; otherwise interpreted TMI – too much information. Such overflow of content is what Solomon expressed in Ecclesiastes 12:12,

> "...my son, be warned: the writing of many books is endless, and excessive devotion to books is wearying to the body."

With that sentiment realize Solomon never encountered Youtube. Today, with modern man's never ending expansion of facts and figures, theories and opinions, percentages and principles it is all the more important for people to discern the knowledge that is truly essential for living. It is in that arena of essential, necessary, relevant knowledge God determines to impart to man in Proverbs; i.e., the fundamental guidance to live life well - not in the by and by, but in the here and now, or as existential relativists refer - the living day.

So what actually is the essential knowledge given to humanity in Proverbs?

In Proverbs 1:2a we discover the da'at, the yada, the knowledge of Proverbs is two-fold:

"to know wisdom and instruction"

It is the combination of **wisdom and instruction** that forms the core of content God desires to impart to man in Proverbs. Both are distinct knowledge components. The Hebrew term for wisdom is **hokmah**. Hokmah (wisdom) presents the information of God's performance skills in order to excel in living. The Hebrew term for instruction is **musar**. Musar (instruction) coaches man in the morality of human decency. This ethical component of musar is clearly identified in Proverbs 1:3, the third purpose statement of the book which states:

> "to receive instruction in wise behavior, righteousness, justice, and equity..."

> For clarity here's the verse with the Hebrew definitions in parenthesis:

> "to receive instruction (musar – moral coaching) in wise behavior (haskel – how to live successfully), righteousness (sedek- the pinnacle of God's perfections, the Mt. Everest of human

experience), justice (mispat- correction; i.e., when mispat is used with sedeq in the same phrase or sentence, mispat takes on the meaning of the restoration of righteousness), and equity (mesharim – fairness).

To gain insight into the moral implications of musar think if we as a nation had implemented God's ethics of righteousness, justice, and equity with African Americans at the inception of our nation. Imagine how different things would have been and would be today.

Understand how proverbial wisdom and moral coaching work in unison

It is in the actualization of both performance skill and human decency which our heavenly Father determines to teach humans through His "Buyer Buys" and "Buyer Bewares" of Proverbs. Working together the two knowledge components of hokmah and musar are crafted to transform personal, family, and societal living in the present.

Consider the partnership of the wisdom (hokmah) and moral discipline (musar) of Proverbs like a well thrown combination in boxing. Followers of boxing know that almost all great punchers possess a dominant knockout hand – either left or right. Joe Frazier owned a potent left hook – ask Jimmy Ellis or Muhammad Ali. Rocky Marciano a devastating right cross – ask Jersey Joe Walcott. Very few fighters possessed dynamite in both hands such as a Joe Louis, George Forman, and Mike Tyson.

While attending the International School of Theology with Campus Crusade for Christ, I ministered as a Christian Education Director at Community Church of God in San Bernardino, California. There I became good friends with Assistant Pastor, Reverend Maynus. Reverend Maynus was a former middle-weight prize fighter. Even then in his early fifties, he stood a muscular block of a man. I asked him about his boxing career, "Reverend Maynus, how good were you? Did you possess a knock-out punch? What was your dominant hand?" He replied, "Brother Howard, I packed dynamite in both hands."

Like Reverend Maynus, Proverbs packs God's power of knowledge in both hands. His right hand communicates His wisdom while His left hand instructs people in moral discipline. Together this right/left combination is revealed by God not to devastate man on the canvas, but to lift him up above the fray to greater heights of human living as Proverbs 3:13-18 states:

> 13 "How blessed is the man who finds wisdom, and the man who gains understanding. 14 For its profit is better than the profit of silver, and its gain than fine gold. 15 She [wisdom] is more precious than jewels' and nothing you desire compares with her. 16 Long life is in her right hand; in her left hand are riches and honor. 17 Her ways are pleasant ways, and all her paths are peace. 18 She is a tree of life to those who take hold of her, and happy are all who hold her fast."

With all its wonderful benefits offered to humanity I submit such proverbial data is the missing link of present expressions of Biblical Theism. In the same manner the knowledge of how to run that 100 meter race was there for the taking, but Lauren's coach failed to communicate essential data to her, so Christian teachers have not adequately coached up the Body of Christ to actualize the truths and goodness of proverbial wisdom and moral coaching. As a result believers are trying to live with insufficient understanding of how life is designed to work. There are gaps in the Biblical data base.

We are not adequately coached up (discipled) in the knowledge of God's wisdom and moral teaching to live successfully, rightly, justly, fairly before the Lord and with one another.

As a result, there is failure to actualize God's wisdom and His ethical discipline. This lack lessens the actualization of human potential. Furthermore, I assert that modern man's resistance and refusal to discern and implement proverbial knowledge is the underlying cause for the breakdown in the quality of people's lives, the dysfunction within our families, the poor performances of our schools, the collapsing of our economy, the decaying morality among our people, the ineffectual governing of our nation, and all the other myriad of troubles that afflict us today in America as well. Today we across our nation are all suffering the negative consequences from data deficiency. Our failings as persons, families, and a people are witnessed by the global community.

Just how missing is proverbial knowledge across our American experience today?

In order to expose the degree in which God's data of wisdom is absent across our American experience, I will demonstrate this fault not by focusing upon obvious cases of secularism such as: agnosticism, atheism, or anti-theism. These examples of dismissing God's wisdom are too numerous and too easily made. Also, I will not give attention in this chapter to how Biblical wisdom is being bypassed, shunned and even over ruled by modern liberalism whether by persons, movements or institutions inside or outside the Church. Instead, I will make the case of wisdom's absence by means of historic Christian fundamentalism – Christian conservatism - Evangelicalism.

In this regard, would it not be fair to postulate that if any group of Christ professing people should have actualized the truths and goodness of Proverbs it would be the Biblical conservative? After all does not Christian fundamentalism assert that the Bible is to be interpreted literally and followed faithfully? Therefore, if we establish that proverbial knowledge is missing in present and historic forms of Christian conservatism then I submit we solidify the premise that the knowledge of God's wisdom is absent in all arenas of American culture as well.

Let's Start with my Alma Mater

In pursuing my graduate studies at Dallas Theological Seminary, I studied extensively the writings of Dr. Lewis Sperry Chafer, the founder of DTS. During my last year at the seminary, I made a personal commitment to listen over and over to all of Dr. Chafer's tapes that the library contained. It was unmistakable the love and devotion this man possessed toward the Lord and His Word. His teachings especially concerning the grace of God and Spirit filled living marked me.

In discussing Dr. Chafer with the older professors who sat under his teaching, I discovered how deeply loved and respected he was by his former students. I remember speaking with Dr. Dwight Pentecost, head of the Bible Exposition Department of my enjoyment in listening to Chafer's tapes. As we spoke, tears welled up in his eyes as he expressed his love and respect for Chafer and the impact the founder of the seminary had upon his personal life and ministry. On another occasion, Dr. Howard Hendricks spoke fondly of how Chafer regularly would have students over to his home for times of friendship, prayer and discussion. On one visit to his home, Hendricks said a couple students discovered that Chafer and his wife had an empty refrigerator. In discussing this later the students realized that Dr. and Mrs. Chafer sacrificed financially even to the point of going without food to help establish the seminary. From that moment on students would secretly leave bags of groceries at their door. Make no mistake when it comes to Dr. Chafer we are dealing with a man who truly desired to honor the Lord. He marked his men and they loved him for it.

Now, Chafer's establishment of Dallas Theological Seminary in 1924 proved seminal in the formation and advancement of the conservative, fundamentalist Christian movement. The impact of DTS over the years in training Bible believing pastors, teachers, professors, missionaries, para-church leaders throughout America and around the world is undeniable. Millions have benefited from the intense equipping of this God honoring institution. If you have been blessed by the teachings and writings of a Dr. Donald Campbell, Dr. Jackie Deere, Dr. Tony Evans, Dr. Gene Getz, Dr. Howard Hendricks, Hal Lindsey, Dr. J.P. Moreland, Dr. Dwight Pentecost, Dr. Ramesh Richard, Dr. Charles Ryrie, Dr. Ray Stedman, Dr. Chuck Swindol, Dr. Bruce Waltke, Dr. John Walvoord, etc., then you have benefitted from a DTS graduate.

Chafer the Theologian

During his tenure as president of Dallas Theological Seminary, Dr. Chafer penned a formidable eight volume, two thousand seven hundred and fifty-two page work on Systematic Theology. In this endeavor, he disclosed his undeniable devotion to Christ and in depth knowledge of Christian dogma. As with all systematic theologians, Chafer sought to categorize and systematize the teachings of the Christian faith in their entirety, and present these truths in a logical, organized manner so that people might know the meaning of the Word, come to Christ, and live rightly before God. In Volume One, Chafer defined Systematic Theology when he wrote:

> "Systematic Theology…incorporates a complete consideration…of the essentials of each [Biblical] doctrine with due recognition of the relation of each doctrine to every other doctrine."

> Preface. viii, Vol. 1
> Chafer, Systematic Theology, Vol. 1, p. 17.

Specifically, in this magnificent work Chafer spelled out the great doctrines of the Christian faith such as: Anthropology, Bibliology, Christology, Ecclesiology, Eschatology, Pneumatology, Soteriology, and Theology Proper. Chafer wrote extensively concerning the deity of Christ, His death and resurrection. He offered solid evidence for the infallibility and inerrancy of Scripture. He wrote of man's desperate need for saving faith and instructed believers in Spirit filled living. He challenged the Church to evangelism, prayer, and missions. In each of these areas, Dr. Chafer presented the Word of God with clearly defined meaning and application to the personal condition of the human experience.

(Theology = ology means study, theos means God- theology therefore means study of God; anthropology – anthros = man, study of man; Bibliology – study of the Bible; Christology – study of Christ; Ecclesiology- study of the Church; Eschatology – study of the end times; Pneumatology – study of the Spirit; Soteriology, study of salvation; Theology Proper – study of God Himself.)

Certainly the size and scope of Chafer's effort, as with all Systematic Theologies, is truly honorable and beneficial to the study of God and His will toward man. For those of us who embrace the Biblical God and His Word the founder of Dallas Theological Seminary produced a most admirable work indeed. I thank God for my years under the teachings of DTS.

However, there remains potential pitfalls to an endeavor aiming to "incorporate a **complete** consideration...of the essentials of each [Biblical] doctrine with due recognition of the relation of each doctrine to every other doctrine?" One such danger lies in the consequence that occurs if there is error (and what human does not err) in the knowledge presented in the systematic theology itself. Inaccuracy in handling Scripture can occur by what is taught and what is not. Error can arise from either commission or omission.

If a certain Biblical principle is absent from the data base of Systematic theology then its truth is not considered, and if it is not considered then it is not defined, and if it is not defined then its meaning fails to be connected to any of the other doctrines. As a result, the missing truth does not influence the reasoning of the theologians; it is not studied in the seminaries; it is not defended by the Biblical apologists; it is not preached from the pulpits; it is not communicated in the discipling of believers. Therefore with respect to that missing theological component that form of Christianity is not accurately defined, believed, and practiced by believers within that sphere of teaching. There emerges a knowledge gap between the actual Biblical kerygma (content), the communication of the Word (exposition), and the conduct of the saints (experience). Minus the dissemination of this revealed Scriptural truth actual Christian thinking and living becomes marred.

Please note that nowhere is this distortion the fault of Scripture. The problem lies in man's misinterpretation and misapplication of the Bible. As a result, if the theological construct contains error, no matter how slight, the inaccuracy will negatively affect the beliefs and behaviors of the people, denominations, and institutions connected to that particular teaching.

Such an interpretive and implementational flaw would be especially harmful to the teachings of conservative Christianity for fundamentalists proclaim that their exegesis and exposition of the text represents the pure, literal meaning of the Word of God. As a result of this declaration of truth, many people view conservative theology to represent what the Bible says in its most straightforward, literally defined form.

Chafer and Proverbs

Now, with awareness of such consequences let us consider Dr. Chafer's work with respect to the knowledge of God in the book of Proverbs. In Chafer's eighth volume, the key Biblical verses used throughout his two thousand seven hundred and fifty-two page work are cited. One discovers in perusing this section that the verses cited from the book of Genesis are extensive, taking up an entire page of the index. From the multitude of verses used there is no question that Chafer drew heavily from the data of God from the Book of Genesis. His inclusion of Scripture is even more weighted from the book of Romans which verse citations fill up a page and a half of the index. One also discovers that Chafer analyzed thirty-eight key verses and passages from the book of Revelation giving intensive study and declarations concerning the end times. However, when one comes to the book of Proverbs, there are no verse citations whatsoever - absolutely none – nada – zilch – zero.

Therefore, in Chafer's two thousand seven hundred and fifty-two pages of Systematic Theology, the principles and practices disclosed by God in the book of Proverbs are absent – they are not there. There is no definition of the meaning or detailed application of God's wisdom to any other doctrine of Scripture or insights into how Proverbs affects Christian living and societal goodness. In other words, what Proverbs brings to the table in the revelation of God to man remains missing. The place of Scriptural wisdom is absent in Chafer's most formative conservative work. As a result people under the guidance of this form of Systematic Theology have a missing, absent data deficiency when they line up to run the race of glorifying God. The practical, temporal wisdom and moral teachings of the Lord, explaining the day in and day out living of the faith lies dormant, even displaced in his fundamental construct of dispensational systematic theology. As a result, the wisdom and moral coaching of our Creator in guiding man in the marketplace of human activity becomes removed or relegated to lesser relevancy in such a theological paradigm.

Fundamentalism and Proverbs

Please realize that this lack of connecting Proverbial wisdom and goodness to doctrine and deed is not limited to the writings of Chafer for this void is characteristic in other theological works of early American Christian fundamentalism. Take for instance the most foundational work of the conservative movement titled: The Fundamentals, a twelve volume series originally published from 1910-1915. Of this work, Dr. Warren W. Wiersbe, former president of Moody Bible Institute, writes concerning the purpose of the original scholarly proponents of fundamentalism:

> "From May 25 to June 1 1919, six thousand people met in Philadelphia at 'The World Conference on Christian Fundamentals.' W. H. Griffith Thomas chaired the Resolution Committee, and among the fifteen well known speakers on the program were W.B. Riley, R. A. Torrey, Lewis Sperry Chafer, James M. Gray and William L. Pettingill. Delegates came from 42 states and most of the Canadian provinces, as well as seven foreign countries." Said W. B. Riley in his first address, 'The future will look back to the World Conference on Christian Fundamentals…as an event of more historical moment than the nailing up, at Wittenberg, of Martin Luther's ninety-five theses. The hour has struck for the rise of a new Protestantism."

In 1958 Kregel Publications updated this conservative twelve volume work in its newer edition of The Fundamentals. This condensed work contained 64 chapters, expanding over seven hundred pages of theological writings, explaining the doctrines of conservative Christianity. The work is a formidable, intelligent, theological treatise putting forth the positions of "literal" Biblical dogma. It is a work well done.

However, when it comes to the book of Proverbs in its 710 pages of theological teachings there is only one verse cited from the entire book of Proverbs. Think of this omission: one verse paraphrased from Scriptural wisdom implanted on page 679. Think of the absence of this - just one verse in a sixty-four chapter theological treatise defining fundamental Christianity.

As a result, the guidance of Proverbial teachings addressing proper ethical human behavior including personal integrity, neighborly living, community responsibility, and social justice fell outside the sphere of fundamentalist concern and became muted, undisclosed in the essentials. The complete fundamentals of the faith have missing data. There is a lack of bringing before Bible believing people the knowledge that God affords to man in Proverbs.

Now please note: in this historical exposing of Systematic Theology's lack of handling the wisdom of Proverbs properly, this author finds no contradiction or confusion over the well-defined doctrines of orthodoxy. These are accepted. They are not challenged. The fundamentals as exposited uphold clearly defined teachings of the Word once delivered to the saints. The truths about Christ, salvation, the Bible are to be embraced, endorsed and enabled.

However, with that established, let it be noted there is a serious flaw in American conservative theology concerning its handling of the wisdom books and writings of Scripture. When fundamentalism missed the Proverbial knowledge that God determined to impart to man in the marketplace of human interaction, certain teachings of Scripture were missed or relegated to lesser status in the Christian expressions of literalists – the very people who should have exegeted and exposited the marvelous truths of God's design for human day by day living.

When I posit this assertion let it be noted that it is not that fundamentalists failed to write commentaries on the wisdom books, however, the wisdom books and writings of Scripture are not included in the systematics themselves. The wisdom teachings are not embedded in the systematic platform of Protestant orthodoxy. They are excluded from the discussion of Biblical thought and congruent behavior. As a result, the wisdom writings become inconsequential to the actual play calling of conservative theologians. The teachings of the Bible concerning the eternal destiny of man were uplifted, exegeted and exposited while the teachings of the Word concerning the temporal were neglected even dismissed. The wisdom books came to have a second class status among God's revelation to man.

To begin to correct this error the wisdom writings must be given their proper status in Systematic Theology and how their principles are divinely crafted to influence the practical everyday outworking of living rightly, justly, and fairly before God and man. To overcome this knowledge deficiency, one does not subtract from the fundamentals of the faith that have been analyzed, but one does need to add at least two more fundamentals (more on this later).

A legitimate question arises as to why the knowledge of Proverbs is so lacking in the fundamentals of American conservative Christianity. Why did literalists fumble the guidance of God's wisdom in the practical day by day actions for human living? One historical reason is that American fundamentalism arose to defend the Bible against the atheistic and liberal attacks of their day which denied orthodox doctrines such as: the existence of God, creation, the deity, death and resurrection of Christ, the infallibility and inerrancy of the Word, the call for personal salvation, etc. In their determination to defend the Savior and the Scriptures, fundamentalists limited their focus of apologetics primarily upon one's individual relationship with Christ, the authority of the Bible, and the eternal issues concerning salvation.

However, because of conservatives single mindedness to defend the faith against liberal and atheistic attack, because of their focus upon individual salvation and personal Christian experience, I submit this is one reason why the wisdom writings, such as the book of Proverbs, which focused on present needs and deeds rather than eternal dogma fell into a state of doctrinal irrelevance. If as the old gospel lyric "the world is not my home I'm just a passing through" truly represents the actual condition of spiritual living then why the need for a practical daily guidebook for living in the present?

Now, this line of reasoning gives only partial explanation for why the wisdom writings were not included in conservative's defining and delineating of the fundamentals of the faith. There is a disconcerting reason that arises to one's awareness. Why weren't the wisdom teachings of God inserted and applied to areas of our American way of living that were in violation of the truths and goodness of Scripture? If the wisdom and moral goodness of God would have been preached, taught, and communicated it certainly would have revealed actual disconnects even violations between Biblical truth and practices. Practitioners of such clearly defined wrongs, when confronted by their iniquitous ways would have had to deal with their sin. However, when the truths are not exposited then the teachings of God's wisdom and moral coaching, which are still relevant in the age of the Church would have countered such iniquities and called for the repentance of Christ's followers. However, untouched, they are left unspoken, non-preached, irrelevant, even unknown by "Biblical" followers. We have a problem here. With such missing knowledge concerning the Lord's revelation, are we knowing the Biblical God as He has truly revealed Himself to be and are we seeing, experiencing true Christian living?

I submit, the fundamentalist, the conservative Christian movement failed in proclaiming the temporal principles and practices of the wisdom books and writings of Scripture. As a result, there was a flaw in the way Evangelicals handled the Word of Truth in this particular disclosure from the Almighty. They failed in bringing the revealed wisdom and moral guidance of God into the actual marketplace of man.

With this said, please realize that just as there are eternal consequences in failing to trust in Christ there are temporal consequences in failing to apply the wisdom of God in the here and now. Therefore, when conservatism missed the knowledge of what God determined to impart to man in Proverbs there was a distortion of actual Biblical living by the followers of the Lord.

For instance, the knowledge of Proverbs would have provided the conservative movement with a more Bibical sense of community responsibility. Literalists would have possessed God's divine guidance to address and overcome societal dysfunction and evil as well as personal piety. Think with me on this, if the knowledge of Proverbs had been taught concerning caring for your neighbor, treating the poor, and connected with the New Testament call for believers to serve one another as co-equals and partners in the body of Christ, if these truths would have been articulated and applied during the eras of American slavery and segregation would not the mandate of Scriptural obedience have immediately called all members of conservative White evangelical Christians, Churches, and denominations to stop the racial bigotry and wrongful actions against African Americans?

However, whether through ignorance or willful refusal the Biblical teachings discovered in the wisdom and moral coaching of Proverbs, as well as other wisdom writings such as the Sermon on the Mount failed to appear on the conservative plate to guide its doctrines and deeds. Wisdom's directives were muted on these and other vital personal and social issues.

When did the bypassing of God's wisdom in the here and now enter into Protestantism? Realize that the seminal seed of the lessening of the wisdom writings and their contribution to human living can be traced all the way back to the originations of Protestantism itself. This can be attested by Martin Luther's dissing the relevancy of the New Testament wisdom book of James which he relegated its significance in the canon as having the theological weight of straw. Therefore, in lowering the status of the wisdom writings, fundamentalist theologians, continuing in the way of Luther and the originations of Protestantism, relegated the wisdom Scriptures to second class citizenship in the Biblical canon.

However, since a major thrust of American fundamentalism was founded and fostered in the southern states, a serious concern arises whether the void of applying Scriptural wisdom to societal wrongdoing was left muted because of other reasons besides Biblical interpretation –such as racial bigotry. Tragically, when the evidence is presented I submit it is not unthinkable to arrive at the conclusion that cultural preference and racial bias provided an underlying reason for the absence of implementing Scriptural wisdom and moral teachings clearly defined in the New Testament such as "Love your Brother" fairly and equally toward African Americans.

It is historically affirmable that conservative believers in our nation's past were not challenged by the applications of the very Scriptures which would have exposed and countered such harmful human practices in the evils of American slavery and segregation. However, divorced from the Scripture's which would have called individual believers and the Church as a body to confession and correction, many white fundamental believers, their Churches and denominations remained indifferent, oblivious, even hostile to blacks suffering under iniquitous human evils.

As a result, conservative theology and practice, absent of the principles and practices of Proverbial wisdom, proved to be an unfaithful "friend"; even a contrarian to the wellbeing of blacks weighed down by unjust societal structures and oppression. Worse still fundamentalism not only fell prey to the sins and shortcomings of the past and the status quo of the present, many in the movement, even the theologians and the institutions themselves participated and led in the continuation of the wrongdoing.

Sadly, this serves to demonstrate that when believers adopt the mores of a surrounding culture they often will adjust the meaning of the Word and bend its applications to fit the contemporary view, or what benefits their group. To justify their personal bias and social position conservatives and liberals alike fall prey to such improper handling of the Scriptures. Conservatism falls prey to the wrongful practices of the past while liberalism falls prey to the wrongful thinking and "progression" of the present. In their violation of Biblical truth and goodness both lead to a lessening of life; i.e., the life the Lord intends for man to experience.

Please realize the problem is not God. The wrongness does not lie in the Scriptures. The error lies with man. There is so much more the Lord intends for humans and society to experience than the present paradigms of conservative, liberal, and moderate Christianity. Deviation from the Lord and His Word through any of those failing paradigms results in misrepresentation of the actual meaning of Scripture as well as a continual lessening even suffering incurred by people under such wrongful interpretation and implementation.

Let it be established then that the wisdom books of Scripture such as Proverbs and the New Testament Epistle of James, the wisdom writings such as the Sermon on the Mount, are revealed to teach believers how to be earthly good while they are headed for their glorious eternal destiny. The wisdom writings call Christians to combine the call of the Good News of forgiveness and eternal life to all those who trust in Christ to also take meaningful action for personal and social righteousness and justice in the now. As a result, we as redeemed believers, freed from eternal consequences of sin and of death, are to represent the goodness, justice, fairness and righteousness of God in standing up for the outcast, the hurt, the needful, the innocent.

For instance, consider how Scriptural wisdom speaks concerning the most public parts of societal living such as its directives in treating the poor and the needy. In this analysis realize the degree of recovery and refinement the wisdom and moral coaching of Proverbs offers to the disadvantaged among us. In this regard there are at least twenty-seven directives given from chapters ten to thirty-one concerning the poor. The following lists only the sayings designating a person's right and wrong behavior toward the downtrodden.

> "...blessed is he who is kind to the needy." 14:21
> "He who oppresses the poor shows contempt for their Maker, but whoever is kind to the needy honors God." 14:31
> "A generous man will himself be blessed, for he shares his food with the poor." 22:9
> "Do not exploit the poor because they are poor and do not crush the needy in court." 22:22
> "A ruler who oppresses the poor is like a driving rain that leaves no crops." 28:3
> "The righteous care about justice for the poor..." 29:7
> "If a king judges the poor with fairness, his throne will always be secure." 29:14
> "[There are those]...whose jaws are set with knives to devour the poor from the earth, the needy from among mankind." 30:14
> "Speak up and judge fairly, defend the rights of the poor and needy." 31:9
> "She extends her hand to the poor; and she stretches out her hands to the needy." 31:20

Just a simple reading of these sayings reveals that a righteous person engages in respecting and helping the poor and afflicted in their need. Such moral coaching coincides with other teachings of Scripture establishing that the virtues in assisting disadvantaged people lie inherent in actual Biblical Theism. Thus, the Christian who engages such behaviors follows the way of their Master as Christ portrayed Himself, giving evidence to John the Baptist that He was the Messiah in Luke 7:20-23:

> 20"And when the men had come to Him [Jesus], they said, 'John the Baptist has sent us to You, saying, 'Are You the Expected One, or do we look for someone else?' 21 At that very time He cured many people of diseases and afflictions and evil spirits; and He granted sight to many who were blind.
>
> 22 And He answered and said to them, 'Go and report to John what you have seen and heard; the blind receive sight, the lame walk, the lepers are cleansed, and the dear hear, the dead are raised up, the poor have the gospel preached to them. 23 And blessed is he who keeps from stumbling over Me.'"

Throughout the Bible the God of creation, the God of eternity, the God of the here and now, the God who brought salvation to man through the death and resurrection of Christ carried out His ministry of caring for the needy, the afflicted, the poor, the disadvantaged. He died in the place of sinners; i.e., sinners like you and me, and he ministered to people in need.

The book of Proverbs then provides all believers in Christ, and people everywhere a playbook of much needed knowledge. It is time to fill in the missing knowledge and coach up the saints in the wisdom and moral coaching of God. As a result, there is great need to bring the wisdom of the Lord into the discipleship of believers. There is great need to bring the moral coaching of God into the center of our Republic.

Now, please realize in this work there is not an attempt to go back. In this determination many of our conservative citizens argue that our nation needs to go back to its roots. However, for many other Americans the past is not a safe or desired place to be. What Native American would desire to replay the genocide march of Andrew Jackson's "Trail of Tears?" What African American would want our nation to return to its iniquitous era of slavery or segregation? Who among the poor would relish the yesterday of child labor when their precious eight year old sons and daughters suffered twelve hour shifts deep down in our nation's coal mines?

While the call to return to the past or retain the status quo of the present may appear grandiose for those who profited under the old system such a call to return to our glory days of yesteryear is undesirable, even detestable for the many who suffered during those same era's. For many Americans the past is something best left behind. However, this does not mean that we "throw the baby out with the bath water." So much of our American experience should be heralded, embraced, and engaged such as our Declaration of Independence which presents the best virtues of our Republic when it states: "All men are created equal" and that "it is undeniable that God has given to man inalienable rights of life, liberty, and the pursuit of happiness."

Yes, proverbial knowledge heralds the virtues of Biblical Theism, cleaning up the mistakes of the past and leading us forward to better living. In the same manner the data of how to run that 100 meter race was there for the taking, but Lauren's coach failed to communicate essential data to her, so our Christian teachers have not adequately coached up the Body of Christ to actualize the truths and goodness of proverbial wisdom and moral living. As a result we are trying to live out our lives with insufficient understanding of how life is designed to work. We were not prepared in the principles of God's wisdom and moral teachings revealed in Proverbs. There are gaps in our understanding of how life works. We are not adequately coached in Proverbial knowledge by our Christian teachers in how to live successfully, rightly, justly, fairly with one another in the now.

Therefore, when it comes to the knowledge of God's wisdom from one degree to another all American's suffer from inadequate coaching. We come out of the blocks absent of revealed knowledge given by our Lord in how to live in the here and now. We are void of pertinent data relevant in how to run our race of life well. How we need the knowledge of God's wisdom and moral guidance. We suffer from a case of missing knowledge. With this said, let us now begin to define what Proverbial knowledge really is, how it works, and how if engaged will better our lives, families, communities, and country.

While there is nothing new about man missing knowledge, if the data is actually available to address and overcome our present state of personal and communal cacophony, then the absence of actualizing that particular data is unnecessary and the resulting human harm and subsequent debilitating of human progress is preventable.

Therefore, like Lauren misfiring in her sprint, the problem does not lie in the available data base but in the dissemination of the knowledge that exists. In these cases the problem is not one of existing knowledge but a failure of coaching in the necessary information. We are not being taught in what is already known. If the knowledge exists in how to guide humans to live well both personally and socially, if this is accurate then do not all people, all communities, all nations need this coaching to implant into the activity of human thought and action such information for living well?

Would this not be especially the case if the Almighty God, the Creator God, the God and Savior of our lives actually shared with man His wisdom, His coaching in how people, communities, even nations are to live well? However, where do we gain the coaching to improve our condition as a nation? I submit that such divine knowledge is available to people and is discovered in the Old Testament book of Proverbs and the wisdom writings of Scripture.

In our secular experiment today, fully charging our American experience, our citizenry, neighborhoods, institutions, commerce, governance, judges, communities are running the race of life missing key, necessary knowledge that God has disclosed in the wisdom and moral coaching of Proverbs. From the African American to the Caucasian - from the Native American to the Latino, from the Arab to the Asian to the Jew – all of us whether conservative, moderate or liberal, whether Republican, Democrat, Libertarian or Independent, whether believer or unbeliever are running the race of life with a severe case of knowledge lack from a failure to be coached up in the temporal wisdom of Proverbs. The knowledge is there, but it is not being actualized. We are failing to teach the revealed principles and practices of Proverbs in how to live well.

We have given the book of Proverbs away

When I would speak at the Union Gospel Mission, if a man came to Christ I would give him a pocket Bible. One night before preaching at the mission I discovered I had run out of these smaller Scriptures. My wife however, had a nice, white pocket Bible displayed on our family room's mantle. I asked her, "Honey, I don't have any small Bibles to take with me to the mission tonight, can I use your white pocket Bible?" She willingly replied, "Sure, take it with you." That evening a couple of men came to the Savior, and in the counseling room, one of the men looks at me and says, "Howard, I don't have a Bible." I said, "Yes you do." I handed him my wife's white pocket Bible.

Please realize that I am only three months into the marriage. I had not learned that a husband does not give away their wife's things. However, at that moment I didn't think twice about it. A couple of days later my wife asks, "Howard, where is my Bible?" At that moment I internalized, "Oh no! What have I done?" I explained the story to her. Sadly, the situation worsened. My wife then tells me how her Dad, who had passed away the year before, had given that pocket Bible to her when she graduated from nursing school. I gave away the Bible her Father had lovingly given to her.

Wasn't that foolish? Insensitive? Wrong of me? Yes, yes, and yes, and it illustrates what we as a people have been doing with the Word of God. We have given away the Bible not necessarily when it comes to salvation, or when it comes to sanctification, or even when it comes to glorification, but when it comes to the book of Proverbs I submit we have given away the knowledge of our Father's wisdom and moral teaching He has blessed us with. Whether as conservatives, liberals, or moderates we have ignored His data, inserted our own determinations, and lost the temporal benefits of its blessings.

It is time to let Proverbs speak. Personally and as a people we need the "Buyer Buys" and the "Buyer Bewares" of God wisdom and moral guidance right now. For the glory of God and the good of man it is time to actualize proverbial knowledge. Over the next four chapters I will show you how to become a man or woman of the wisdom of God. In so doing I will show us how to actualize the wisdom of the Lord as a people and bring our nation to a better place to be.

Next chapter

Chapter 4: Discovering God's Skill Set

Picture my five year old niece, Celeste, attending her first day of kindergarten. Imagine this little girl, fingers holding tightly to her father's strong, reassuring hand, walking together down the school's long institutionally grey hallways, passing mysterious rooms filled with noisy children and authoritative adults. As Celeste, arrives in front of her classroom, she shows outward mannerisms of anxiousness and uncertainty. Her dad Burt, sensing his daughter's apprehension halts their entrance just outside the classroom door and asks: "Honey, what's wrong?" Celeste looks up at her father's caring eyes and responds, "Daddy, I don't know how to read, I don't know how to write, I don't know how to spell. What am I doing here?"

Although my niece knew she lacked knowledge, she was unaware that the purpose of elementary school was to impart the very skills she needed. In the same manner primary school is designed to instruct students in the basics of reading, writing, and arithmetic, God's book of Proverbs is crafted to impart to man knowledge (da'at/yada) and knowledge of a very specific kind – the knowledge of performance skill (hokmah) and moral discipline (musar). Let us now commence our coaching in actualizing the first element of Proverbial knowledge - wisdom. We discover this component in Proverbs 1:2a:

> "The proverbs of Solomon the son of David, king of Israel:
> to know **wisdom…**"

I submit the failure to properly actualize proverbial knowledge is the primary cause for dysfunction within our personal lives, families, education, and all the other myriad of ills that afflict us as a people. This is certainly true of Biblical wisdom. If the wisdom of the Word would be inserted into the individual and institutional outworking of our citizenry it would unleash the necessary principles and practices to bring dramatic recovery and betterment to our American experience. Life would dramatically improve for the better.

Therefore, let us now focus our coaching upon Biblical wisdom, what it is, how it works and the difference it will make in our personal and public living as Proverbs 3:13-18 asserts:

> 13 "How blessed is the man who finds wisdom, and the man who gains understanding. 14 For its profit is better than the profit of silver, and its gain than fine gold. 15 She [wisdom] is more precious than jewels' and nothing you desire compares with her. 16 Long life is in her right hand; in her left hand are riches and honor. 17 Her ways are pleasant ways, and all her paths are peace. 18 She is a tree of life to those who take hold of her, and happy are all who hold her fast."

What actually is proverbial wisdom?

The Hebrew term for wisdom in Proverbs as well as through the entire Old Testament is **hokmah**. Hokmah describes a person masterful in performance. One hundred and two times in the Old Testament the word hokmah is used to identify people who were skilled as sailors, craftsmen, counselors, singers, administrators, teachers, movers, diplomats, warriors. If a person excelled in their performance or produced a most exquisite product they were known as a hokam – a person of wisdom. Thirty-nine times the term hokmah is used in Proverbs. The hokmah in Proverbs aims to guide people in living life with skill.

In Scripture a person who performs with excellence and produces a most exquisite product to be known as a hakam – he/she is a person of performance skill. The expertise to live skillfully is the first knowledge component that Proverbs determines to produce within you. Through Proverbial knowledge God wants to develop you to be a person of skill.

It is easy to identify people who lack hokmah.

One of my favorite comedians is Bob Newhart. Newhart once declared that since the invention of the blue tooth it is getting harder to identify the psychotics. Why? Today everybody seems to be speaking to themselves. However, while it is getting harder to identify the psychotics today, it is still easy to identify an individual who lacks hokmah. In this consider the plight of the "Hit and Run" painters.

Phil Mead, my roommate at Spring Arbor University, and I decided to paint houses one summer to make money to help get through another year of college. Now, I had never painted a house before, but Phil assisted in painting a few homes and exuded confidence. We contacted a woman's add in the newspaper who sought painters for the outside of her home. After our analysis of her home we made our "official" bid. The house was quite large. The front of this home was a two story, but the back, due to the slope of the yard became three-stories with an overhanging porch. On the north side of the home was a long, thin green house built right against the main structural wall.

Now, Phil and I had never bid on painting a house before. However, our bid was accepted. We got the job! Thus began the escapades of the hit and run painters. After we were hired the woman told us that she was recently divorced, and her former husband was a professional house painter. When this man heard of the ridiculously low bid these two college students offered to paint his ex-wife's house he drove over to meet us. Throughout our painting venture he regularly stopped by to check on how we were doing.

On the first day in preparation for our painting we rented an extremely large and heavy ladder. We weren't sure of the size so we got the biggest ladder the rental store owned. This ladder resembled a fireman's ladder. It was huge and heavy. In fact, it was way too big for the size of the house. In our initial day of scraping the old paint off the home, we attempted to carry the behemoth ladder fully extended down the slope on the side of the home, it started to fall. We couldn't stop it. With "perfect" timing the woman's former husband, the professional painter comes around the corner as we are bouncing this monstrous ladder off of the electrical wires. Then BOOM it crashed to the ground. After that episode he called us boys. "Hey boys, come here!"

The second day we decided to paint the window sills. In order to do this we had to remove every outside storm window on that old 1940's house. So that morning we took all the storm windows off and laid them very carefully across the front yard of her home. We spaced these twelve two by three foot glass panes equally apart so that we would not step on them as we worked. Throughout the day we painted the window sills and then in the evening replaced the storm windows. We felt good about our progress.

The third day we arrived to the greeting of her former husband who awaited our coming. He said,

"Hey boys come here. You painted the storm windows yesterday, didn't you?"
"Yea, how did you know?"
"Look at the front yard."

We looked at twelve perfectly shaped burnt two by three foot rectangles of dead brown grass. Everywhere we had placed one of those glass panes the sun's rays were magnified and torched the grass. We created a wonderfully designed checkerboard in that woman's front yard.

On the fourth day, Phil and I are painting the front of the house. Phil is actively painting the left side of the home, and I am mindlessly painting the right side. We were both doing what we "thought" was a fine job. We finally felt good about our progress. Then the painter drives up and calls us over to his car, "Hey boys, come here." As we sauntered over he musingly declared,

"Take a look at the house. See anything different?"
Dumbfounded we responded, "No, not really."
He smiled, "Look again. Look more closely. Do you notice the right side of the house is kind of shiny, but the left side of the house is kind of dull? You are painting with two kinds paint. The one on the right (that was me) is painting with porch paint, while the person on the left (that would be Phil) is painting with flat paint."

On the fifth day we decided to tackle the north side of the home which had that long and narrow greenhouse running along the side. This presented us a challenge for we had to get our gigantic ladder inside that glass structure and somehow position the ladder through the windows of its roof. Anyone observing Phil and I trying to get that ladder into that long thin green house and through the windows we would bring that ladder in one way. That didn't work. We would try a different angle. Failure again. Over and over again. Laurel and Hardy or Dumb and Dumber could not have done it any sillier than Phil and I. Finally after about the fifth attempt we figured out how to accomplish this feat. It took quite an effort but I then painted the side of the home moving that ladder at least six times through different windows of that greenhouse. Each time Phil and I had to take the ladder down and over one or two of the windows. What a task, but I completed the work.

On the sixth day, we arrived and saw the woman's ex-husband surveying our work. He called us over to the north side of the home. He had us look up at the wall. All across the high part of the wall were identifiable smudge marks caused by the ladder's end which had rubbed against the painting. To save time when I was painting high up on that ladder I would paint on both sides. However, because of this when we repositioned the ladder it would rest on a part that I had previously painted, leaving two well defined marks. As a result there were at least twelve such markings. So Phil and I had to bring that ladder back into that green house and repaint those marks.

On the seventh and following days we didn't rest but we eventually "finished" the job. Now let me ask you this question: were we men of hokmah? Of course not! In fact, as the summer went on we started to call ourselves the "Hit and Run Painters". Our motto was, "We do work!" We felt it was unncecssary to refer to the quality of our work. You see, it is easy to identify an individual who lacks hokmah because the proof lies in the pudding; i.e., in the performance and quality of the product. If an individual fails to perform with excellence, they are **not** a person of "Hokmah". If the product they produce is inferior, inadequate, insufficient, they are **not** a person of "Hokmah."

It is easy to identify people who possess hokmah.

Just as it is easy to identify people who lack hokmah it is also easy to identify a person who possesses "Hokmah". Why? The proof is in the pudding. This is certainly the case in sports. In this regard was there ever a more excellent performance in collegiate pigskin history than Vince Young against USC in the 2006 Rose Bowl? It was incredible to view Young give one of the finest, maybe the most excellent of all college performances in the history of bowl games. However, there is another pigskin performance that I believe compares with Young.

In the 1950's, Bobby Lane quarterbacked the University of Texas in the Cotton Bowl against Missouri. At the end of that contest Bobby Lane had three rushing TD's, passed for two more, caught a touchdown pass and successfully kicked four extra points. He was responsible for every single point by the Longhorns that afternoon. Texas won 40- 22 against Missouri. After the game the Missouri coach entered into the Texas locker room to shake the hand of Bobby Lane and proclaimed to him, "Son, that was the greatest performance I have ever seen on a football field." In American sports from pee wee football to the pro's, when the game is on the line you want the ball in the hands of a player with hokmah.

American's respect people of hokmah

If a person performs with excellence and produces an exquisite product, they have "Hokmah." When it comes to hokmah it is not hard to identify a person who possesses skill in a particular aspect of living. One recognizes hokmah when one sees it. For instance, in the African American community one can identify the performance skills in the inventive genius of a George Washington Carver, the reasoning and rhetoric of a

Frederick Douglass, the cunning and bravery of a Harriet Tubman, the incomparable oratory, bravery, and leadership of a Dr. Martin Luther King, Jr. One can recognize the great skills of the teaching style of a Marva Collins or the historical writings of a Juan Williams. In music one relishes the performance excellence of a Lena Horne, a Nat King Cole, a Louis Armstrong, a Sammy Davis Jr., a Diana Ross, a Stevie Wonder, a Michael Jackson, a Whitney Houston. In movies one can admire the writing and directing of a Spike Lee or the brilliant acting of a Sidney Pottier, a Cicily Tyson, or a Denzel Washington. In sports one watched amazed by the hokmah of incomparable athletic feats of a Joe, Louis, a Jackie Robinson, a Wilma Rudolph, a Jim Brown, a Willie Mays, a Muhammad Ali, a Michael Jordan, a Kobe Bryant, a Lebron James, a Kevin Durant, a Steph Curry, or a Tiger Woods. Each mentioned person exemplifies a specific occurrence of hokmah in their area of expertise.

In this regard, consider the communicative hokmah of many African American preachers. Trust me many African American pastors exude a freshness, a uniqueness, a connection, a communicative flair that often surpasses the oratory of their white counterparts. Using a negative metaphor to make the point – many black preachers preach us white pastors under the table.

I know this all too well in my own experience. My father-in–law, Reverend Robert Ray Williams opened up his pulpit to me many times before his death. Each time I got up there as a young man and preached the Word. Before hand, I agonized over the sermons. I prayed. I studied. I sought the power of the Spirit. However, no matter what I did. Regardless of how I trusted, after every sermon the same scenario played itself out. At the conclusion of my sermon, Rev. Williams would look at me, pat me on the shoulder and thank me for the message. It was as if he was saying, "It's ok, you did the best you could. I understand your limitations."

One of the most historic examples of an African American pastor preaching a white pastor under the table happened on a shared Easter service with black and white pastor's communicating sermons on the resurrection of Christ. First, a renowned white preacher got up and delivered a wonderful sermon, presenting the historical evidence of Christ rising from the dead. The message was well defined – well thought out – communicated with expositional preciseness. What a message. The congregation received the sermon with affirmation and admiration. Then he walked back to his seat.

As the white pastor walked back to his seat, the African American pastor next in line to preach, turned to him, touched him on the shoulder, and said, "That was good, now watch this." He then preached one of America's most famous sermons, "It's Friday, but Sunday's Coming!" The entire fellowship of believers both black and white exploded: "Wow! What a message!"

What was the difference? While I do not have the time to go into detailed analysis let me make one point. I submit a skill of historic African American preaching is the active engagement of the listener in the personal, congregational, and societal experience of Scripture's truth far more than the traditional sermons delivered by the Anglo preacher. The black preacher connects the Word with the pain, history, and exhilaration of the listener. Throughout the preaching experience the congregation feels the immediate relevancy of Scripture to their present situation. From beginning to climatic end the listener encounters an emotive identification with the Scriptures communicated from the pastor to the person in the pew.

Please note: when the meaning of Scripture is communicated accurately (what the Bible actually says), and the application of the text is presented clearly (how the passage actually works), when this preaching is delivered by Spirit filled men with vital communicative style an electricity occurs in the congregation that one has heard the Word of the living God. Is this not what we want in our sermons?

Like you, I want to know what the Word says; i.e, the meaning. I want to know how the Word works; i.e., its application. In this communication I desire to know the relevancy of the Bible with the reality of my life. When those ingredients connect through the power of the Spirit the sermon exudes Scriptures aliveness. One hears from God.

Yes, whether it be singing, painting, athletics, counseling, hunting, preaching hokmah is identifiable. Hokmah is discovered in the quality of performance and the exquisiteness of the product. You know it when you see it. You recognize it on the field of play. You know it when you hear it. How we need men and women of hokmah today in all arenas of American life.

When you have a job to do you want a person of hokmah

Consider the case of my three brother in laws, Bobby, Bernard and Burt. These men possess hokmah in many areas of their lives – but as ranchers? At the time of this story they didn't quite have that skill down. My wife's side of the family owns land in Giddings, Texas. On our property were twelve unbranded cows. So Bobby, Bernard and Burt, decided to put on their cowboy hats, put on their jeans, their boots, and go out there and brand some cows. Now they had never branded a cow before. The first cow they tried to brand they tied to their pickup truck. By the time they finished branding that cow, they had broken that cow's neck. Now, if you were the next cow in line? You certainly wouldn't want to be branded by those guys. You would want a rancher with some hokmah.

Believe me if you are going in for brain surgery you don't want Mr. Bean to operate on you - you want a masterful surgeon. When life matters most you need a person who possesses hokmah. This holds true whether one needs a Doctor, a lawyer, an accountant, a teacher, a parent. When life matters most you need people with hokmah to get the job done right.

For instance, when the Lord commanded Moses to build His tabernacle in the wilderness (Exodus 31:1-11), He commanded Moses to pick men of Hokmah for the construction.

2 "See, I [the Lord] have called by name Bezalel, the son of Uri...and I have filled him with the Spirit of God in wisdom (hokmah), in understanding, in knowledge (yada), and in all kinds of craftsmanship...6 And behold, I Myself have appointed with him, Oholiab, son of Ahisamach...and in the hearts of all who are skillful (hokmah), that they may make all that I have commanded you..."

(The craftsmen were to build: the tent of meeting , the ark of testimony, the mercy seat, the furniture, the table and its utensils, the pure gold and its utensils, the altar of incense, the altar of burnt offering with all its utensils, the laver and its stand, the woven garments, the holy garments for Aaron, the garments for his sons, the anointing oil, the fragrant incense for the holy place)

As the Lord required men of hokmah to build His tabernacle in the wilderness so too when Solomon constructed the Temple in the Promised Land he also surrounded himself with men of great skill. In the planning and construction of the Temple, Solomon sent word to Hiram, the king of Tyre (1 Kings 5:1-18) to hire the Sidonians to cut down and deliver Cypress and Cedar trees from the mountainous slopes of Lebanon to secure the proper lumber for the building he specifically requested that Hiram hire the Sidionites for this task. Why? Solomon's assessment provides the answer:

> "...for you know [Hiram] that there is no one among us who knows how to cut timber like the Sidonians..." (1 Kings 5:6b)

It is not difficult to recognize people with hokmah. It is evident in their decision making, their craftsmanship, and ultimately the excellence of their product. Notice Hiram's immediate identification of the hokmah in Solomon's request:

> "And when it came about when Hiram heard the words of Solomon, that he rejoiced greatly and said, 'Blessed be the Lord today, who has given to David a wise (hokam) son over this great people.' So Hiram sent word to Solomon, saying, 'I have heard the message which you have sent me; I will do what you desire concerning the cedar and cypress timber.'" (1 Kings 5:7-8)

As this demonstrates the entire planning and construction of the Temple from its inception to completion was entirely undertaken by men of hokmah. As God built His Temple with wisdom so too the Lord wants to construct you. He desires to make you into a person of hokmah to impart to you the necessary knowledge to perform in life with skill.

Hokmah and the capacity to do things well

One day during High School football practice, our punter Steven Rupe was missing so I inserted myself and stepped in to punt. I shanked the ball off the side of my foot and it travelled only ten yards down the field. I tried it again only to see the ball travel about fifteen yards past the line of scrimmage. After practice I got into the car with my dad to drive home. My dad who viewed this sorry episode, said to me: "Son, don't do what you don't do well."

This is the wonder of Proverbs in hokmah. The entire book is written to develop you to do things well. Specifically the book offers its teachings, addressing over 480 identifiable topics. For instance the hokmah of God in Proverbs instructs us in...

> How to balance your check book, work smarter, work harder, plan, organize, lead; how to be a better husband, wife, son, daughter, a kinder neighbor, closer friend, how to make good decisions, live fairly, administer justice, know righteousness; how to discover God, discern goodness, be delivered from evil, protect yourself against sexual harm; how to navigate successfully through life, improve your schools, communities, and country, and on and on and on...

God's Hokmah is there for your taking

God desires you to exercise His hokmah. With Scriptural wisdom you have the Creator God imparting His advice on how to improve the performance of His creatures and the condition of humanity. God gives to man His personal knowledge on how to live better. Think of this, the same wisdom that God used in creating the universe is there for you to actualize as revealed in Proverbs 8:22-31:

> 22 "The Lord possessed me [wisdom –hokmah] at the beginning of His way, before His works of old. 23 From everlasting I was established, from the beginning from the earliest times of the earth, 24 when there were no depths I was brought forth, when there were no springs abounding with water. 25 Before the mountains were settled, before the hills I was brought forth; 26 while He had not yet made the earth and the fields, nor the first dust of the world. 27 When He established the heavens I was there, when He inscribed a circle on the face of the deep, 28 when He made firm the skies above, when the springs of the deep became fixed, 29 when He set for the sea its boundary, so that the water should not transgress His command, when He marked out the foundations of the earth; 30 then I was beside Him, as a master workman; and I was daily His delight, rejoicing always before Him, 31 rejoicing in the world, His earth, and having my delight in the sons of men."

Think of what people have in their knowledge bank of Proverbs. God's creative principles that formed the universe is there to better the finer aspects of human living. Hokmah equips man to reach their God given potential. Hokmah provides positive instruction in how to speak, how to listen, how to build friendships, hot to be fair with people, how to handle money, marriage, love-making, child rearing, teaching, decision making, justice, fairness, kindness, leadership, discipline, employment, success, all those principles and more are identified in the Book of Proverbs.

Do we not need people actualizing the hokmah of God in every aspect of American life today? Do we not need husbands and fathers, wives and mothers practicing the hokmah of God in their marriages and child rearing? Do we not need educators and administrators who possess hokmah developing our curriculum and teaching our children? Do we not need people of hokmah sitting as judges on our courts, or people of hokmah as our political leaders initiating and passing legislation? Yes, in every area of American life, we need men and women who possess and practice the wisdom of God.

The hokmah of God is there for your taking. Just as an athlete would do well to follow the refinements of a most excellent coach so too a person would do well to follow the directives of the hokmah of the Creator God. Think of the wonderful advancement humans would gain if they learned and followed the advice of God's hokmah. Hokmah is what God wants to do for you in Proverbs. He wants to impart to you excellence in living right now. Oh, if we only lived with the same performance skill as Gale Sayers once ran with the football. Hokmah is the source of knowledge the Lord imparts to man in the first purpose of Proverbs. He wrote this book for you to come "to know wisdom". Proverbs was crafted to impart to you the performance skills of God.

The realization of this should stop once and for all the idea that God is holding out on you. Nothing could be further from the truth. Our Lord cares about your eternal destination. He went to the cross to give you the opportunity to gain life forever. In this God demonstrates His own love for you in that while you were yet a sinner Christ died for you. He cares about your life in the here and now. The principles of hokmah are not black, brown, red, white, or yellow principles they are God's principles. They are revealed by the Lord for all people to actualize. They are divinely crafted to develop you into the person He intends for you to be.

Some people carry the misconception that God purposely hides Himself and His will from man. Humans, as a result, are left to futilely search for guidance destined only for uncertainty, even despair. In this view people see God's will like a man going through a forest in quest for the discovery of God, but only coming to the end of his exploration hearing God laughingly exclaim. "Ha-ha!! You never did find Me did you?" The book of Proverbs gives the lie to this sentiment for in its pages God reveals directives to live life well, to live with performance skill How wondrously detailed this book becomes in clearing up mistaken paths and refining performance. This is the sophistication of Biblical wisdom. How we need this knowledge today as individuals, families, communities. How we need His hokmah. The da'at of Proverbial hokmah aims to equip you to become a man/woman of wisdom to know life as God designed it to be and to put that knowledge into practice throughout your life.

Wisdom is a matter of time

When I was soccer co-captain at Spring Arbor University with Nate Mains, the first meeting we ever had with the team I asked our players this question: "What is it we have in common with every team we will play next year and the use and misuse of this will determine the winner of those games?" Some of the guys responded, "We all have two legs." "We all play with eleven players." "We all use our heads." After they had exhausted their fun and knowledge I replied, "What we have in common with every team we play and will be the ultimate determiner of which team will be victorious is the use or misuse of time. What we will do with the amount of minutes in the days of preparation before the game begins – the use of time."

All of us have 365 days in a year, 24 hours in a day, 60 minutes in an hour – now what are we going to do with the time we have – this is the great definer of men – the use or misuse of time. With respect to time men are not equal; i.e., in terms of quantity and in terms of quality. Time is the great divider and determiner of human existence. How does one decide to use the minutes one is given upon this earth.

As a college freshman I went to the musical "Stop the World I Want to Get Off". In that musical the main character "Littlechap" during times of intense pressure, times of discouragement, times of loss of life, times great grief he would cry out in the middle of the scene "Stop the world!" And everything would halt, the people frozen in their stances, and then he would walk to the front of the stage and soliloquize. He would talk about the existential moment, his hurt, the pain, the grief, the despair. However, this is exactly what one cannot do with time – it cannot be stopped. Time keeps going and once it's gone it's irretrievable.

Even with a bad heart I remember my dad trudging up and down the sidelines with the yard markers during our high school football games. I went up to him after the first time he did this and asked him, "Dad, why are you doing this when you know it is not good for your health?" He responded, "Son, I do this because I love you and I want to be as close to the game as I can when you play."

What do you do for a man like that? You love him back. Six months after that conversation my dad died. A few years after his death I watched the movie Brian Song about the relationship between two Chicago Bears teammates: the great Gale Sayers and the running back Brian Picolo. The movie displayed the closeness of their friendship.

Sayer's deeply grieved after the death of Picolo who died of cancer. Emotionally moved from this movie I went out to the track at Spring Arbor University and I began to sprint around that oval until I fell to the grass on the infield exhausted. I wept deeply because of the grief I had from the loss of my dad.

At the hospital within minutes of his passing I remember dad asking me, "Son, I have a golf game set up this weekend and I'm not going to be able to play. I want you to play that game in my place." I said sure dad I'll do that. I walked out of that room and by the time I came back he had passed away. I always wished that I had told him one more time that I loved him. Time had gone.

When my wife's dad, Pastor Williams was in the latter stages of his cancer, I visited him in the hospital. Over a period of occasions I observed all different types of ministers who came in to see him with many praying for his healing. As his health continued to fail and I could see he was closing in on his departure. I went in and said to him, "Pastor Williams it is possible that God may heal you, but He may chose not to. Pastor, now's the time, now's the time, now's the time to tell your wife what she means to you, now's the time to express to your children how much you love them. Now's the time."

Many of you reading this are fathers and mothers. Love, discipline, and care for your children. When my kids were babies and toddlers I told my wife, "Honey, let's do whatever we need to do in getting the kids ready to sleep, but once they are prepared for bed I want to go in there last." Upon entering their rooms, I would first sit down in a chair with them, holding them in my arms, and I would read to them. Then after the story I would walk with them in the room still holding them in my arms and sing songs of praise to the Lord with them. Finally, I would lay them down in their bed and pat them on the back as I prayed. The last thing I said to them was, "Stephen, Philip, or Lauren, God loves you, God loves you and daddy loves you too." Then I would depart and close the door. I can still recall as if it was yesterday one night after telling Stephen, "Stephen, God loves you, God loves you, and daddy loves you too." That before I took two steps away my little son responded, "And Stephen loves daddy."

Now is the time. This is your moment. What are you going to do with it in terms of relationships? The book of Proverbs gives you principles in how to be a loving spouse – a caring parent. The Book of Proverbs gives instructions in how to relate with your parents. Time goes by quickly. As I am writing this chapter, my other son, Philip, is getting ready to leave for Church camp. When he returns he has two weeks before he takes off to Australia for a year of development in worship with Hillsong International. After dropping him off for camp all the way home I'm weeping because I'm internalizing his departure for a year. We only have our wives, our kids, our friends for a moment.

Consider the profundity of Psalm 90

Psalm 90 is the oldest psalm in the Old Testament Psalter. Written by Moses, Psalm 90 is a wisdom psalm contrasting the permanency of the everlasting God with perishing human beings. Here is the wisdom Psalm in its entirety.

1 "Lord, Thou hast been our dwelling place in all generations. 2 Before the mountains were born, or Thou didst give birth to the earth and the world, even from everlasting to everlasting, Thou art God.

3 Thou dost turn man back into dust, and dost say, 'Return, O children of men.' 4 For a thousand years in Thy sight are like yesterday when it passes by, or as a watch in the night. 5 Thou hast swept them away like a flood, they fall asleep; in the morning they are like grass which sprouts anew, 6 toward evening it fades, and withers away. 7 For we have been consumed by Thine anger, and by Thy wrath we have been dismayed. 8 Thou hast placed our iniquities before Thee, our secret sins in the light of Thy presence. 9 For all our days have declined in Thy fury; we have finished our years like a sigh.

10 As for the days of our life, they contain seventy years, or if due to strength, eighty years, yet their pride is but labor and sorrow; for soon it is gone and we fly away. 11 Who understands the power of Thine anger, and Thy fury, according to the fear that is due Thee? 12 So teach us to number our days, that we may present to Thee a heart of wisdom.

13 Do return, O Lord; how long will it be? And be sorry for Thy servants. 14 O satisfy us in the morning with Thy lovingkindness, that we may sing for joy and be glad all our days. 15 Make us glad according to the days Thou hast afflicted us, and the years we have seen evil.

16 Let Thy work appear to Thy servants, and Thy majesty to their children. 17 And let the favor of the Lord our God be upon us; and do confirm for us the work of our hands; yes, confirm the work of our hands."

In contrasting the everlasting God with dying man, Moses states that people have seventy years to live or by reason of strength 80, but the time is quickly gone. The days of human beings fly away. Ecclesiastes tells us that present life is but a vapor. The wisdom book of James tells us that man's life is but a puff of smoke. James further states that a person doesn't even know if he/she will have a tomorrow. Tomorrow in this life is not promised to anyone and with every day that goes by each individual has one day less. Death awaits us all. There is no escaping.

With respect to the fragile nature of human life Moses challenges you to do some addition and subtraction and "number your days so that you might get yourself a heart of wisdom."

A reverse calendar

If you would come to my office, as you enter, on your immediate left you'd discover a reverse calendar. Over the past twenty years I have been doing some addition and subtraction – mostly subtraction. Applying some simple arithmetic I figured a normal life span of 70 to 80 years and added up the number of days I might still have left according to Psalm 90. Here's the count…

> One year ='s 365 days (leap year 366 days)
> Ten years ='s 3,652 days
> Twenty years ='s 7,304 days
> Fifty years ='s 18,260 days
> Seventy years ='s 25,564 days
> Eighty years ='s 29,216 days

Make yourself a reverse calendar. Calculate where you are in your earthly sojourn. How old are you? Do some addition. Total up the number of days you have lived _____. Now, subtract this number from the total number of days for 70 years. What is the number of days you have left _____? Do the same thing for eighty years. What's your number? (_____) You have just identified your life expectancy upon earth based on the wisdom Psalm of Moses.

Our days are dwindling. As of the writing of this paragraph here's my count. So far I have lived for 22,454 days. If I live to the age of seventy I have 3,110 days, left. If I live to eighty I have 6,762. At the close of each and every day I subtract; i.e., I cross out one of my remaining days. Each day that goes by I mark that day off my reverse calendar. You might be saying that's morbid! No, in the words of Dr. Howard Hendricks,

> "That's not morbid! That's motivational! Men, you don't have eternity to live down here. You only have a small slice of time. And each day that goes by you have one day less! That is the motivation to apply your heart to wisdom to accomplish the work that God has called you to do."

My reverse calendar is made up of years with the days identified in boxes. Here's an example of a year with 365 days. After each day I mark off one of the squares. Here's a one year example:

J																														
F																											?	X	X
M																														
A																														X
M																														
J																														X
J																														
A																														
S																														X
O																														
N																														X
D																														

The Death Clock

If you want a more startling and immediate fix google up "The Death Clock." The question the Death Clock seeks to answer for you is: "When are you going to die?" The Death Clock is described as "The internet's friendly reminder that life is slipping away." To discover the day of your death the Death Clock challenges you to "use [their] advanced life expectancy calculator to accurately predict the date of your demise." You will insert information such as age, body mass index, etc. Once submitted the death clock gives you your expectant moment of death, including the day, the month, and the year. The clock then begins to tick backwards subtracting second by second of your life expectancy till the end of your earthly time.

Quotes from www. deathclock.com/

A friend told me about "The Death Clock" after I shared with him Psalm 90. He explained the process and said his clock gave him 74 years of life expectancy and how his clock ticks down second by second the time he has left. His eighty year old grandmother tried it. After she inserted her personal data The Death Clock responded, "Sorry, but you have run out of time!"

Maximize your Days

The Book of Proverbs was written that you might become a man or woman who maximizes your days. Now, in light that you do not eternity to live down here go and get the wisdom to live life well. Let wisdom work for you. Moses concludes His wisdom psalm with this directive:

> 14 O satisfy us in the morning with Thy lovingkindness, that we may sing for joy and be glad all our days. 15 Make us glad according to the days Thou hast afflicted us, and the years we have seen evil. 16 Let Thy work appear to Thy servants, and Thy majesty to their children. 17 And let the favor of the Lord our God be upon us; and do confirm for us the work of our hands; yes, confirm the work of our hands."

Think of this, God wants you to become a person of His wisdom. He calls you to be a hokam; i.e., a man or woman of performance skill. He desires that you exercise His principles of performance right now in order to live life well. Wherever you are, whatever you are doing, God calls for you to discover and exercise His wisdom. The blessing of actualizing the Lord's hokmah in your life awaits as Proverbs 3:13-18 states:

> 13 "How blessed is the man who finds wisdom, and the man who gains understanding. 14 For its profit is better than the profit of silver, and its gain than fine gold. 15 She [wisdom] is more precious than jewels' and nothing you desire compares with her. 16 Long life is in her right hand; in her left hand are riches and honor. 17 Her ways are pleasant ways, and all her paths are peace. 18 She is a tree of life to those who take hold of her, and happy are all who hold her fast."

However, like Celeste maybe you are standing on the outside of the door of the classroom looking in. While my niece called to her father "I don't know how to read. I don't know how to write. I don't know how to spell. What am I doing here?" The answer to Celeste's lack of learning was right in front of her. Her dad brought her to the right place for learning. All she needed to do was enter through that door and the process of gaining those skills would commence.

God does not leave you uninformed. He gives you His knowledge to come out of the blocks, run your race down the stretch and finish well. However, you must enter the door, open up the book of His Proverbial learning and gain the wisdom that is divinely revealed to excel your human experience. Make a commitment to gain the hokmah of God. Make a determination to become a hokam – a man or woman of wisdom. Learn and live from the wisdom of the Lord who created all things and who fashioned you in the womb.

We pray for wisdom. Now go out and get her.

Chapter 5: Acquiring Wisdom

Moments before the opening kick-off of the 1986 American Football Conference Championship game between the Cleveland Browns and the Denver Broncos, Cleveland's head coach Marty Schottenheimer gathered his players on the sidelines for one last challenge. Huddling his team around him he delivered the following charge: "There's a gleam men. There's a gleam. Let's go get the gleam!"

The gleam that Schottenheimer challenged his men to possess was the highest glory offered by the National Football League – the chance to play in the Super Bowl and win the Vince Lombardi Trophy, the most coveted crown of professional football. Once they possessed that gleam no one could ever take that prize away from them. Forever, they would possess the Lombard award, that shining silver trophy symbolizing them as the world champions of their sport. That Sunday afternoon, with just one more victory separating the Browns from the opportunity to play for that glory, coach Schottenheimer delivered his charge.

Now, as Schottenheimer challenged his team to gain the gleam of the Lombardi Trophy, Proverbs challenges you to go out and get the glories of God's wisdom for yourself. This is the charge in Proverbs 4:5-9 when he states:

> 5 "Acquire wisdom [hokmah]! Acquire understanding! Do not forget, nor turn away from the words of my mouth. 6 Do not forsake her [wisdom], and she will guard you; love her, and she will watch over you. 7 The beginning of wisdom is: acquire wisdom; and with all your acquiring, get understanding. 8 Prize her [wisdom], and she will exalt you; she will honor you if you embrace her. 9 She will place on your head a garland of grace; she will present you with a crown of beauty."

In this passage Proverbs stands before us today and coaches us, "There's wisdom men! There's wisdom women! Go get the wisdom!" However, unlike the Browns who fell two minutes short of the super bowl thanks to John Elway's ninety-eight yard "the drive," the benefits of becoming a person of hokmah, God's wisdom lies within your reach. She is there for your taking. But how?

How does one acquire wisdom?

In this chapter I want to ask and answer the question: how does one become a person of performance skill? More specifically, how does one actualize the Lord's knowledge of skillful living in the here and now? How does someone become a hokam – a man or woman skilled in living well? More personally, how do you go out and get the gleam of God's wisdom for yourself?

The Hebrew term for **acquire** in Proverbs 4:5-9 is (qanah: kaw-nah). The meaning of qanah is to "to get" "to obtain", "to pursue", "to buy", "to purchase for oneself."

Hebrew and Chaldee Dictionary, (# 7069, 'to procure especially by purchase... to own: -attain, buy)

Four times in this passage Solomon uses the term qanah to challenge you to go out and gain the performance skills of the Lord for yourself. Kidner states: "What it takes [to acquire wisdom] is not brains or opportunity, but a decision. Do you want it? Come and get it."

Kidner, Proverbs p. 67; Source: Waltke, Vol. 1, p. 281

However, please note, the Scriptures do not say go out and get it as if wisdom were an object, Solomon charges you to go out and possess her. Throughout Proverbs wisdom is personified by means of female pronouns. In fact, fifty-four times the pronoun "she" is used and one hundred and three times the pronoun "her" is used for wisdom in Proverbs. Take our present passage of Proverbs 4:5-9 for example when Solomon states,

> "Do not forsake **her** [wisdom] – and **she** will guard you,"
> "Love **her** – and **she** will watch over you,"
> "Prize **her** – and **she** will exalt you,"
> "**She** will honor you if you embrace **her**"
> "**She** will place on your head a garland of grace"
> "**She** will present you with a crown of beauty."

Ten times the female pronoun is used in this passage for wisdom. Each of these gleams of wisdom Solomon highlights by means of the wonder of man's natural attraction for a woman and the glories that result from a committed, loving marital relationship. Solomon uses the natural attraction of males for females to communicate that humans are to strive after wisdom with the same intensity and priority that a man strives to win the hand of the woman he loves.

A question that arises is why does Solomon craft the argument of wisdom as feminine and not depart from this line of reasoning throughout the entire book? This is perfectly understandable when one realizes that while Proverbs is applicable to every individual Solomon addressed this writing to his son(s). He personalized the book to equip his son to become the king of Israel. The book serves as a curriculum of father to son, man to man mentoring. Twenty-six times in Proverbs the term father is used and forty-six times the term son or sons' is utlilized. Here are three such examples:

"My son, if you will receive my sayings and treasure my commandments within you..." (Prov. 2:1)

"Hear, O sons, a father's instruction, and be attentive, that you may gain insight." (Prov. 4:1)
"Hear my son, and accept my sayings, and the years of your life will be many." (Prov. 4:10)

Now, this connection helps explain why wisdom Biblically is personified as female. Keep in focus that a major reason Solomon wrote Proverbs was to equip his son(s) for leadership – more specifically to be King of Israel. No surprise should disturb one's cognitive domain that the books motivations are predominantly male in nature. Observation of proverbial content demonstrates the book is crafted as a guide for father/son mentoring. Its principles and practices are tailor made for guiding young men to better living. As a result, the book of Proverbs is crafted for the development of people and especially men.

Specifically maleness pervades the sayings and commandments of the writing as exemplified by the use of the feminine pronoun for wisdom – her. Thus underscores why the challenge to possess wisdom is crafted by means of the feminine pronoun. As a result, it should come as no surprise that the pronouns used to motivate men to acquire wisdom are feminine. In following this line of reasoning let us analyze the acquiring of wisdom by means of the male-female attraction.

First, acquiring wisdom requires pursuit.

Inherent in the Hebrew term qanah (acquire) is the idea of pursuit. As males pursue females so too people are to pursue the gleam of wisdom. The male-female pursuit is God created within the human being. Solomon seeks to build upon this natural desire to construct his argument of how a person is to seek after wisdom. Therefore, Solomon instructs people to pursue the acquisition of wisdom; i.e., the gleam of God's hokmah, as a man pursues the woman he desires to marry.

Scripture presents the natural bent of a man is to woo and win a woman. This Biblical principle was seconded by comedian Jerry Seinfeld who remarked,

"What do men want? Men want women. Where there are a group of women, we have a man on the job. He may not know what he is doing, but at least he is out there trying."

This whole rigmarole of the male pursuit of the fairer sex begins at a very early age. I remember during first grade recess how we boys attempted to impress our six year old female classmates with our strength by carrying them across the playground. The goal was to carry the girl all the way to the fence without dropping her.

However, let it be noted that before we could carry the girls we first had to catch them. This required another display of our maleness – speed. The problem we encountered was that the girls at this age of maturation were faster and larger than we were. So, in retrospect they really had to want us to catch them. I don't think any of us guys contemplated the psychological reasoning behind why we were doing this feat of strength and speed, but I do know somehow we thought this would impress the girls. I guess this was our literal interpretation of what it meant to "pick up girls."

One Saturday that year my older sister Pam invited her eight year old friend Diane Zowlezi over to our house to play. Now, this act of friendliness affected me little, except for one exciting difference, along with Diane came her little six year old sister Linda. Linda was my first grade heart throb. As she entered into our home, she now came upon my turf. Through that door appeared the little girl of my dreams. I now had the opportunity to personally put the approach of impressing her by strength into action. However, since I had already tried out my recess routine with the fair Miss Zowlezi, I needed something different – a new shtick.

So this time, when everyone had gone their own way, suddenly Linda and I found ourselves in the family room alone. What did I do? I got behind the couch and pushed that behemoth (not Linda, but the couch) all the way across our living room floor. Did it win the heart of Miss Zowlezi? I don't think so because after I had accomplished this feat of strength, she ran to tell my mom what I had done. When mom appeared and saw the displaced couch she sent me to my room. In retrospect this was a wise move on mom's part for who knows how many pieces of furniture I would have displaced that afternoon to win the affection of the most fair but less loyal Linda.

As one can tell, during my elementary years, my determination at wooing women involved brawn over brains – at least I was trying, but I really didn't know how. Regardless, I was in the act of "acquiring" for I was striving to win her affection. However, there is a missing component or person in this story, for I assure you if dad had been home he not only would have understood my efforts of masculinity he would have applauded them. "That's my son!" What's more he could have taken me aside and provided this neophyte with some instruction: "Son, let me tell you how to win the heart of that little girl." Better still if he had come into the room he could have spurred me on by saying, "Son, what about my TV chair? Are you strong enough to move that?" Such reveals the prowess of males before women.

Do you need a Biblical example of a man seeking to impress the heart of a woman by means of strength? Think of Jacob's pursuit of Rachel. Consider their initial encounter as recorded in Genesis, chapter 29:

> 1 "Then Jacob went on his journey, and came to the land of the sons of the east. 2 And he looked, and saw a well in the field, and behold, three flocks of sheep were lying there beside it, for from that well they watered the flocks. **Now the stone on the mouth of the well was large.** 3 When all the flocks were gathered there, **they** would then roll the stone from the mouth of the well, and water the sheep, and put the stone back in its place on the mouth of the well."
>
> And Jacob said to them, 'My brothers, where are you from? And they said, 'We are from Haran."
>
> 5 And he said to them, 'Do you know Laban then son of Nahor?" And they said, 'We know him.'
>
> 6 And he said to them, 'Is it well with him?' And they said, 'It is well, and behold, Rachel his daughter is coming with [Laban's] sheep."
>
> 10 And it came about, when Jacob saw Rachel...
>
> [It was said of Rachel in Genesis 29:17 that she "was beautiful of form and face...."]
>
> **[that]...Jacob went up, and rolled the stone from the mouth of the well, and watered the flock of Laban..."**

Now, Jacob, didn't carry Rachel across the playground, he didn't push the couch across the living room, instead he went up to that huge stone and moved that massive rock by his own initiative. He displayed his strength before the lovely shepherdess and then he went further and watered her dad's flock. Why? The exact reason I aimed to win the heart of fair Miss Linda, young Jacob, determined to impress Rachel with his manhood. At the sight of Rachel, Jacob was smitten. He immediately became a man, shall we say "in hot pursuit."

The reader can gain some wonderful stories of romance by engaging in conversation with couples concerning how the man pursued his wife. Here's the story of my pursuit of the fair Miss Betty Williams.

From the moment my eyes met Betty, when I unknowingly sat next to her in Church, I became a man in pursuit. The first thing that struck me was the beauty of her face – her eyes and smile. My efforts began subtly with a few comments concerning the pastor's sermon – which she tried to ignore; i.e., my wit not the sermon. Later I discovered she was brought up not to talk during Church.

During Rev. Rowe's sermon I noticed a tear coming down her cheek. My pursuit took form with the giving of my handkerchief to dry away her tear. It intensified as I took one more quick glance as she walked away from the Church toward her car. I still remember this moment as if it was today. Believe me, there was a gleam men! There was a gleam! And, her name was Betty!

My pursuit continued with some research. I sought out Mrs. Brooks, who sat next to Betty on that life changing Sunday. Now, I knew Mrs. Brooks. She was a gracious, respectful and kind woman. The next Sunday I asked her a few questions: Who was Betty? What was her family like?

First and foremost Mrs. Brooks impressed upon me that she came from a highly respected Christian home. Her dad was Revered Robert Ray Williams, pastor of Good Hope Baptist Church in Round Rock, Texas. Her mom worked in the public school system of Austin as Head of the cafeteria responsible for the feeding of 400 children each and every school day. Mrs. Williams was also one of the leaders of the women in the African American Churches throughout Austin. Betty's older sister, Linda was also a graduate of TWU, a teacher and soon to be vice-principle. Her younger brother Bobbie was in the Army, and her youngest brother Bernard worked for Dell Computers. Mrs. Brooks then told me that Betty was a Registered Nurse, also a graduate of Texas Woman's University who now worked the graveyard shift at Parkland Hospital in Dallas.

OK, with round one of research completed, I then sought out information from one of my fellow teachers in the singles class, Darryl Nelson. Darryl was dearly beloved by Betty's family and a close friend of hers. I asked him questions about Betty. "Darryl, what is Betty like?" Out of his mouth came glowing reports about her personality. She was "smart, funny, and sassy." I understood the first two but in thirty years of marriage, I am still acquiring the meaning of sassy.

Satisfied with my initial research I decided it was time for a few close encounters. So after one of the singles classes I initiated conversations with her and started to see Betty's qualities for myself. A month later I decided to ask her for a date. After a class I asked her to go out, she kindly replied, "No, thank you." At least three different times that year we danced her waltz of polite but certain rejection. Smiling, I would ask her to go out. Smiling, she said no. Finally, after twelve months she relented and said yes.

Now, I had a predicament. I had sold my car to get through the second year of seminary. For transportation I drove an old vehicle that had been hit on the driver's side. Its trunk was held down by a bungee cord. Its passenger door could only be opened by the outside handle. Even I knew this form of transportation would fail to impress the fair maiden. So I sought out Martin Puryear. Martin owned a 280 Z. Being a great friend he gave me the OK to use his sports car. I owe Martin deeply.

Driving up to her apartment in that 280 Z I was speedily in prayer. Then we went out. The question that I needed answered in my mind and heart during that date was: did Betty actually have a vital relationship with Christ? Did she truly love and desire the Lord? As we sat down to eat, she glowingly began to talk about her love for Jesus and her reinvigorated commitment to follow after Him. She was beautiful to behold and exciting to be with. I was hooked.

Once her love for Christ was cemented that proved to be all the fuel I needed. I was off and running. With my determination peaked and my soul energized, I decided: "OK, let's go!" What was so refreshing is after our first date Betty was as fully energized to build the relationship as myself. She too had found someone who shared her passion for the Savior and zeal for life. Within two weeks we were an inseparable couple. Now, there is something wonderful when a man and a woman long to be with one another. Let the romance begin and it did with...

> Dinners-Musicals-Plays-Parks-Walks-Trips-Phone calls (Oh, those wonderful phone calls!)-Presents-Flowers...Acts of kindness...signs of affection...hugs and kisses. Does life get any better?

On one occasion I wanted to surprise her with a gift when she returned from her graveyard shift at the hospital. I went to her apartment door and left a stuffed animal – a cute little bear named Russ. I put a rose into his arms which he held lovingly in place. I then put a sign above him taped to the door which read: "Just for Betty!" That depicted my pursuit of life with her: "Just for Betty!"

From the moment of our first date we began to pray together. We started to study the Word of God together. I would bring her to my seminary classes and together we learned about Christ. We also began to minister together. I had organized a ministry to reach people around the seminary. It was called Inner-city Bible Ministries. We even started a fledgling Church which met on the seminary grounds on Sunday. In the projects we went out and shared the gospel with children and their parents. Twenty-six Bible studies were set up within the community involving African Americans, Hispanics, Anglo's and Asians. Seven marriages to seminary students emerged out of that ministry of which Betty and I were one. We were married on May 21st, 1983, at Good Hope Baptist Church, where her dad was pastor.

Trust me, there was a gleam men! There was a gleam! And her name was Betty! Here's the point: if we only pursued after the Word of God with the same intensity we sought after the woman we married we would all become spiritual giants. This is precisely the charge Solomon presents to us in Proverbs 4:5-9.

> 5 "Acquire wisdom [hokmah]! Acquire understanding! Do not forget, nor turn away from the words of my mouth. 6 Do not forsake her [wisdom], and she will guard you; love her, and she will watch over you. 7 "The beginning of wisdom is: acquire wisdom, and with all your acquiring gain understanding. 8 Prize her and she will exalt you; she will honor you if you embrace her. 9 She will place on your head a garland of grace; she will present you with a crown of beauty."

In this passage Solomon calls out to us: "There's a gleam men! There's a gleam! Come and get her!" Therefore, pursue after wisdom as a man pursues the woman of his longing. Pursue wisdom to possess her for your very own.

See the gleam!

However, far too many people fail to see the gleam of Scripture. As a result, many approach the acquisition of the Word of God as a chore. Like the young high school student who was asked by his teacher to explain the difference between ignorance and apathy. He replied, "Who knows and who cares!"

However, if the inner motivation is there; if the desire comes from within, if a person catches the gleam, then a whole different scenario plays itself out. Now, a person carries an intrinsic want to from the inside that moves him/her to action. This is why the Lord sets before a person the gleam to see the benefits for themselves.

Think of the effort God demonstrated to show Adam the gleam of Eve! Think of how God drove the need for a woman into the soul of Adam. He initially revealed to Adam his great need for a mate in the naming of the animals. Each male animal had a partner. For every male there was a female, but not for Adam. Adam was alone. Then the Lord put Adam to sleep and fashioned the woman from his side. When Adam awoke and saw Eve he said, "This is now bone of my bone, flesh of my flesh." In other words as one speaker explained: Adam said, "Wow! Where have you been all my life? Wrap her up Lord. I'll take her! On second, thought don't wrap her up I'll take her just the way she is!" Yes, God showed Adam the gleam of Eve! This was a concerted plan in the mind of God to reveal to Adam his need for Eve.

The challenge of Proverbs chapters 1-9

As the Lord impressed upon Adam his need and desire for Eve in the same fashion Solomon demonstrates great effort in setting before man the qualities of lady wisdom. In the first nine chapters he lays out the gleam of wisdom before you. Almost $1/3^{rd}$ of the book displays her benefits. Even in his conclusion in Chapters 30-31 Solomon sets before you the glorious banquet table of wisdom and calls you to come and eat. His plea is that you cannot live without her. He seeks to awaken the passion of a person to possess hokmah as a man desires to embrace the woman of his longing. Once the hunger is ignited in the heart of man for lady wisdom he will seek after his heart's desire.

In the same manner I researched Betty and began to see her beauty, her brilliance, her benefits, so too Solomon displays the glories of wisdom as Proverbs 3:13-18 states:

> 13 "How blessed is the man who finds wisdom, and the man who gains understanding. 14 For its profit is better than the profit of silver, and its gain than fine gold. 15 She [wisdom] is more precious than jewels' and nothing you desire compares with her. 16 Long life is in her right hand; in her left hand are riches and honor. 17 Her ways are pleasant ways, and all her paths are peace. 18 She is a tree of life to those who take hold of her, and happy are all who hold her fast."

However, as asserted previously in this book modern Christianity fails to capture the gleam of the wisdom writings of the Bible. Where is the attraction of wisdom presented in the teachings of American Christianity whether conservative or liberal? Where is the demonstration of wisdom's glory that invites a man to pursue after her? Where is the intrinsic passion in the heart of men to acquire God's wisdom for today? Where is the level of intent and determination that cries out "I have to have her, to possess her, to make her my own?"

I submit Protestant failure to teach the glories of God's wisdom for present day living can be traced all the way back to the Reformation. During the Reformation Martin

Luther tagged the wisdom book of James a "Strawy epistle." I further submit the neglect of teaching the wisdom writings of the Word continued through the Fundamentalist movement of conservative American Christianity. While Evangelicals did a superlative job of upholding the eternal glories of Christ and the orthodox doctrines of the faith they relegated God's teachings in the wisdom books to second class citizenship.

As a result, fundamentalists did a disservice to that particular revelation of God's Word. This proved detrimental to the full development of Christ followers for many remained ill equipped for the day in and day out living in the here and now. Minus the relevancy of wisdom's teaching in the now, unbelievers came to view the Lord as less caring in people's struggles in the present. People came to view the Saving God, the Biblical God to be concerned about eternity but less about the present day.

For some theologians the gleam of the wisdom writings were subordinated under the jurisdiction of the Law rather than fully relevant in the age of grace. As a result the principles and practices were relegated to be of an age long ago – something in the past outdated and trumped by New Testament teaching. Still others relegated the wisdom of God such as the Sermon on the Mount to the future millennial kingdom and therefore its principles and applications were not binding or relevant in the here and now.

I submit that these are theological errors blocking the relevancy of wisdom and hiding its gleam in the present. Instead of the treasures of wisdom its practical guidance came to mean a nice, interesting, curious set of ideas and implementations enjoyable and thought provoking but non-binding, and certainly not life changing. Such handling of the wisdom books and writings fails to capture the imagination and implementation of Biblical adherents. Minus the igniting of a person's inner desire followers of Scripture fail to pursue her glories. Being non-motivated by wisdom one becomes the disinterested student who was asked the question what is the difference between ignorance and apathy? He answered "Who knows and who cares!"

American Christianity failed to polish and present the gleam of God's wisdom and her vital teachings became muted and marred. As a result there was little attention brought to exegete and exposit the benefits of Proverbs which would spark people's interest and ignite their hunger and thirst to actualize the Lord's hokmah.

It is time to go and get the gleam of wisdom

There is a real need to display before people the gleam of God's wisdom. Christian teachers, institutions, and denominations need to present before the entire populace of the American people: believers and unbelievers, conservative and liberal alike need to be equipped in the wonders of the wisdom writings.

Do you want to change a man all out of recognition? Let him catch the gleam of wisdom for himself for when a person internalizes the gleam pursuit is triggered. A completely different man emerges when his inner desire is detonated.

This is the effort Solomon affects to create within you a pursuit of wisdom's gleam. Throughout Proverbs Solomon charges you: "There's a gleam men. There's a gleam. Go get the gleam!" The gleam here is the wisdom that God has revealed for man to gain in the practical arena of human belief and behavior. The benefits of possessing such wisdom is detailed in Proverbs 8:6-21:

6 Listen for I [wisdom] shall speak noble things; and the opening of my lips will produce right things. 7 For my mouth will utter truth; and wickedness is an abomination to my lips. 8 All the utterances of my mouth are in righteousness; there is nothing crooked or perverted in them. 9 They are all straightforward to him who understands, and right to those who find knowledge. 10 Take my instruction, and not silver, and knowledge rather than choicest gold. 11 For wisdom is better than jewels; and all desirable things can not compare with her....

17 I love those who love me; and those who diligently seek me will find me. 18 Riches and honor are with me, enduring wealth and righteousness. 19 My fruit is better than gold, even pure gold, and my yield than choicest silver. 20 I walk in the way of righteousness, in the midst of the paths of justice, 21 to endow those who live me with wealth, that I may fill their treasuries....

32 Now, therefore, O sons, listen to me, for blessed are they who keep my ways. 33 Heed instruction and be wise, and do not neglect it. 34 Blessed is the man who listens to me, watching daily at my gates, waiting at my doorposts. 35 For he who finds me finds life, and obtains favor from the Lord. 36 But he who sins against me injures himself; all those who hate me love death."

The blessings of wisdom delineated in this passage are:

> Nobility
> Truth
> Protection
> Deliverance
> Righteousness
> Honesty
> Wealth
> Honor
> Justice
> Life
> Favor

These are just some of the benefits Proverbs presents to human living, and Solomon extols such glories of wisdom far exceed the riches of pure gold and choicest silver. Furthermore the blessings of God's performance skills await the man or woman who determines to go out and possess her – who makes wisdom his own. It is time we begin to push those couches, move those stones and pursue after the benefits of the wisdom of God.

To become a person of wisdom you pursue after her with the same intensity a man pursues after the woman of his dreams. You pursue wisdom to possess her. Dear women marry a man who pursued you - who pushed those couches, picked up the stones, who strove to win your heart. So too Solomon says pursue after wisdom and make her your own. This brings us to the second component of becoming a person of wisdom.

Second, acquiring wisdom requires a purchase.

Inherent in the Hebrew term "qanah" is also the idea "to buy". In Proverbs 4:5-9 "qanah" calls one to purchase the Lord's hokmah for one's own possession. A person is to make the decision to obtain the wisdom of God and pay the price to obtain her. Now, we as Americans know all too well the great attraction of buying things we want. We are notorious for buying a lot of stuff. We purchase our toys, our jeans, our sneakers, our cars, our education, our homes. If possible day after day we buy more things.

Like the pursuit of women the determination to purchase items we desire lies inherent in the soul of males. This is certainly evident in our city of Midlothian. When Betty and I arrived in our community, we quickly recognized we now lived in a town filled with man toys: tractors, lawn mowers, motorcycles, four wheelers, boats, pools, acreage sheltering horses, dogs, cattle, goats, Lamas - play things.

Baby Boomer men remember well the old Boys Life magazines for scouting. One of the first things we'd do when our monthly subscription arrived was to open to the page of things to buy. This was the Sears Robuck, the Montgomery Ward's catalog, the E-bay for scouts. Immediately we'd see the scout knife, sleeping bag, utensils, camping stove, pup tent, and a whole lotta other stuff all containing the official scouting logo. Wanting to be a super scout these pictures inflamed our interest to possess those items.

Then we would look at the cost – not in terms of dollars and cents but in terms of man power or shall we say boy power. Why? You could not purchase the item with money - only with effort. Keep in mind while girl scouts sold cookies, boy scouts sold cards - not the popcorn of today. Therefore, as boy scouts we had to discern exactly how many greeting cards, Christmas cards, and birthday cards we would have to sell to our neighbors, friends, and family members (thank God for family members). The question we had to address was did we possess the purchasing power and relationships to obtain that coveted item? Could we convince our parents that they would not be saddled in buying the entirety of the boxes? Of course our parents knew precisely how the dance worked; in the end mom and dad would eventually pick up the cost of any unsold items, but they engaged willingly.

Now, like the Boy's Life scouting items, the gleam of Scripture's wisdom is prominently displayed throughout the pages of Proverbs. Consider for instance Proverbs 3:1-4:

> 1 "My son, do not forget my teaching, but let your heart keep my commandments; 2 for length of days and years of life, and peace they will add to you. 3 Do not let kindness and truth leave you; bind them around your neck, write them on the tablet of your heart. 4 So you will find favor and good repute in the sight of God and man."

The wealth of wisdom such as "length of days," "years of life," "peace" combined with "kindness and truth" and "favor and good repute in the sight of God and man." are to be pursued and purchased. Once acquired these blessings will improve your character, endeavors, marriages, child rearing, profession, communities, and country - talk about bang for your buck. There's a prize to be gained.

What's more in Proverbs 4:5-9 Solomon reveals you have the purchasing power to acquire the blessings of wisdom for yourself, but the benefits will cost you. The means of better living lies within your reach. However, you must purchase her blessings. As you determined to go out and get that pocket knife, sleeping bag, or pup tent Proverbs tells you to make a decision and go out and get the performance skills of God. Make the purchase whether by money or by effort.

A Price to Pay

Now, knowing there is a price to pay to acquire wisdom is not confusing to a person of achievement for there is effort behind any worthwhile acquisition. Before the

New York Giants played the Bills in the 1991 Super Bowl, coach Bill Parcell's said to his players, "Men, this is why you do all those push-ups men. This is why you lift all those weights, run those sprints, go to the meetings. This is why you do all those things."

If there is something or someone a man wants it is within his nature to put down the dollars and put forth the discipline to possess it (her). He will willingly pay the price to acquire the longed for object - the qanah of a wife. Men are wired to pay the price. In fact, if such effort is short circuited I submit the maturation process for a man becomes stunted. He must learn to gain possession of a prize through effort. He must learn to earn the prize. So too in his pursuit of his desired wife, in the Hebrew system a man had to pay to a price for her. There was a cost involved. She did not come cheaply. She had to be possessed with effort. Men are made to pay that price.

The "qanah" of a wife

In Solomon's days a man paid a price to marry the woman he pursued. While we Americans know well the process of purchasing an item, most of our citizens would be repulsed with the thought much less the practice of paying dollars to gain the woman of our dreams. In fact a renewal of this custom would probably create a gender revolt across our country led by both males and females. Therefore, because the monetary practice of the Old Testament culture is so foreign and distasteful to our American style of love and marriage, let us gain a better understanding of its purpose and practice in matrimony.

During the time of Solomon the betrothal and marriage of a woman to a man involved the Father of the bride setting the value upon his daughter to be married. This was called a **mohar**. The mohar was the price the suitor had to pay to the Father to secure the hand of the selected woman he desired to marry. Unless the pursuer paid this agreed upon sum or service there would be no marriage. He had to earn the woman he longed for. He had to work for her hand.

After preaching a sermon on the topic of a mohar, an African family came up to me with great smiles. The man shook my hand and pronounced that was exactly the custom he encountered in gaining his wife. He had to work for her for twelve years. He then presented to the father of his bride gifts. I asked the woman how she felt about this custom. She answered: "I felt important." Today many American women give themselves over to a man for a Coke and a movie. There is a cheapening in the price. A man is not required to work for the woman he longs to marry. The value is lessened.

Consider the mohar required for Jacob to marry Rachel. The agreed upon price for Rachel was mutually set by Jacob and Laban:

Jacob said, "I will serve you seven years for your younger daughter Rachel." Genesis 29:18

"So Jacob served seven years for Rachel and they seemed to him but a few days because of his love for her." Genesis 29:20

Jacob saw her gleam and he worked long and hard for her hand. He was more than willing to pay the price to possess her. However, after the seven years of labor there was a devious twist to Jacob's possession of his sought after bride for Laban deceived him. On the wedding day Laban pulled a switcheroo. Instead of Rachel, Laban presented to Jacob Leah, her older sister.

It took another commitment to gain Rachel – another seven years of labor under Laban. However, this time he had to wait only seven days to marry Rachel, but Jacob had to serve Laban for an additional seven years...." Think of that, fourteen years Jacob served Laban. This was the mohar Jacob faced to gain the hand of Rachel in marriage.

In the age of Solomon the mohar demonstrated that the man who wanted the woman of his dreams would work to obtain her for himself. The principle as shown by Jacob is that a man would do whatever it takes to gain the hand of his beloved.

There are at least three blessings the mohar brings to the marital union.

First, the mohar proved the man.

The mohar revealed a suitor's commitment to the woman he desired to marry. It demonstrated that this man not only wanted the woman but would work to gain her hand. The mohar gave assurance to the female that this male pursuer was authentic in his passion for her.

In this one can see Jacob's passion to possess Rachel was not just a fleeting infatuation or passing lust. The mohar proved the authenticity of his pursuit. Fourteen years of serving Laban demonstrated beyond any question that he wanted her. Jacob really desired Rachel. He proved he would work for her. As a result the mohar showed that his pursuit was authentic. Today a woman must discover other means to determine the quality of a man's intentions for her.

In Solomon's age marriage involved both a pursuit and a purchase. – he had to want her. Marriage involved a price – he had to work for her. The mohar protected the woman against lustful males. In this regard, what's the price to gain a woman and her body today? For some it's the repayment for taking her to Red Lobster. Women, don't give yourself away cheaply... make the man pursue you... make the man earn you.

Some women will spend all their life trying to get the man to pursue her. Rachel never had to question Jacob's determination to possess her. Does he really want me? The desire was authentic. She felt important.

In Biblical times the mohar not only proved the man's intentions but was strategic in the maturation of the man himself. It forced the young man to take responsibility and demonstrate his ability to provide for the woman of his dreams. The mohar showed both the father and frauline that he was suited to be a husband and a father. It evidenced that he was a man who would get his house in order, he had a job, he could save, he would work to provide. He would fulfill his obligations. The mohar proved the man before he got to the altar. This man not only wants you but will work for you. This man will provide for you. He was a man with proven character and conduct. He could carry responsibility.

In our present system of love and marriage the woman is vulnerable because men come to the altar unproven. Betty told me of an instance when our son Philip as a kindergartner took a walk on the school playground with little Brittany. She told me that they were discussing how they would marry one another. I don't know about that little girl, but I know my son. I guarantee he took that conversation seriously. He was figuring out how this could work. Let's see I have no money, no job; however, I can color within the lines and I have just learned to ride my bike without training wheels. Hmmm... I think I can make this work.

Sadly, today we have far too many five year olds getting married. Our societal system does not adequately prepare our young men and women for marriage. As a result, too many women marry boys and not men. In this, the mohar acted as a prevention. The mohar matured the man and proved his pursuit was not infatuation. Therefore, in Biblical days a woman did not hope she would marry a man who would provide for her she knew he did. In this her father helped make this a surety, requiring the suitor topay the price demonstrating a track record of accomplishment. The mohar produced a better man for marriage, family, and community.

Something negative happens when things come too easy for males. Comfortableness, effortlessness, undemanding pursuits stunt the maturing process in males. In modern American pursuit of love and marriage a man is left untested, unproven, under developed. As a result many men enter into marriage today with the tag – "assembly required." Marriage today is too easy and the woman entangles herself with a boy not yet matured. Worse still for women today it is unnecessary to marry to possess a woman. A man can live with a woman. Enjoy the fun of sex without any binding connection.

When marriage or partnership comes too easy for the male the woman finds herself connected to an immature man. She connects herself to a male who has failed to grow up. He has not learned responsibility. Now, he will passionately play with you but he is not prepared to provide for you. The mohar proved the man's intentions and provided a societal means to mature him for the responsibility of marriage and family. The mohar also protected the woman against lustful and slothful males. Women if you embrace a man who doesn't work, and all your life you will end up trying to get that man to achieve. The Lord intended from the man's creation in the Garden until today for males to work. Make sure the man is willing to pay the price – for his sake – for your sake – for our sake. Find a man who will pay the price to provide. Find a man who will work for you.

Second, the mohar protected the woman.

The mohar provided security for the new bride. Although the father received the payment, the dad was to keep the money for his daughter in times of need. The mohar served as security if the marriage ended in divorce or the husband died. At that misfortune the father then gave the entire mohar, or a major portion of it back to the daughter. A dad who kept the mohar for himself was viewed negatively in the culture. The mohar was the social security for the father's daughter, but unlike the way our system works it was not to be spent on other matters, but reserved for the very purpose in which it was given.

It served as a form of social security for the daughter. If something happened to her husband it served as a will. The mohar insured security for the woman. It put the dollars aside if something happened to the man or the marriage dissolved.

Today women are out there with little societal security. There is little pursuit and no purchase price. Women are giving themselves over to boys and not men. The boys are bedding the women without cost and our children are being aborted out of the womb or being born out of wedlock. Minus the security of a married couple, a beloved wife and a mature dad there is little stability in our homes. There is little cost to the man in the present American style of love and marriage.

Third, the mohar produced societal stability

The mohar provided societal cohesion and wellness. It provided an environment conducive to personal wellness and family togetherness. The mohar gave security for the family unit and for society as a whole.

It built men. Today we operate in a society that fails to produce men of pursuit who know the cost and pay the price. We don't ask enough of our men and weakness enters into the male population when a man is not asked to rise to a challenge. Something negative happens when we don't ask enough of men – there is a failure in maturation process which cripples male responsibility and leadership.

It gave security to marriages. Here's a question to ponder: Is the present means of courtship actually better? Today, women must discern the true intentions of a man without the societal protection of a mohar. However, the mohar made a man pay the price. When the man saw the gleam no amount of effort and price was too high. For him she had to be gained. She had to be worked for.

There is a popular sound bite: "Whatever it takes." The mohar proved this actuality in the completion of the mohar. While we met in Church as for my wife Betty it took a year before she agreed to go out with me. We then dated for a year and were engaged for six months. During our courtship I was a full time graduate student at Dallas Theological Seminary, preparing for full-time ministry. I made a commitment to get up at 4:00 each morning to study before attending my courses beginning at 7:30 P.M. To help pay for my studies I worked the maximum time the seminary allowed for a full-time student, twenty-four hours a week as a security guard for the school between 5:00-1:00 A.M. Between rounds I would again hit my books in study. Betty on the other hand worked as a full time RN on the graveyard shift from 11:00 to 7:00 A.M. On the evenings I worked we only had a small slice of time to see one another so she would come over to meet with me at the seminary. About 4:45 p.m. I would have to go to get ready to fulfill my duties as a security guard for the school. On the days I didn't work I would immediately pick her up and we would spend the late afternoon and early evening going out on dates and returning in time for her graveyard shift.

On the weekends when we didn't work we would go out to plays, musicals, parks, etc., On Saturday's we ministered together in a project area in Dallas, on Sunday's we led a Sunday School class together, and she would hear me preach in the evening service. For a year and a half I averaged about four hours of sleep a night, but mastered the art of fifteen minute power naps to keep going. For a year and a half we waltzed that dance. As seven years was just a moment for Jacob to possess Rachel so too that year and a half blurred because I was with her. There was a gleam men! There was a gleam! And her name was Betty!

So too there is a price to pay for becoming a man or woman of wisdom

The first time I met Doctor Howard Hendricks, head of the Christian Education department of Dallas Theological Seminary, national speaker, author, and chaplain of the Dallas Cowboys was when he was the guest lecturer for a Spiritual Leadership course I took at Campus Crusade's International School of Theology in San Bernardino, CA.

At the time I worked the graveyard shift as security guard to help pay for my graduate studies. After staying up all night, I would immediately go to my morning classes. I can't fully explain the excitement I had to sit under this man and learn. However, I was filled with personal questions that a class could not answer. So, as security guard, who knew where the guest speakers were lodged, later that afternoon I made my way to Prof's room and knocked on his door.

For over an hour and a half I talked with Dr. Hendricks about one subject: How does one become a man of the Word of God? I plied him with questions. One question I asked was, "Dr. Hendricks, how do you personally study the Bible?" He spoke that apart from his daily hours of preparation as a professor at DTS and apart from the study required to fulfill his weekly national and global speaking engagements, he told me that he spent one hour every day in his own personal study of the Word of God. He explained how he studies through the entire Bible every six years with his one hour per day. I asked him how many times he had accomplished this six year schedule. He replied "Over five times." Quickly multiplying the variables I calculated that to be over thirty years.

Now, as a "snotty" nosed upstart I asked him, "Prof, how many days have you missed?" He answered, "Not a one."

With that I began to realize what makes Dr. Hendrick's - Dr. Hendricks, and what makes me – me, and you- you. He then continued, "Howard, people say to me, 'Prof. I wish I knew the Bible as well as you.' Now, I am a gracious person please understand, but sometimes I want to say – 'No you don't for if you did you would discipline yourself to become a person of His Word.'"

He then challenged me saying, "Howard there are only two things that God will ever save from this planet - the Word of God and people. You will never waste your life, by building into the lives of people or becoming a man of the Word."

With that statement Hendricks set before me the gleam of Scripture to become a man of the Word. So to Solomon charges us: "There's a gleam men. There's a gleam. Go get the gleam!" It must be understood that to gain the wisdom of God it will cost you something.

The price to be paid, the effort to be extended in becoming a person who possesses God's wisdom is explained in Proverbs 2:1-4 which states:

> "My son, **if you will** receive My sayings, and treasure My commandments within you, 2 make your ear attentive to wisdom, incline your heart to understanding, 3 for **if you** cry out for discernment, lift your voice for understanding, 4 **if you** seek her as silver and search for her as for hidden treasures;"

In this passage there are three conditions that must be met for a person to become a man or woman of the wisdom of God. In Volume IV of this series titled: "Transforming America through Proverbial Coaching" I break down each of the conditions and give eight lessons from this passage in how to become a person of the Word of God. However, here let us take a glance at condition three:

> "If you seek her [wisdom] as silver and search for her as for hidden treasures."

Many Christians try to acquire the knowledge of the Word without cost. Proverbs tells us that one must get into the Word and dig out the nuggets of truth for oneself. The gold and silver of wisdom are in the book but you must get in this book and get them for yourself. In this the possession of the Word of God cannot occur without pursuit and purchase.

How does a man acquire wisdom? The possession of wisdom is equated to a man who pursues the woman he longs for. In order to gain possession he pays a set price and proves himself as a man and his commitment to her. A person is to acquire wisdom in the same manner a man is to pursue and pay the price for the woman he longs to marry. How does a man acquire wisdom? It is like a person who seeks after the precious metals of silver and discovers the map that leads one to treasure.

Scriptural wisdom is not free

Now, please realize there is a distinct difference between salvation and Scriptural wisdom. There is a purchase price necessary for hokmah. Salvation is a work of grace. You cannot earn salvation. Christ paid the entire price on the cross. You receive His gift of forgiveness and eternal life the moment you place your trust in Christ. You receive salvation by faith. Salvation costs you nothing.

However, unlike your salvation the possession of God's wisdom will cost you something. There is a price to pay to possess her benefits. To acquire wisdom you pursue and make a purchase. Are you willing to pay the price to possess her? Yes, throughout Proverbs Solomon charges you: "There's a gleam men. There's a gleam. Go get the gleam!"

There's a gleam men! There's a gleam women! One must pay the price to possess her for oneself. What about you? What price are you paying to become a man or woman of the wisdom of God? You must pursue wisdom for yourself and pay the price to make her your own as Proverbs 23:23 states:

> "Buy truth and do not sell it, get wisdom and instruction and understanding."

Third, acquiring God's wisdom requires prizing

After the pursuit and the paying of the mohar, a man gains possession of his wife, but the wooing and winning of her is not to end with the purchase. There is another crucial element involved in acquiring wisdom that can be explained through the male's relationship with his wife. A man is to prize wisdom just as he is to prize his wife. Solomon explains this in Proverbs 4:7-9 when he states:

> 7 "The beginning of wisdom is: acquire wisdom, and with all your acquiring gain understanding. 8 **Prize her** and she will exalt you; she will honor you if you embrace her. 9 She will place on your head a garland of grace; she will present you with a crown of beauty."

The Hebrew term for "prize her" is salseleha. Salseleha means "to esteem", "to set a high value on," "to raise something up." Other Biblical examples of salseleha involve the building up of a highway in Isaiah 62:10, and the uplifting of God in worship as shown in Psalm 68:4.

> "Go through, go through the gates; clear the way for the people; build up, build up the highway; remove the stones, **lift up** a standard over the peoples." Isa. 62:10

> "Sing to God, sing praises to His name; **cast up** a highway for Him who rides through the deserts, whose name is the Lord, and exult before Him." Psalm 68:4

Prizing means you are a one woman man

Of the seven billion people who roam our earth, three and a half billion of these humans are women. That's a lot of women. However, of all these females your wife is to be set apart- lifted up – valued higher than any other woman. She is to reign supreme and next to the Lord your wife is to take prominence over all other relationships.

For over a year a pastoral friend of mine kept a framed picture of his wife on the floor in a corner of his study. In contrast to her portrait pictures of friends, kids, family members were prominently displayed on the walls and in strategic locations on his book shelves. His favorite professional football team was bannered on a wall with a bobble head sitting at the front of his desk. However, week after week, month after month, the picture of his wife stayed alone, collecting dust in the corner.

At one time I joked about the picture hoping this would motivate him to prominently display her portrait in his study. This had no effect. A few months later I indulged in a deeper question by asking him what this communicated to his wife every time she walked into his office. Even after discussing this he never moved the picture of his wife from that location. She never attained to the status of his pro team.

Then he switched to a larger more prestigious office. Even then, after arranging his pictures, awards, diploma's and team banner he once again curiously placed her picture alone, on the floor near a corner of the room. What was even stranger is that right next to his picture of Jesus was an open space and peg to hang a prominent picture. It seemed to be the perfect spot for his wife's portrait. I mean is there another location better suited than to be resting right next to the Lord? Yet this peg remained empty. Nothing hung from it. As far as I know her portrait still picks up dust on the floor.

We pursued, we purchased, but do we prize? Scripture tells us we are to prize wisdom. We are not to forget her. We are not to forsake her. As Rogers and Hammerstein's musical South Pacific asserts when Emile Debeck sings "Some Enchanted Evening" to Nellie: "Once you have found her never let her go."

When Betty and I were dating we fell into a routine. I would come to pick her up for our date. Upon entering she looked magnificent and I would ask, "Honey, are you ready?" To which she always replied, "No, not yet." Then I would customarily respond, "That's alright honey! Take all the time you need." Upon which she would disappear back into her room and I would sit on the couch and wait for her second appearance. There was no hurrying after all I would soon be with her. However, now after thirty years of marriage I'm out of the driveway and down the road before I realize she's not in the car. Today so many of us men are forgetting and turning our affections, our commitments away from the wife of our youth. After ten, twenty, thirty years we look for a greener pasture, a younger woman. Where is the commitment to the woman who stood with us through the growth, the raising of our children, the battles we faced together?

Worse still many men are forsaking the wife of their youth. At the beginning of the 1900's only 1/10th of 1 percent of all Americans had experienced a divorce. Recently I heard John Trent disclose that in 1950 only four married couples out of 1000 had experienced a divorce. However, this year alone there will be more divorces than marriages. Sometimes our marriages do not even last down the aisle. We are failing to prize her in our older days. Prizing her enables you to continue to see the gleam.

> 5 "Acquire wisdom [hokmah]! Acquire understanding! Do not forget, nor turn away from the words of my mouth. 6 Do not forsake her [wisdom], and she will guard you..."

Solomon asserts that as we are not to forget, turn away from, or forsake our wives so too we are to lift up and esteem the wisdom of God. The terms forget, turn away, and forsake portray a negative digression away from actualizing the wisdom of the Lord. This downward divergence of apostates begins with forgetting, moves into a conscious moving away from Scripture, and ends with an actual forsaking of her truths.

Culturally one can see this downward prizing of wisdom in our more recent generations. As with our wives, wisdom is not to be forgotten, turned away from, or forsaken. In analyzing our recent American generations we discover that the GI Joe generation determined to follow the paths of Christian upbringing. However, this was not true of the Baby Boomers.

Eerily similar is how people fail to esteem, to value, to lift up the Word of God. The Scriptures, instead of being prized and prominently displayed in our hearts and lives often lie dusty, unused unnoticed. Like this man's picture of his wife the Word is left on the floor while the lesser avenues of life take prominence. We spend our lives in so many activities fixated on lesser causes, things, ventures, people, but take little time to get into the Word and manifest its truths for ourselves.

The benefits of acquiring wisdom

This is just the opposite of Solomon's charge to acquire wisdom through prizing. So continuing our analogy of a man's relationship with his wife let us answer how one is to lift up and esteem the wisdom of the Word. Let us engage the passage of Proverbs 4:5-9 again.

> 5 "Acquire wisdom [hokmah]! Acquire understanding! Do not forget, nor turn away from the words of my mouth. 6 Do not forsake her [wisdom], and she will guard you; love her, and she will watch over you. 7 "The beginning of wisdom is: acquire wisdom, and with all your acquiring gain understanding. 8 Prize her and she will exalt you; she will honor you if you embrace her. 9 She will place on your head a garland of grace; she will present you with a crown of beauty."

Acquire the wisdom and she will…
"guard you,"
"watch over you,"

"exalt you,"
"honor you"
"place on your head a garland of grace"
"present you with a crown of beauty."

These are just some of the benefits Proverbs presents to human living. Solomon extols such glories of wisdom far exceed the riches of pure gold and choicest silver. Furthermore the blessings of God's performance skills await the man or woman who determines to go out and possess her – who makes wisdom his own.

However, when we disconnect the hokmah of God, when we place her on the floor as we pursue other avenues of expression there is a loss that occurs to the human experience, but if wisdom is esteemed, loved, and embraced she is crafted to bring to the expressions of man a most full and wonderful life. She exalts the one who prizes her and brings honor to her possessor. She offers a most abundant reward of grace and an enduring trophy of beauty which awaits the person who actualizes her attributes.

These are just some of the benefits Proverbs presents to human living. There is such a prize for you. Why miss wisdom's gleam? Solomon extols such glories of wisdom far exceed the riches of pure gold and choicest silver. Furthermore the blessings of God's performance skills await the man or woman who determines to go out and possess her – who makes wisdom his own.

"There's a gleam men. There's a gleam. Let's go get the gleam!"

Becoming a person of wisdom involves acquiring.
Make a commitment to acquire the Lord's hokmah!

Chapter 6: Giving Attention to Wisdom

Many times during elementary school, as my teacher waxed eloquently about the lesson and fellow students sat seemingly enthralled by the learning process, I would be daydreaming about anything else. On one such occasion, I was creating (doodling) offensive plays on a piece of paper for my Saturday's upcoming Little League football game against the mighty, undefeated Badgers. While I was exploring my abilities as an offensive coordinator, Mrs. Walters, my fifth grade teacher at Wing Lake Elementary stood leading the class in discussing our weekly vocabulary list. As for me, I really didn't have a clue to the words she was pronouncing and their definitions because I was actively working behind the scenes on a game changing play.

All of a sudden, Mrs. Walters uttered the one word every daydreamer dreads to hear. She called out my name. "Howard!" Immediately I snapped back into attention. Awakened and now fully cognizant of my vulnerable educational situation I internalized that this existential happening was probably not going to end well. Mrs. Walters then did the second thing daydreamers fear the most she asked me a pointed question concerning the lesson: "Howard, how do you pronounce this word?" I lifted my eyes to observe her pointing to a term on the blackboard containing seven letters "a-n-t-i-q-u-e". Having failed to hear a single consonant of the class discussion, and to the best of my knowledge, having never encountered this word in its written form before, I was dumbfounded. How do you pronounce a-n-t-i-q-u-e? Instantly, I began to whirl around in my mind my knowledge of phonics.

Standing up, as we were required to do, I responded, ever so slowly and deliberately the following: "Ann -- ti -- cue (as in cue ball). As I said this, I knew this could not be right. My error was spontaneously confirmed by the raucous laughter of my classmates and one student saying: "Ann -- ti – cue?" On the positive side, although I sufficiently embarrassed myself in front of my peers, I did possess a real neat set of plays for Saturday's game. Let's face it those Badgers were tough.

What happened? The problem lay with inattention. I simply failed to focus upon what my teacher was communicating. I had turned my attention to other matters. In so doing I did not hear what she was saying. I did not know the answer.

Now, there is nothing unique about my non-hearing episode. You've done the exact same thing. You too can share personal examples of inattentiveness and the negative outcomes that occurred. In fact, you may be experiencing a moment of mental distraction right now as you read this chapter.

Such stories of inattentiveness mirror what so many people do to the Word of God. Even when we open the pages of the Bible we often find ourselves doodling our plays, contemplating our strategies, and focusing our minds upon coming events. Engaged by such personal excursions, we fail to hear what the Lord is saying. Like I tuned out Mrs. Walters, we have turned our ears away from the Scriptures to engage what we think are more pertinent, relevant, exciting, immediate concerns.

However, please realize there is an infinite difference between human fancies and the content of the Bible. The Bible does not communicate an inventive curriculum of vocabulary lists, geometry, physics, or chemistry, neither does it present the latest collection of human theories or the newest advent of cultural conjectures, instead the Scriptures declare that its teaching is the actual revelation of the Lord God and His will to man. In this assertion the Bible is unmistakable. Over three thousand three hundred times in the Old Testament alone is the equivalent saying, "Thus saith the Lord." From Moses to the Prophets, from Matthew to Paul to Peter to John, the human authors of Scripture all attest that their writings are the very Word of God.

Now, if this is so, if God has spoken, if He has actually revealed Himself and His knowledge to man in the Bible, then there is nothing more important, more essential, more necessary than to hear what He has said. This is precisely Solomon's command in Proverbs 2:2a when he states: "make your ear attentive to wisdom."

So how do you give attention to wisdom?

First, set your ear to hear.

Throughout Proverbs the learning gate for gaining the knowledge of God's hokmah is the ear. The ear, like an intake valve must be opened for the Lord's wisdom to flow into the life of the receiver as the following verses attest:

> "He whose ear listens to the life-giving reproof will dwell among the wise." (15:31)
> "... he who listens to reproof acquires understanding." (15:32b)
> "He who gives attention to the word shall find good..." (16:20a)
> "...the ear of the wise seeks knowledge." (18:15b)
> "Incline your ear and hear the words of the wise, and apply your mind to my knowledge;" (22:17)

Please note: Solomon places the responsibility of hearing the Lord's hokmah directly upon you. No one else can do this for you. It is your choice. It is your decision. You are to set your ear to hear the wisdom of God. So what catches your ear? What do you give your ear to hear?

When it comes to hearing we all have personal preferences. For instance, as a young boy, my favorite football team was the Cleveland Browns. I was born in Berea,

Ohio where the Browns practiced. We lived in North Olmsted located thirty minutes from Browns stadium. We lived there from 1950-1962, moving the same year Paul Brown was fired. My heart broke when we moved that infinite distance of one hundred twenty-five miles from Cleveland, Ohio to Detroit, Michigan. For the first few years in Detroit even when my Dad took me to the Lions game all I wanted to do was listen to the Browns.

We had one radio in our house that picked up the broadcast of Cleveland's games. The radio was in our kitchen. I would sit at a little desk next to that radio, and for three hours I would move the little knob back and forth during the game, so I could keep the game going on. During commercials, I would make and eat pickle sandwiches and drink chocolate milkshakes. I was in dog-pound heaven, because I was listening to my Browns.

This was my personal preference. I longed to hear those radio broadcasts. How many of you would spend three hours on a Sunday afternoon with your ear plastered to a radio station requiring the constant moving of a dial to stay connected to a faint, distorted signal while gaining sustenance by eating pickle sandwiches for the specific purpose of hearing the Cleveland Browns? For me it was a matter of preference, I had to listen to the Browns.

Then I got into music. Music for me involved Bob Dylan, The Moody Blues, Neil Young, Richie Havens, James Taylor, Cat Stevens, Gordon Lightfoot, Donovan, Harry Chapin, Jim Croce, Buffet St. Marie, John Denver, Joni Mitchell, Judy Collins. I went to sleep with my headphones on listening to such music. Many nights I slumbered to the sounds of the Moody Blues. This practice explains why I have difficulty hearing over the crickets and high pitch sounds rumbling in my ear today.

Following my passion for such music, I learned to play acoustic guitar and strove to excel in the musical venue of folk. I wrote songs, practiced rifts, played at small Christian colleges and coffee shops and customarily serenaded my dates. Following this mode of courtship, on the third date with Betty I invited her to come to Dallas Theological Seminary. We sat in the stairwell of Lincoln Hall. I pulled out my Martin D-28 and began to sing. After the third song, Betty touched my arm and said, "Howard, I'm really not into John Denver."

At that moment I discovered Betty's listening preference for music did not mirror mine. On the other hand she did possess a musical preference for during her college days my wife was really into Motown especially the Temptations. The degree of her motivation to hear her favorite singing group evidenced itself when the Temptations came to Texas Woman's University during her sophomore year. She waited hours and hours in line to be the first one to purchase tickets. During the concert she sat in the front row. After the concert she successfully snuck behind the stage to meet the group. What was the difference between the Temptations and John Denver? For "My Girl" Betty it was a matter of preference she just wasn't into "Rocky Mountain High." Fortunately we both loved musicals.

You see, when it comes to things we hear, we all have personal preferences. With professional football some people listen attentively to the Cleveland Browns, others the Detroit Lions, maybe the Dallas Cowboys or the Pittsburgh Steelers. So too people exercise preference in their music: some favor Beethoven others Bach, some enjoy

Sinatra others Nat King Cole, some like the Beatles others the Supremes, some sit spell bound by Neil Young while others turn their ears to Snoop Dog.

Going beyond the entertainment scene of music and sports there are a multitude of diverse voices calling out for your attention such as: philosophies, religions, pursuits, professions, CNN, Fox News, the Drudge Report, talk radio, math, conservatism, liberalism, youtube, even theological programs such as Gilligans Island or the Kadashians. So what captures your attention? What catches your ear? What do you turn your ear to hear? With all of these listening options, Proverbs commands you…

"to make your ear attentive to wisdom."

The Hebrew term for "make" in Proverbs 2:2a is the infinitive - lehaqsib. Lehaqsib comes from the primitive root (qashab – kaw-shab') which means " to prick up the ears, i.e, hearken:-- attend, (cause to) hear, give heed, incline, mark (well), regard."

Strong's Hebrew and Chaldee Dictionary, p. 105, #7181

In the same manner one chooses to hear a certain speaker, a teacher, a musician, a politician, or a favorite sports team Proverbs commands you to make a determinative decision to tune your ear to hear the wisdom of God. This directive is precisely the thrust of Solomon's teaching in Proverbs 3:32-35 which states:

> 32 "Now, therefore, O sons, listen to me [wisdom], for blessed are they who keep my ways. 33 Heed instruction and be wise, and do not neglect it. 34 Blessed is the man who listens to me, watching daily at my gates, waiting at my doorposts. 35 For he who finds me finds life, and obtains favor from the Lord."

Therefore, to become a hokam, to become a person of wisdom Solomon proclaims you are to turn your attention away from the volume of lesser voices and make a cognitive, volitional decision to put on your headphones, set your ear inserts and focus your listening to hear every note, every verse, every refrain of the wisdom of God. So how do you make your ear attentive to wisdom?

Consider the great Johnny Unitas. At one time all NFL quarterbacks called their own plays. Every player in the huddle paid strict attention to the play calling of their QB. There was to be no talking in the huddle except for just one player - the quarterback. All the offensive players were to hear ye him. Every eye and ear in that huddle was wide open to his voice. Everyone in that huddle needed to hear the voice of the quarterback for in his call each player knew the precise play, the purpose of the play and their individual part to run it successfully. The greatest QB of that era was Johnny Unitas. In the huddle no one spoke but Johnny U. Every ear was turned to listen to him. All the players knew it was Unitas' huddle.

So too Proverbs commands each of us to set our ears and listen to the play calling, the wisdom of the Lord in living life well. Like the players who huddled up and turned their ears to hear the great Johnny Unitas, so too you are to enter the huddle of God's hokmah and hear the wisdom of the Lord.

If you want to be a man or woman of wisdom Proverbs commands you to turn your ear and hear the hokmah of God. In this regard you are to be in the huddle of hokmah and acquire the precise play call. You are to set your ear to hear the Lord's hokmah. Is this true of you? Have you made a determinative decision to set your ear to hear the wisdom of God? How do you make your ear attentive to wisdom? First, you set your ear to hear His hokmah.

Second, you give preference to wisdom's principles.

Principles matter, and in the same vein people are advantaged or disadvantaged in sports by physical attributes: some humans are fast - others slow, some are strong - others weak, some are tall - others short; so too in the game of life humans are advantaged or disadvantaged not as much by stature (ask Napoleon) or strength (ask David), but by the principles they adhere and advance. You see, principles matter, and if a person or a people apply a lesser set, an inferior collection, an impotent gang of principles there will be a lowering of human and societal performance in that area of living.

To better grasp this principle, consider my misfortune in mimicking the kicking style of Lou "The Toe" Groza. Lou Groza was the All-Pro Offensive tackle and kicker for the Cleveland Browns from 1946-1967. During his twenty-one year Hall of Fame career Mr. Groza played in more final championship games (13) than anyone in the history of professional football. However, he acquired the nickname Lou "The Toe" Groza because this 270 lb. man did all his kicking (field goals, extra-points, kick-offs) with his toe. He was by far the best field goal kicker of his era.

So as a child living near the Cleveland area in the 50's and early 60's I wanted to kick like Lou" the Toe". I watched Groza kick, I studied his style, I read about his principles for kicking. I avidly practiced his method. Although I never was very good for eighteen plus years I kicked Lou "The Toe" Groza style. I kicked the ball with my toe.

After graduating from high school I attended Texas Christian University in 1970 and tried to walk on the "Horned Frog" team as a defensive back. The freshman coach informed me that I was too small and too slow for TCU football. By the way too small and too slow is not a good combination for a football player. After all the "heart" can only compensate for so much. The coach then refused to let me walk on. Once back into my car I wept deeply.

Eventually I transferred to Spring Arbor University with four of my closest friends. This small Christian college didn't have a football team, but they did have a soccer team. So I purchased a pair of soccer shoes and went out for the team. Immediately they stuck me on a wing because even though I wasn't fast enough for TCU football I was plenty fast for that Christian college soccer team. For them I could really run.

Now, for those who play soccer you should recognize instantly that I encountered a problem, because when you kick the soccer ball, it is improper, less effective, even anathema to kick with the toe. In soccer one kicks with the instep and power shots boom from the front part of the foot – sledgehammer style. As a result, all my years of learning to kick, a lah "Lou the Toe" Groza worked against me. To excel in this new sport Mr. Groza's principles had to be reversed. I had to relearn everything to successfully kick that soccer ball. It took me two years to overcome my performance disability and become proficient in kicking, crossing, passing with my foot – not my toe. I never really mastered it.

I submit this is what happens when people, when communities, when movements, even country's practice inferior principles whether kicking a ball, learning to read, running a business, or leading a nation. People and communities waste a lot of time, energy and dollars learning inadequate principles and then engaging these impotent principles into programs and practices. What is happening is that the inadequate principles themselves teach people to kick with their toe when they should be kicking with their instep. Worse still the more these lesser directives are ingrained in the culture the harder it is to correct the misalignment and manifest what is truly best. We keep engaging, teaching, leading with the insufficient even harmful set of convictions. As a result, there is a continuation of lesser conduct by individuals and populace who mistakenly or wrongfully prefer the proliferation of such inadequate principles.

However, if a person or a people embrace, engage, and enable correct principles there will be a bettering of life. In this Proverbs seeks to build the human experience of individual, families, communities, even countries by injecting life excelling principles into the souls of people and the fabric of society. In so doing Proverbs declares that its principles will improve your personal life [3:13-15], better your relationship with God [2:5-8]. improve your interaction with others [2:9-11] and bring honor, goodness, righteousness and success to living as Proverbs 8:4-21 speaks.

> 4 "To you, O men, I [wisdom] call….6 Listen for I shall speak noble things; and the opening of my lips will produce right things…8 All the utterances of my mouth are in righteousness; there is nothing crooked or perverted in them. 9 They are all straightforward to him who understands, and right to those who find knowledge.

> 10 Take my instruction, and not silver, and knowledge rather than choicest gold, 11 for wisdom is better than jewels; and all desirable things cannot compare with her….18 Riches and honor are with me, enduring wealth and righteousness. 19 My fruit is better than gold even pure gold, and my yield than choicest silver. 20 I walk in the way of righteousness, in the midst of the paths of justice, 21 to endow those who love me with wealth, that I may fill their treasuries."

If this is accurate then man possesses a divinely revealed mother lode of principles to guide the human experience to better living. Such principles of God's wisdom give to humanity a bank of great wealth. To better understand how rich God's wisdom truly is, compare and contrast the silver and gold of hokmah to the legend of the Lost Dutchman's Gold Mine.

One of the most geographically rugged and historically rich locations in Arizona is the Superstition Mountains. In exploring this mountain range many a person has mysteriously disappeared. However, even with the casualties people keep venturing into the preserve. One reason for this attraction is the legend of the Lost Dutchman's hidden stash of gold. In Arizona lore an old prospector discovered the mother lode of gold in the 1800's somewhere in those Superstitions. However, he never disclosed the location of his treasures to family, friend, or foe. As legend records he died hoarding the riches to himself. The mother lode of gold is still there.

Even today, there are people who enter the Superstitions searching to discover the Dutchman's mine and gain the gold for themselves. Some prospectors take this search deadly serious. Hikers who venture off the established trails have been shot at when they get too close to people who are aggressively seeking to find the Dutchman's treasure. In this regard, one needs to be cautious of a person who hoards or seeks wealth for oneself.

Now, like the Dutchman, Solomon too had discovered the mother lode of gold, but his stash contained the riches of the wisdom of God as Proverbs 3:13-15 attests:

> "How blessed is the man who finds wisdom, and the man who gains understanding. 14 For its profit is better than the profit of silver, and its gain than fine gold. 15 She is more precious than jewels; and nothing you desire compares with her."

However, unlike the Dutchman he chose to disclose his riches to others, even to the point of drawing a precise map (Proverbs), directing any willing person to the precise location to obtain the treasures for themselves. In this disclosure, he demonstrated his benevolent intention, for it is possible for an individual to hoard knowledge in the same manner one hoards material wealth.

In fact, the more valuable the data the more one might be tempted to keep the knowledge to oneself, especially if such information provides an advantage over others in gaining or maintaining wealth, power, and prestige. Essential knowledge possessed by any person or group provides such a person(s) with an enormous advantage over their contemporaries. This is true whether one is placing a bet, running a business, waging a war, leading a nation. The advantage goes to the one who holds the knowledge while the disadvantage falls upon the person lacking such information.

On the other hand, Solomon chose not to restrict his knowledge to a select group of people. He advocated an equitable system of learning irrespective of a person's upbringing, social class, culture, or nationality. Solomon cried out, "Here are God's treasures! Listen to her riches! Make a determination to gain her wealth for yourself!"

With this conviction, the knowledge of Proverbs extends far beyond the nation of Israel and functions as a book of common grace, for Solomon in his writings made a commitment to teach God's practical skills and moral guidelines to every person, every people group, every nation willing to hear.

> "To you, O men, I call, and my voice is to the sons of men..."
> Proverbs 8:4

Therefore you can go to the bank of God's wisdom and make a withdrawal of its principles. The hokmah of God is in there. God's wisdom speaks to our marriages, our child rearing, our business decisions, and on and on and on. Yes, principles matter and there is a huge difference in the presuppositions and precepts people adopt to live life. With respect to principles what do you prefer? Do you prefer the hokmah of God or human whim? Proverbs tells you to make your ear attentive to God's wisdom. Do you give attention to the principles of God's hokmah?

The bank account is full. The gold is there. Dig out its riches and make a withdrawal of God's wisdom for the area of life you need it the most. Therefore, when a person makes their ear attentive to wisdom it means they volitionally set their learning capacities to understand the principles of the wisdom of the Lord.

Now, picture yourself being in the huddle with the great Johnny Unitas in what many NFL historians call the greatest game ever played, the Colts 1958 championship game against the New York Giants. In overtime the Colts have the ball and begin driving down the field to win the game. Unitas calls his play. In that play you have coded every piece of information for each and every offensive player. The play includes all the details necessary for each and every player to know precisely his place and action to make that play successful. Everyone knows exactly what to do. You know what you are to do.

Now, this doesn't mean that the wide receivers gdidn't have a preference of a particular play – down out and up. Certainly the half back preferred a sweep around the end or the fullback, a run between the tackles. You see, everyone had a preference, but in that huddle when Johnny U called the play – each player willingly submitted their desires for the sake of the team.

So too in your present situation, circumstance, problem, joy, grief, decision it is inevitable that you have a preference- you have a play you want to run, but in the heat of the game, when Johnny U calls the play you commit to that play. When God's hokmah calls a play in the game of life, you commit to that play. Hear the play call, understand its meaning, and commit to give preference to it. What is true of us as individuals is also true for us as a people. Give preference to wisdom's principles.

Doesn't this make sense? Think of God's hokmah in terms of creation. What is this wealth that the Lord has stored up for us to draw upon throughout our lives? Solomon tells us that hokmah is the very wisdom that God used in creating the universe as Proverbs 8:22-31 asserts:

> 22 "The Lord possessed me [wisdom] at the beginning of His way, before His works of old. 23 From everlasting I was established, from the beginning, from the earliest times of the earth. 24 When there were no depths I was brought forth, when there were no springs abounding with water. 25 Before the mountains were settled, before the hills I was brought forth; 26 while He had not yet made the earth and the fields, nor the first dust of the world. 27 When He established the heavens, I was there, when He inscribed a circle on the face of the deep, 28 when He made firm the skies above, when the springs of the deep became fixed, 29 when He set for the sea its boundary, so that the water should not transgress His command, when He marked out the foundations of the earth; 30 then I was beside Him, as a master workman; and I was daily His delight, rejoicing always before Him, 31 rejoicing in the world, His earth, and having my delight in the sons of men."

Think of that, hokmah is the precise knowledge God used in initiating and guiding the magnificent structure and complexities of the universe. From the creation of the stars to the developing baby in the womb all evidence the Lord's wisdom. Hokmah rejoices in fulfilling her designed purpose to guide humans to better and bountiful living. This is the work of wisdom, and God rejoices in her compositional masterpiece.

Think of it in this manner. My step dad, Ken Beaser, was an architect. He communicated with me about a meeting his division attended for a presentation of a construction company that successfully built one of the largest domed football stadiums in the NFL – the Silverdome. Ken told me that in this man's presentation he explained the intricacies and challenges of building this mammoth seventy-thousand seat coliseum. At the end of his presentation he declared: "If our company can successfully build the Silverdome. We certainly can build your structure." With that proven background Ken's company hired them.

Now, if wisdom can build the universe, just as that company can construct a building, so wisdom can build your life, marriage, family, business, even society for the better. The principles of hokmah are constant principles. In whatever you are going through, hear ye the wisdom of the Lord and give preference to her principles.

How, does one make their ear attentive to wisdom? First, you set your ear to hear, second, you give preference to the Lord's hokmah, and...

Third, you run the play

The Hebrew term for "attentive" in Proverbs 2:2a "make your ear attentive to wisdom" is ('ozneka). 'Ozeneka carries the idea of hearing with the commitment to heeding. As a result, a person who gives attention to wisdom purposes "to know" and "to do" the hokmah of God. Therefore, attending to wisdom does not conclude with the accumulation of a bucket full of principles, or a complete set of notebooks, or a well-defined declaration of truth, attending to wisdom concludes with the actual doing. People give attention to wisdom when they heed its directives.

The essential component of doing the Word of God rings throughout Scripture and is a distinguishing mark of an authentic believer. Throughout the Bible the only proper response to God's word is to hear and heed the Word of the Lord.

Consider Moses' challenge to Israel

1 "Now this is the commandment, the statutes and the judgments which the Lord your God has commanded me to teach you, that you might do them in the land where you are going over to possess it, 2 so that your grandson might fear the Lord your God, to keep all His statutes and His commandments, which I command you, all the days of your life, and that your days may be prolonged. 3 'O Israel, you should listen and be careful to do it, that it may be well with you and that you may multiply greatly, just as the Lord, the God of your fathers, has promised you, in a land flowing with milk and honey.'"

Deuteronomy 6:1-3

Consider the call of Joshua

"Only be strong and very courageous; be careful to do according to all the law which Moses My servant commanded you; do not turn from it to the right or to the left, so that you may have success wherever you go. 8 This book of the law shall not depart from your mouth, but you shall meditate on it day and night, so that you may be careful to do according to all that is written in it; for then you will make your way prosperous, and then you will have success."

Joshua 1:7-8

Consider the words of Jesus

"Therefore, everyone who hears these words of Mine, and acts upon them, may be compared to a wise man, who built his house upon the rock. 25 And the rain descended, and the floods came, and the winds blew, and burst against that house; and yet it did not fall, for it had been founded upon the rock. 26 And everyone who hears these words of Mine, and does not act upon them, will be like a foolish man, who built his house upon the sand. 27 And the rain descended, and the floods came, and the winds blew, and burst against that house; and it fell, and great was its fall."

Matthew 7:24-27

Consider the wisdom book of James

"But prove yourselves doers of the word, and not merely hearers who delude themselves. 23 For if anyone is a hearer of the word and not a doer, he is like a man who looks at his natural face in a mirror; 24 for once he has looked at himself and gone away, he has immediately forgotten what kind of person he was. 25 But one who looks intently at the perfect law, the law of liberty, and abides by it, not having become a forgetful hearer but an effectual doer, this man shall be blessed in what he does."

James 1:22-25:

So too, Proverbs asserts that people are to turn their ears to hear and heed the wisdom of the Lord. This is the meaning of making your ear attentive to wisdom. You hear the principles in order to put them into practice. Once the principles of wisdom are properly identified then the behaviors are to follow suit. Therefore, it is essential to understand what the meaning of the Scripture actually is and how the application of that meaning is to actually work. Both meaning and application are necessary. Get the principles down and then put them into practice. Therefore, one does not give attention to the Lord's wisdom until the principles are properly put into practice.

Nine time major golf winner Gary Player set a goal to practice his sand trap shots over and over again until he sank five shots – he then concluded his practice. Gary knew the right principles. He knew how to hold the club. He knew how to dig his feet in the sand. He knew how to swing the wedge. He knew all those things, but then he practiced them, and practiced them, and practiced them. As a result he became undeniably one of the greatest sand trap artists in the history of the game. However, please note: Gary practiced precisely the proper principles to hit a sand shot. You see practice only makes perfect when you practice the precise principles.

As Gary excelled in his wedge play by practicing his shots over and over again this is the process by which God intends for you to actualize in Proverbs. The Lord reveals His principles. You hear them. You prefer them. Then you put them into practice. As a result, your life is changed for the better in whatever area of life you apply His knowledge. You begin to become a man or woman of performance skill. Your life begins to be transformed – God's style. This transformational change is there for you in whatever area of life you actualize the principles of God's wisdom whether your speech, manners, marriage, decision making, etc.

Therefore, in whatever enterprise one enters, a person would do well to investigate the knowledge of God's hokmah in that particular expression. Compare the directives of hokmah with the present set of guidance you are giving your ear to hear. What principles are you actually heeding? Are you following the principles of hokmah or have you deviated into lesser dogma? Commit yourself to unlocking the principles and the practices of the Lord's wisdom. Then put them into practice in your marriage, your business, even to the social issues and challenges of our day and watch God work.

The end result of hokmah is not measured by glowing promises or pledges but by excellence of performance and exquisite products. Hokmah is actualized in the true quality of the expression and the ultimate end of a matter. Take a good look at your life. With respect to hokmah how are you doing as a person? How is your personal life? What about your marriage? How's your business? As a nation how are we doing in educating our children? How's the economy? How are we doing in building our citizenry? What are the conditions of our relationships with our neighbors? How's our nation's infrastructure? How are we doing in building men? What percentage of our men are in prison? How's our economy? What percentage of our population lives in poverty? How's the defense of our country? How are we doing in taking care of the most innocent, fragile, persons among us?

However, it must be clearly understood that making your ear attentive to wisdom does not conclude with the acquisition of principles it concludes with the actual doing of the wisdom.

Let us now conclude our Johnny U. analogy. Imagine Unitas calling a play in the huddle and then he says, "Ready break!" However, instead of the players breaking the huddle to run the play, the offensive center verbalizes, "Johnny, that was one great play you just called. In fact, it was tremendous! Call another one!" Mesmerized by the quality of that particular play call the players stayed in the huddle instead of running the play. The fans were stunned. The coach confused. The players simply stayed in the huddle. Johnny U. then gathered his players back into the huddle and called another play. This time the tight end stated, "Johnny that play call wasn't quite up to your standards, try another one. I think you can do better." Then Johnny U. called a third play, the halfback states, "I liked the first play you called better. The third one was OK but that first one, whew! Now, that was something!" Throughout the game on and on and on – the players stayed in the huddle only hearing the play calling of Johnny U. Is this not a picture of Christianity today?

The play of God's wisdom is called to run the play. The judgment is not the quality of the play call by our pastors and Christian leaders, the judgment is whether people are running the play. How, do you make your ear attentive to wisdom? First, you set your ear to hear the wisdom of the Lord; second, you give preference to wisdom's principles, and third, you then run the play.

Hokmah gives specific guidance in the how to's of living life according to the will of God. In Proverbs one encounters the principles and practices that need to be actualized for the wellbeing of people both personally and in society. In this many of us acknowledge the Lord but fail to follow His advice in the specific aspects of living life. The hokmah of God is to be known and implemented. Isn't it time we prefer the hokmah of God both personally and publicly? It is time we run the plays.

It is time we pay attention to the wisdom of God

While pastoring and working as a professor in Phoenix I hiked and jogged the mountain preserves of the Valley of the Sun for seventeen years. More specifically my excursions covered three primary trails measuring from two to six miles - up, down and around South Mountain, Shaw Butte, and North Mountain. In my jogging experience I encountered various snakes (garter, gopher, about fourteen rattle snakes), reptiles, animals (foxes, ring tails, horses, dogs, donkey's, coyotes, javelina). Over the years, averaging 4 times a week, I logged thousands of miles (calculated 14,144) throughout the preserves without a single attack (although one time I jumped over a startled rattlesnake). During my hour to an hour and a half on those paths each day I prayed, listened to spiritual tapes, studied, memorized Scripture, and enjoyed God's creation. My goal was to seek the Lord and stay in shape. I never worried about the condition of those trails I trusted in those man made paths. Besides, once navigated I knew precisely where they were taking me. Even after moving from Phoenix to the Dallas area twelve years ago I can still visualize the bends, the terrain, the subtle nuances and sudden elevation changes of those three circuits.

However, at least six times I fell by not paying attention to the path. My falling never occurred going up or down an incline, but each time happened when I was on a straight and flat part of the trail. Feeling secure in my direction my mind and eyes would drift from the trail to view the scenery. Inevitably, I would hit a rock with my toe and then sprawl to the ground with my hands taking the brunt of the fall. My flesh on my hands and knees would tear from rocks and then I would finish my jog for that day bleeding profusely. Each time the fall occurred after I took my eyes off the path. Few things in life are as embarrassing as confidently jogging past someone, lifting one's hand in recognition of their presence only to fall flat on your face in front of that amused hiker.

This author submits that the dysfunction and wrongdoing we presently experience across our country directly correlates to shifting our eyes off of the Lord's and His trails of wisdom. It is time to acquire, set our attention upon, and actualize the Hokmah of our Creator and Savior.

In this the Lord's Proverbial playbook of wisdom benevolently aims to connect His performance skill and moral coaching to improve the human condition both personally and socially in areas including but not limited to…

Abortion	Abuse	Adultery
Anger	Animal Care	Animosity
Anxiety	Attitudes	Bad Company
Behaviors	Business Ethics	Character
Cheating	Child Rearing	Commendation
Contentment	Correction	Creation
Criticism	Cruelty	Death
Decision Making	Deception	Depression
Devotion	Diligence	Discipline
Dishonor	Drunkenness	Economics
Education	Equity	Encouragement
Entertainment	Environment	Envy
Ethics	Evil	Failure
Fairness	Faithfulness	Fathering
Fear	Foolishness	Friendship
Generosity	Gluttony	God
Good Company	Goodness	Governing
Greed	Hatred	Honesty
Honor	Hope	Humility
Husbands	Hypocrisy	Ignorance
Impurity	Injustice	Integrity
Joy	Justice	Kindness
Kings	Knowledge	Laziness
Leadership	Leisure	Listening
Love	Lying	Marriage
Mercy	Money	Mothering
Morals	Murder	Need
Neighborliness	Obedience	Order
Orphans	Peace	Pleasure
Poverty	Pregnancy	Prostitution
Rebellion	Rebuke	Rejection
Relationships	Righteousness	Ruling
Sadness	Self-control	Service
Sex	Shame	Slander
Soberness	Speech	Stealing
Strife	Success	Teachableness
Thinking	Trust	Truth
Unfaithfulness	Unfriendliness	Virtue
War	Wealth	Wickedness
Wisdom	Wives	Worry

Worship

Portions of the above list came from The Bible Knowledge Commentary, Old Testament, Vol. 1. p. 905

Each aspect of the Lord's trails in Proverbs aims to lead man away from attitudes and actions which lower and harm human experience while bringing the human journeyer to upward and onward paths leading to goodness and excellence of living. Therefore, each specific trail of the Lord's hokmah, whether it be how to be a successful businessperson, to how to be kind to a neighbor, to how to raise one's children can be actualized to improve that particular area of human existence. It is time to actualize the wisdom of God.

Chapter 7: Actualizing God's Performance Skills

It Worked for Me! Such is a title of a parenting book which provides practical insights by mom's who discovered ways to better rear and relate with their children. In like manner, the book of Proverbs is populated with principles and practices that will work for you. Keep in mind these directives are not derived from the whims of man. They are not black principles, they are not white principles, they are not Asian, Latino, or Native American principles, they are Biblical principles written by God for man's wellbeing.

With this in mind let me demonstrate how God's wisdom worked for me in becoming a better teacher. Now, I have spent over thirty-five years studying Scriptural insights in how to teach. The most significant part of my discovery lay in seeking to know how Christ taught people. I mean if you want to become an effective communicator does it not make sense to study the greatest teacher in the history of mankind? Regardless of what you might believe about His divinity, can you question His ability to communicate?

Now, in this chapter **I will share just one principle** of teaching from the book of Proverbs. There are many more. As you read how I applied this performance skill to my teaching experience, consider how this single piece of educational hokmah would renovate the teaching experience and bring dramatic improvement to our schools. As you think through this one principle, image the wonderful difference it would make for the American experience if we gave full attention to the skill set of God.

Student teaching at Detroit Northern

During college at Spring Arbor University, I majored in Social Science, minored in Psychology and gained a Secondary Teacher's Degree. In order to earn certification for middle and high school teaching I needed to successfully complete twelve weeks of student teaching experience. I requested and received permission to teach at Detroit Northern High School, an inner city school which at that time was ninety-nine percent African-American.

I was assigned to teach twelfth grade Psychology and eleventh grade American History. The American History class included thirty-nine students, thirty-two were guys and seven had been referred to that class because of behavioral problems. This class was located three stories up, the furthest classroom away from the office.

My college supervisor was Dr Sickmiller, a leading professor in Spring Arbor's Education Department. The first time Dr. Sickmiller arrived to observe my teaching he drove around the school three times before mustering up the confidence to exit his vehicle and enter the premises. An armed policeman patrolled the halls. A year after my teaching internship a student was shot to death in the cafeteria. Detroit Northern was exactly where I wanted to be.

Before stepping into those classrooms I spent my college's six week Christmas break preparing to teach my classes. My primary motivation in this effort was to become the best teacher I could be for the sake of the students. I sought to discover answers to the following question: "What is the best that can happen in the life of my students while they are in my class?" A primary source of my study was the book of Proverbs.

In my six hours of daily preparation, I committed one hour per day to study what Scripture had to say concerning class conduct. In so doing by the time I walked into my class I had spent 36 hours studying Scriptural principles on establishing respectful class behavior. In this pursuit I supplemented my Biblical study with secondary source materials from Christian leaders to formulate a set of standards for effective class control. A few of my resources included two books by Dr. James Dobson's: Dare to Discipline and The Strong Willed Child. A tape message by Dr. Henry Brandt titled: "The Nature of Human Nature", and a series of messages by Josh McDowell concerning Law and Grace from the Book of Romans. Adding to this my study concerning teaching included a six part series on "Communication" by Dr. Howard Hendricks. It was also this time when I began my personal study in how Christ taught men.

A question might arise as to why I spent such significant time studying discipline? My impetus to discover keys for establishing respectful class conduct came out of personal experience. I knew myself. Here's one example: As an eighth grader I could be a real pain in the behind with teachers I didn't like. I remember, Mr. Damaan, my junior high math teacher, who challenged us during one class period to try and beat him in a math game. One by one students would go up to the board only to walk away defeated by the superior mind of Mr. Damaan. Finally I had seen enough and with disgust stood up and loudly pronounced, "Damaan, the only reason you can beat us students is because math is the only thing you've got going in your life!" I cringe even today when I think of the disrespect I directed at him. However, at the time I really didn't care. I intended to hurt that man by my statement.

From my own disruptive behavior I knew there were students out there just like me. In fact during eighth grade these guys were my closest buddies. Rules, regulations, good intentions, reasoning, didn't mean a thing to us. We wanted to disrupt the class. That was our objective. Based upon the knowledge of my disruptive behavior and my fellow delinquent cohorts, the question that I had to address was "how do I handle a person such as me?"

Within the first hour of my research in the Book of Proverbs I discovered my former "donkey behind" behavior fit the description of a mocker. The term mocker or scoffer is used twenty times in Proverbs. Applied to education a mocker is not the class clown. A mocker does not intend to delight but to disrupt. A mocker aims to resist the rules of a class and lead others in rejecting the order of the teacher. A mocker agitates for glory and seeks to create class rebellion. Yep, that was me in eighth grade.

Here's a few proverbial principles concerning mockers

21:24b "The proud and arrogant man---'Mocker' is his name; he behaves with overwheening pride."
1:22b "...mockers delight in mockery..."
29:8a "Mockers stir up a city..."
13:1b "...a mocker does not listen to rebuke."
15:12 "A mocker resents correction..."
9:7-8 "Whoever corrects a mocker invites insult... 8 do not rebuke a mocker or he will hate you..."
19:29 "Penalties are prepared for mockers..."
21:11 "When a mocker is punished, the simple gain wisdom..."
22:10 "Drive out the mocker, and out goes strife; quarrels and insults are ended."

As I began to ponder and research these principles of hokmah on the subject of discipline I became better equipped in understanding human behavior from a Scriptural point of view. As a result, based upon preferring this revelatory knowing over contemporary educational theory I rejected the permissive style of class behavior set forth in the 1970's.

Through personal experience I knew the permissive style foisted upon the educational landscape of that day especially the inner-city, minority schools failed to address this type of individual in fact it encouraged and multiplied their numbers.

For instance, as a requirement in preparation for my student teaching experience I had to observe a number of teachers in the public school system in Detroit. On one such observation I entered a middle school math class in the inner-city. I arrived before the bell, introduced myself to the teacher and took a seat in the back of the class which was now beginning to fill with rambunctious students. For the entire 45 minutes of class time I observed the teacher explaining the lesson, putting equations on the board, giving the reasoning to the various problems, but no one appeared to be listening. In fact, the students were getting up from their seats, conversing with each other, throwing paper at one another, flicking the back student's heads, shooting spit wads. All the while the teacher stood in front of the class and uttered instructions on how to do math problems. The instructor never corrected the behavior, never confronted the talking, never required the students to listen to his remarks. He continued throughout the chaos to verbally explain how to do the problems. At the end of the class I went up to thank the teacher for allowing me to observe his class. Before I departed he made this statement to me, "Howard, this is how you must teach these students."

Please realize that the permissive manner of class control, propagated at that time and continuing throughout the public school systems of today fails to provide answers for relating to a mocker. In fact the educational establishment lines up against the wisdom of Proverbs. With respect to class conduct the hokmah of God has been removed from the public educational system. However, has the education of our young citizens improved by ignoring or violating the hokmah of God?

Therefore, based upon my research of hokmah concerning discipline I set up what I believed to be the necessary rules for my class and established an enforcement system that in my judgment was clear, fair and reasonable.

So what happened?

After navigating three flights of stairs I entered Mr. Tank's American History class. I prayerfully kept focus on my introductory remarks. After Mr. Tank officially turned the class over to me, as he was making his way to exit the class, one of the students, Steven Riley, loudly called out, "Tank, can he teach Blacks?" Mr. Tank, gave me one final encouraging glance and out the door he went. I was on. Immediately I passed out a three page syllabus and began extolling the exciting adventure of learning American history.

Within this challenge I carefully explained the rules of the class. For instance: when I was teaching verbally to the class there was to be no talking or moving from one's seat unless the student raised his hand and I gave the individual permission to do so.

After articulating the rules I pronounced, "Now, I know what some of you are thinking. You don't like Mr. Tryon's rules. I understand that. I was a student once too. So let me tell you what will happen if you choose to break the rules. The first, thing I will do is look at you- just to let you know, that I know that something is wrong. Second, if you continue in the behavior I will then verbally confront you. Third, if that does not correct the situation then you will be dismissed from the class for the day with an F, and not allowed back into this class until I have had a personal discussion with you, and/or with your parents."

The first day went great! I remember returning to that inner-city home in Detroit and thinking "Man, I got through the first day!" Second day was super, but then came the third day.

I began the third day by lecturing my students on the historical method, using an overhead projector to identify key points in my verbal teaching. Suddenly out of the corner of my right eye, I saw Alan Bishop stand up. Alan was about 6'2", big fro. Alan was eventually kicked out of school because he beat a kid into unconsciousness. Alan, got out of his chair, walked directly toward me and removed the acetate off the overhead projector, saying "I don't want to do this."

Now, I'm contemplating "Well, I think we have gone past number one. There's no use in me standing here just looking at him." So immediately I proceeded to number two and said, "Alan, whether you want to do this or not you need to sit down and take notes." Alan, again articulated, "I don't want to do this." I then reached into my shirt pocket and pulled out a behavioral form. Alan, looked at the form and astonishingly said, "Hey man, that thing is already filled out!" I said, "That's right." And signed his name to the completed disciplinary form. As I handed it to him I said, "Alan you are dismissed from the class for the day with an F, and not allowed back into this class until I have had a personal discussion with you and with your parents". He swore at me, went out and slammed the door.

Trust me, at that moment I was internally praising the Lord because with all my preparation I hadn't come up with a step four. Within the next five minutes I removed three other students from that class. The second to go was Eugene. Eugene was 6'3", 260 lbs., recruited by the University of Tennessee as an offensive lineman. Third to leave was Steven "Can he teach blacks" Riley, and last but not least - Hugh Turner. Within the first five minutes of that class I removed four young men. Each time I reached into my pocket and pulled out a completed behavioral form. I just signed their names and they were dismissed. I kept expecting Mr. Tank to re-enter his domain. I will forever be grateful that he allowed me to work this out. By the way I started the class with five disciplinary forms filled out and in my pocket. I had one left.

Now, did I apply the principle of Proverbs in dealing with a mocker? Yes, four times within five minutes. Each occurrence I put into practice the following knowledge:

Proverbs 29:8a "Mockers stir up a city…"
Proverbs 21:11 "When a mocker is punished, the simple gain wisdom…"
Proverbs 22:10 "Drive out the mocker, and out goes strife; quarrels and insults are ended."

The rest of the class period went superbly. No outward resistance, no bickering, no rebellion – only teaching and learning. Upon arriving home I immediately got on my knees and anxiously prayed, "Lord, I had rebellion today. What is going to happen tomorrow? Will this work?" I opened up the Book of Proverbs and read Proverbs 3:21-26:

21 "My son, let them [the principles of wisdom] not depart from your sight; keep sound wisdom and discretion, 22 So they will be life to your soul, and adornment to your neck. 23 Then you will walk in your way securely, and your foot will not stumble. 24 When you lie down, you will not be afraid; when you lie down, your sleep will be sweet. 25 Do not be afraid of sudden fear, nor of the onslaught of the wicked when it comes; 26 for the Lord will be your confidence, and will keep your foot from being caught."

As I contemplated this passage I gained assurance from the Scriptures that I was doing the right thing. I needed to keep going and apply what I had learned. I committed this to the Lord and readied myself for the next class day.

As promised, before class I met with all four students and asked them to explain their inappropriate behavior. One articulated that he did not read or write very well. Another stated that he just didn't get into history. The other two reiterated the sentiments of the latter – they just didn't like history. I responded by saying, "I understand what you are saying and I want you to know I will do everything I can to be the best teacher I can be to teach American History well. If you desire I will work with you outside the classroom. I will do whatever I can to help you succeed in this course, but, you need to know, if you are going to pass this class, if you are even going to remain in this class, you have got to follow the rules."

From that moment on until the end of my student teaching experience I had to remove just one other student from a class session. Two of my original mockers Eugene and Steven Riley became my staunchest allies, providing necessary leadership that worked for and not against the advancement of learning in the class. Hugh hung in there. Alan showed up intermittently.

As the learning continued students would tell me they would come to school just to attend my class. Why, because of the discipline? I submit the class respect certainly didn't hurt. However, once I was able to gain their attention it freed me to really teach. You see there are many more principles concerning teaching than discipline and Proverbs addresses many communicative pearls. However, the application of just one principle of Biblical hokmah, removing the mocker, set the foundation for the rest of the teaching process. As a result everything else I was hoping to accomplish became a possibility. The principle worked and it will work for you.

A more advanced question to deliberate is why did I have the behavioral forms already and appropriately filled out? Scripture gives you an insight into the nature of human nature. This principle and so many more can be studied in Volume IX of this series "Transforming America through Proverbial Coaching titled: Excelling American Education.

However, what would have happened if I hadn't removed the mocker?

Let me demonstrate the negative consequences if the mocker is not removed by my experience in teaching seventh grade Geography to migrant workers kids at Lake Shore Middle School in the Everglades, Belle Glade, Florida. I remember the student council brought in a local rock band for an assembly during school hours. The students were required to sit in the bleachers of the gym and enjoy listening to the music. They were told not to stand up during the concert but to remain in their seats. It was clear that there was to be no dancing during the concert. Dean Darryville stood up and with the microphone spelled out these rules clearly before the student body. Now, the school had two deans who at times functioned like the good cop - bad cop. Dean Darryville was clearly the "bad cop".

The rock band began to play. For the first minute the students followed the rules. Then an eighth grade girl stood up amidst the six hundred students in the gym and began to dance. Every eye in that gymnasium from students, to teachers, to administrators, even the band focused their attention on that gyrating girl. What did Dean Darryville do? He simply walked over to her section of the bleachers and waved her to come down, and then paraded that young girl across the floor, out of the gym for everyone to see. Darryville and the girl never returned. For the next few minutes the students were perfectly content to enjoy the music. However, then another "mocker" took up the dancing gauntlet.

An eighth grade male arose and began to dance. Again, every eye in the gymnasium focused upon this "Footloose" individual. However this time nothing happened. Dean Davis did move. He just stood there watching. Within a minute another student jumped up and began dancing. Within minutes the gymnasium stands were filled with gyrating students. Then a "mocker" went further and moved his swiveling self from the bleachers onto the gymnasium floor. This was quickly followed by an entire group of "dancing with the stars". A significant portion of the entire student body moved from the bleachers to the floor. Total celebratory chaos! What a scene! Yes, "Mockers stir up a city."

Question: what would have happened if Dean Davis had followed Darryville's example and immediately removed the second mocker? I submit the problem would have been solved, the students would have learned from the examples of the "two mockers". As a result the rule would have been set and the situation would have been controlled. However, the deans would have needed to return back to the gym.

Proverbs tells us when the mocker is disciplined; i.e., incurs a penalty that both the simple and the wise observe. Once the discipline is applied, others gain wisdom. Even the "lesser" motivated or shall we say "latent" mockers having also witnessed the negative consequence of their more aggressive brothers acquiesce. Therefore, a reasoning process occurs. When the mocker incurs a just but necessary penalty, the other students begin the process of accepting the boundaries, and turn their attention from testing the rule (dancing) to the event (listening to the music). A cultural principle is adopted by the group which concludes in the individual minds and collective thought "Let's not do that." Once established the individual and group moves on to other matters.

The same is true with learning. When mockers are removed the class moves to accepting the behavioral boundaries and move to the actual learning of reading, writing, and arithmetic, but let me be very clear in this: men and women it is impossible to teach once the mockers are "dancing" in the classroom. However, hokmah tells us that to improve class conduct remove the mocker and out goes strife. Remove the mocker and both the simple and wise learn. Remove the mocker and you also have a reasonable opportunity to turn the mocker himself around.

If removing the mocker worked at Lake Shore it will work at your school as well.

As one might imagine from the previous story, Lake Shore Middle School was notorious for negative student behavior. Many teachers within the school experienced stress from lack of respect and loss of class control. Consider Miss Kriss. Miss Kriss, our team's seventh grade English teacher came into her room, and observed seven of her male students standing near the back of the class facing the wall. As she approached them requesting they get into their seats she discovered all seven were peeing on the back wall. The boys turned exposing themselves to her.

My brother, who was attending the University of Florida, came down to observe my classes. He walked around the school once and saw three fights. Substitutes found the teaching experience to be especially challenging. On one occasion as I was teaching my Geography class I heard a great deal of commotion coming from another classroom. Looking out my modular door I viewed a math class with a male substitute blocking the doorway of his room with arms and legs apart, attempting to keep the seventh graders from exiting in that direction; however the kids instead were making their escape by climbing out of the windows. As he was yelling at them to get back in their seats I observed Sam Kemp, a good natured kid, jumping up and down in his seat. When Sam saw me watching this riotous scene he enthusiastically smiled at me and waived. Whatever was going down in that classroom I guarantee it wasn't arithmetic. I quickly closed the door to my modular and went back to teach my class. The mockers had stirred up the city and the class was "dancing" or in this case escaping.

With stories such as these spreading throughout the teaching community as the year progressed the administration could not secure substitutes. As a result, we the regular teachers were asked or better stated "required" to give up our planning hour and substitute for our "battle weary" instructors.

On one such afternoon I was assigned an eighth grade English class. This class was renowned for its outlandish, uncontrollable behavior. Equipped with my knowledge of hokmah I walked into this class a few minutes before the bell and sat down on the teacher's desk to face my soon to be entering class. Then the students came entering disgruntled, happy, yelling, pushing, moving. When the bell rang to start the class nothing changed.

What did I do? I simply sat on that desk facing the riotous group and just looking at the class. I uttered no word. I showed no signs of displeasure. I sat there and waited them out. I needed to make sure every single student heard clearly my initial words. By the way I gained this principle of communication from Jesus with his encounter of the crowd when the Pharisees brought the woman caught in adultery to Him as told in John 8:1-11. After a few minutes one of the students said to the class. "Hey, be quiet he wants to talk to us." The classroom began to quiet down. During this process I continued my non-verbal demeanor. I waited until every student was perfectly quiet.

Once all the students were silent and looking directly at me I made the following statement. "My name is Mr. Tryon. Most of you know me from teaching in the modular room across the grass. I pointed to my room. Many of you guys have played basketball with me in the gym. I have two rules for this class. First, there will be no speaking or moving from your chair unless you first raise your hand and ask for permission. Second, everyone is to complete the assignment your teacher wrote on the board before the bell rings to end the period."

I continued, "Now, I know what some of you are thinking. Some of you do not like Mr. Tryon's rules. I understand that. I was a student once too. So let me explain what will happen if you choose to break those rules. First, I will verbally let you know that the rule has been broken. Second, you will be dismissed to the dean's office for the remainder of the class period with an F and not allowed to return. I have behavioral forms (I held one up to show the class.) already filled out. All I need to do is write your name on the form. I have spoken to Dean Darryville and Dean Davis concerning this and they are not looking forward to seeing any of you in their office this hour.

I then picked out a student I knew quite well from playing basketball many times with him in the gym. I remember his name to be Michael. Michael was a good guy, a big guy. He could stand on his own. Students respected him. He possessed solid leadership ability. He respected me. We liked one another. I said to him, "Michael, since I do not know some of the students, I want you to be the class monitor and if necessary help identify for me the names of students in the class." He agreed. I then explained to the class the assignment. Instructed them to take out their books and begin the class work.

I went back and sat on the desk facing and surveying the students as they started their work. I knew my mocker would soon reveal himself/herself. True to form within sixty seconds the mocker emerged from the multitudes. A male student on my left turned around and began to speak to the boy sitting behind him. I asked Michael, "Michael, what is his name?" He replied, "Billy." I looked at him and said, "Billy, that's one." Less than thirty seconds later Billy said, "Mr. Tryon" and then said "Whoops!" and raised his hand. I simply responded, "That's two." I pulled out the behavior form, stating: "Billy, you are dismissed from this class for the day with an F. You are to go to the Dean's office immediately." He came over and took the form and left to see either Dean Davis or Dean Darryville. I'm sure he was hoping for Dean Davis.

From that moment on to the end of that class period the behavior of the students was exemplary. They followed the rules. Any questions were properly expressed with a raising of the hand, and by the end of that class period every student in that room had fully completed the assignment. Ten minutes before the bell sounded I added a communicative humorous but pertinent insight into the content of their lesson. With about two minutes before the bell sounded I made this statement. "I want to thank you all for being such a great class today. It was a privilege to be your instructor. When I see your teacher tomorrow I will let her know just how well you did. She has good reason to be proud of you." I then collected the assignments and had them pick up any paper lying on the floor near their desks.

Now, what was the difference between the substitute who was standing with his arms and legs apart holding students in his classroom and my experience in substituting for that English class? The English class had eaten up other substitutes before therefore it certainly wasn't a difference in the potential of disruptive behavior. I submit the difference maker was that I preferred and actualized a performance skill of Proverbs. I simply removed the mocker as Proverbs 22:10 states:

"Drive out the mocker, and out goes strife; quarrels and insults are ended."

Do you want to dramatically change your class? Do we want to improve the private and public schools across our nation? Do you want to transform the education of our American youth for the better then actualize the wisdom of God. Discipline is but one principle from the book of Proverbs that addresses the educational quality of teaching. There are principles that cover curriculum development, teaching style, motivation and the learning ways of students. There is wonderful and enlightening guidelines of God's hokmah to better equip teachers in how to teach better. Do you want to give our children the hokmah advantage? Do you want to dramatically improve our education system for the better? Apply the principles and practices of Proverbial knowledge to the art of teaching. It will work. It worked for me. It will work for you. It will work for us.

(For a fuller rendering of Proverbs and teaching, read Volume IX :Excelling American Education", in this series titled: Transforming America through Proverbial Coaching.)

It is time to actualize the hokmah of God

All of God's principles of hokmah carry an intrinsic potential to improve the human condition if they are actualized. In this regard think of the great inventor, George Washington Carver.

"Most people know that George Washington Carver was a chemist and agronomist. Born a slave in 1860, Carver rose to become director of agricultural research at Tuskegee University in Alabama. He is remembered for developing 118 derivative products from sweet potatoes and 300 from peanuts——including my favorite food, peanut butter. Thanks to his efforts, by 1940, peanuts were the second largest cash crop in the South. But go to his name in the encyclopedia, and you'll find no reference to the most important aspect of his life: how his faith in God inspired his creativity. "I didn't make these discoveries," Carver once said. "God has only worked through me to reveal to His children some of His wonderful providence."

Chuck Colsen: Radio Commentary: The Christ-Inspired Heritage of Black History

If Carver can draw out of a peanut 300 ways to benefit man think of what people can do if they break down each and every Proverb and apply its principles properly in the area of its intended focus. In order to accomplish this each Proverb and its collective cohort of like meaning needs to be studied and implemented issue by issue, situation by situation, remedy by remedy to better the human experience. By actualizing the hokmah of God man and his/her ways whether personal or communal, move upward and onward to better living.

Become a person of Biblical wisdom

Preparing for my student teaching experience at Detroit Northern High School I took my Bible, text books, and notes to a Howard-Johnson's for breakfast. After spreading the material out across the table, three of my college friends walked into the restaurant, and saw me encamped amidst this clutter of papers. As we conversed, Stan Williams asked: "Howard, what are you doing?" I enthusiastically replied, "In two weeks I start student teaching at Detroit Northern and I'm studying Proverbs to learn how to become a better teacher." Stan, with concern on his face, looked at my Bible and then looked directly at me. With a shake of his head he declared, "That's not going to help."

That's not going to help? Think about that statement. Stan was a born again believer. We attended a Christian college. That's not going to help? Nothing could be further from the truth. Proverbs is the very book that God has given to man to help in the practical outworking of life. It was written to help you in your marriage, on your job, the raising of your children, making better decisions, and your professional pursuits. Yes, Proverbs provides the practical guidance necessary to live a better and fuller life, even in the area of teaching.

God wrote the book of Proverbs that you might become a man or woman of hokmah; i.e., you might become a person of performance skill. In so doing Proverbs provides you with a manual to give you wisdom for the now. Make a decision to gain the hokmah of the Lord. Acquire her, seek her, pursue her, prize her. Once she is in your possession pay attention to her. She will bring to you a great blessing. In this acquisition no one can stop you from becoming a hokam but you. Learn the principles and implement her truths and goodness. Inject the hokmah of God into your life and experience the Lord's transformation. Life can dramatically change for the better. It is time to put the principles of Proverbs into practice. Acquire wisdom, give attention to her guidance, and actualize her blessings. No one can stop you but you.

Make a commitment to let the wisdom and moral teachings in Proverbs work for you. Identify the areas of your life where you need His wisdom. Gain the insights. Prefer the principles. Put the guidance of the Lord into practice. Whatever you are doing in your life right now, whether it be in your business, whether it be in education, whatever your circumstance apply the knowledge of Proverbial coaching.

Yes, there is hokmah in this book for you, for your marriage, for your child rearing. Dig out its principles, practice them, and then actualize its product. Discover and study the Proverbs that deal with the matters that most personally affect you. Learn the principles and begin to implement its truths and goodness. Inject the hokmah of God into your life and experience the Lord's transformation. Life can dramatically change for the better both for you and for us. As Bible believing people whether African-American, Arab, Asian, Caucasian, Jew, Latino, Native American it is time to actualize the hokmah of Scripture.

Chapter 8: Team Play

Suppose 97% of the American populace loved the taste of M & M candies. In fact there was such a national craving for the M & M's that virtually every citizen, community, governing, ecclesiastical, and judicial official made it their civic duty to make sure there was an abundant supply of the candies available for every American festival, exercise and public event. As a result those tasty morsels were everywhere. They were in our schools, courtrooms, institutions, governing bodies, and all social activities.

What's more our political leaders stored away a trillion M & M's placing them in a huge national vault for posterity just in case our nation ever suffered a shortage of the candies. They then secured the continuation of the scrumptious morsels in perpetuity by writing into community, state and national laws safeguards to make sure that the production and eating of the M & M's would always remain a necessary part of our United States from generation to generation, unhindered, unabated. After all the eating of M & M's was the overwhelming preference of the American people. The nation believed that the M & M's were an inalienable right of all Americans to enjoy.

However, of the 3% who were indifferent or disliked the M & M's, less than 1/100th of that 3% who loathed their taste grew more and more impatient, intolerant of the continuous diet of the morsels. Although their numbers were extremely small these M & M haters, in spite of the overwhelming public sentiment for the candies, tried time and time again to eliminate the presence of the morsels from public gatherings. Initially their attempts were thwarted. No matter what they tried to do they could not stop the practice. Everywhere they turned the American populace stood united in favor of the M & M's, and the governing, ruling authorities from community to community, State to State, stopped any attempt to change the laws. For the M & M haters there appeared no way to reverse the practice throughout the American system for the public gatekeepers, the politicians, judges, and local civic leaders all enjoyed the eating of the M & M's also. As a result, there appeared no way to change the menu.

Then the M & M detesters discovered a modus operandi that would lead to the eventual elimination of the candies from public consumption. They crafted a "legal" argument that the eating of M & M's was strictly a personal matter and not an ordained public practice. They presented that the established laws guaranteeing our nation's freedom to enjoy the M & M's also guaranteed the freedom not to enjoy the candies. They then sought out the most ardent M & M hater who would take their detesting to the local, state, and national authorities, one particular event, point, situation at a time.

However, in order for this strategy to succeed they needed one more crucial piece to the puzzle. They needed a ruling authority, a judge who would be sympathetic to their cause. Then the pivotal day occurred for after hundreds of years of backing the public eating and distribution of the M & M's a particular ruling authority decided in favor that the freedom for M & M's also meant the freedom from M & M's. As this shift in American law became secured throughout the courts the M & M haters knew it was just a matter of time before the public practice of M & M eating would be eliminated. Not all at once mind you, but one piece of candy at a time.

Thus began a legal process of decisions which favored the detesters over the lovers of the candies. The haters of M & M's presented their arguments, threatened million dollar lawsuits, and won victory after legal victory against the overwhelming M & M eating populace. Each judicial decision resulted in more and more M & M's being confiscated and discarded from public practice.

Year after year, decade after decade, generation after generation the elimination of the M & M's continued. Historical lovers of the candy referred to it as the great candy heist. However, no one appeared able to stop it. As the judges became more and more tolerant of the M & M haters, the detesters, emboldened by the highest courts tolerance of their position then went after the M & M color they detested the most. First, they determined to eliminate all the red M & M's, but since the number of people in America who really enjoyed eating the red ones were insufficient in numbers to stop the theft of their color over the years all the reds disappeared. The thieves then went after the yellows, then the blues, followed by the greens, and finally they targeted the browns. In the end all the M & M's had been taken. There were no more M & M's for the public to enjoy. The national supply of M & M's were stolen from public consumption.

Of course the M & M enjoyers were still permitted to eat their morsels in private or in designated places of dining throughout the communities, but no longer could any eating of an M & M be permitted in public. In fact, if someone actually ate an M & M in a classroom, or a civic affair there were serious repercussions – a threat here – a lawsuit there – a jail sentence here - even imprisonment there. Billions upon billions of dollars were spent to ensure no citizen would be affronted with an M & M. No mercy was shown in enforcing the new form of American discrimination. Whole industries arose to ensure the discrimination would be followed.

This did not mean that the public was void of their desire for chocolate. So the M & M haters with man-made precision scientifically crafted a new norm of candy which they proudly presented to the public. They pledged that this new synthetic morsel would go down smoothly, but once eaten the American public discovered over time that they were left with an unsatisfying, even bitter aftertaste. Regardless the detesters appeared to enjoy the taste, and presented the new concoctions as being the new norm. Despite the glowing marketing propaganda, the American population never developed a real hunger for this replacement candy.

In the end all the M & M's were eliminated from public consumption. As the years past, fewer and fewer M & M lovers were still alive to speak of the days when the candies reigned supreme throughout our life and liberty, when 97% of the public united together to enjoy the taste of those most delicious morsels at every public event, social gathering, and governing practice.

Hokmah and the American Experience

For over two hundred years the way of American private and public life went right through the M & M's of Biblically based hokmah. Historically the M & M's of God's wisdom populated our Republic like the great Buffalo once roamed our land. This assertion is evidenced by our United States Supreme Court in its unanimous (9-0) ruling of 1892:

> "There is a universal language pervading (the History of the United States), having one meaning; they affirm and reaffirm that this is a religious nation. These are not individual sayings, declarations of private persons: they are organic utterances; they speak the voice of the entire people. . . .
>
> If we pass beyond these matters to a view of American life as expressed by its laws, its business, its customs and its society, we find everywhere a clear recognition of the same truth. Among other matters note the following: The form of oath universally prevailing, concluding with an appeal to the Almighty; the custom of opening sessions of all deliberative bodies and most conventions with prayer; the prefatory words of all wills, 'In the name of God, amen'; the laws respecting the observance of the Sabbath, with the general cessation of all secular business, and the closing of courts, legislatures, and other similar public assemblies on that day; the churches and church organizations which abound in every city, town and hamlet; the multitude of charitable organizations existing everywhere under Christian auspices; the gigantic missionary associations, with general support, and aiming to establish Christian missions in every quarter of the globe.
>
> These, and many other matters which might be noticed, add a volume of unofficial declarations to the mass of organic utterances that this is a Christian nation...We find everywhere a clear recognition of the same truth. The happiness of a people and the good order and preservation of civil government essentially depend upon piety, religion and morality. Religion, morality, and knowledge [are] necessary to government, the preservation of liberty, and the happiness of mankind.
>
> [Therefore], no purpose of action against religion can be imputed to any legislation, state or national, because this is a religious people. This is historically true."
>
> ### 1892, HOLY TRINITY CHURCH v. U.S., 143 U.S. 457, 12 S.Ct. 511, 36 L.Ed. 226, February 29, 1892

From the Christian commitments of our early European settlers to the charters of our original colonies, from the constitutions of our original States to the ratifications of our Federal Documents, we as a people set forth, embraced and engaged our eventual national motto: "In God We Trust." As a result, Biblical Theism populated the American way of life, laws, and liberty as set forth in our Declaration of Independence which stated:

> "We hold these truths to be self-evident, that all men are created equal, that they are endowed by their Creator with certain inalienable rights, that among these are Life, Liberty and the pursuit of

Happiness. ....We, therefore, the Representatives of the United States of America, in General Congress, Assembled, appealing to the Supreme Judge of the world for the rectitude of our intentions, do, in the Name and by Authority of the good People of these Colonies, solemnly publish and declare....with a firm reliance on the Protection of Divine Providence, we mutually pledge to each other our Lives, our Fortunes, and our sacred Honor."

Declaration of Independence, 1776

The Declaration reveals the Subject of our American freedoms of life and liberty is the Creator God. President **John Fitzgerald Kennedy** articulated this truth in his inaugural speech on January 20, 1961:

"The world is very different now. . . . And yet the same revolutionary beliefs for which our forebears fought are still at issue around the globe - the belief that the rights of man come not from the generosity of the state but from the hand of God..."

Upon more detailed analysis the dogma of Biblical Theism in our Declaration extended beyond the Subject of our freedoms and is seen clearly embedded in our national virtues such as:

> There is a God.
> Man is not God.
> God is the Creator
> Man is created equal
> God has given to man unalienable rights such as: life, liberty, and the pursuit of happiness (property)
> God is the ultimate judge of the world even upon man's intentions
> Man is dependent upon God
> Man calls out for God's protection

Therefore, throughout our American experience from the founding of our country in 1776 until the mid-nineteen hundreds our judiciary protected, permitted, and propagated the private and public practice of the M & M's of God's hokmah throughout our nation. In fact, one would be hard pressed to discover a single judicial decision in early American history when an atheist or anti-theist actually won their case against Biblical Theism in a court of law. Why? Because the justices knew that while America was not founded to be theocratic; i.e., we were not Israel, we were not the Churchi; we were founded to be theocentric.

Hokmah and the American Advantage

As a result, the United States functioned as a team of Biblical Theists, actualizing Scriptural wisdom to better personal, community, and national living. In so doing our founders set up a system by which the M & M's of the Lord's wisdom would be engaged in every arena of our nation's way of living, being implemented for our personal and community well being. From the moment the Pilgrim's arrived in 1620 the originator's of our Republic expected the hokmah of God to be preached from our pulpits, manifested in our marriages, expressed in our parenting, taught in our schools, practiced in our neighborhoods, engaged in our commerce, implemented in legislation, and carried out by the communal interactions of our populace. It was the wisdom and moral coaching of Scripture's God which gave us the advantage.

If only we had applied the Lord's hokmah rightly, justly, and fairly to African Americans at the inception of our nation think how different our Republic would be today. Yet, even in our national evils of slavery and segregation it took America's two greatest Scripturally based, societal correcting movements of Christian Abolitionism and Christian Activism to bring emancipation and empowerment to African Americans. So today, the realization of social correction and human refinement will find fulfillment through applying the wisdom and goodness of Biblical Theism.

Whether through correction or blessing what has been good and right in the American experience would never have been fully actualized under the dogma and deeds of secularism or any other religious teachings. We never would have arrived at our greatness under the directives of Hinduism, Islam, Buddhism, Shintoism or any other religious dogma and deed. The excellence of our nation resulted from engaging Biblical Theism. Our way of governing and living emerged from our mutual belief in the God of Abraham, Isaac, and Jacob – the God and Father of our Lord and Savior, Jesus Christ. It was the Christian God that our founders based their hope and developed our way of living. It was the implementation of God's wisdom which proved to be the decisive key to our beginnings, the explanation of our continuance, and the prosperous nation we became. It was the actualization of the principles and practice of Biblical Theism which set us apart - it gave us our great advantage.

From the Biblical doctrine that "all men are created equal," to the moral teachings of the Ten Commandments, from the Puritan work ethic to the Christian ethic of love, mercy, grace, and discipline all such teachings gave to the American people guidance and fortitude to enact a society of human advancement. It was the Biblical God, His wisdom and moral goodness which gave us the capacity to create the greatest nation in the history of mankind.

However, today we are going in the opposite direction. In deviation from our Declaration we have relegated the Divine Subject of our freedoms to the back of our public bus. We have removed our Great Difference Maker from interacting in public life. We have displaced His wisdom from social and political relevance. We are presently a nation resisting and rejecting the Lord's "Buyer Buys' and "Buyer Bewares." Furthermore, in our rebellion we replaced His hokmah with secular whim, why, and ways. What are the consequences? What started as a resistant strain against God's glory and goodness now manifests itself in an uncontrollable viral outbreak of human suffering, societal collapse and potential national calamity. The storms of life surround us. They engulf us. We are attacked by enemies from without; we are dissolving from dissidence from within.

> **For the sake of our personal lives, families, communities, and nation,
> it is time for all God honoring, Bible respecting Americans
> to unite and actualize the Lord's wisdom.**

In this regard, consider the words of this author's all-time favorite college football coach - Bo Schembechler. Bo coached the University of Michigan football team from 1969 to 1989. During his 21 year reign the Wolverines achieved 17 top ten finishes, winning 13 Big Ten Championships. In 1982 once again U of M won the Big Ten Championship by beating Ohio State in the deciding game of conference play. Now, entering the 1983 season Schembechler addressed his squad of Wolverine players. Having lost seven players from the previous year to the NFL his team lacked superstars. In fact only two players from this team would make it to the pros. Here is his opening speech to his college team.

"We want the Big Ten championship and we're going to win it as a team. They can throw out all those great backs, and great quarterbacks, and great defensive players, throughout the country, and in this conference, but there's gonna be one team that's gonna play solely as a team. No man is more important than the team. No coach is more important than the team. The team. The team. The team. And if we think that way, all of us, everything that you do, you take into consideration what effect does it have on my team?

Because you can go into professional football, you can go anywhere you want to play after you leave here. You will never play for a team again. You'll play for a contract. You'll play for this. You'll play for that. You'll play for everything except the team. And think what a great thing it is to be apart of something that is the team.

We're gonna win it. We're gonna win the championship again cause we're going to play as a team. Better than anybody else in this conference, we're going to play together as a team. We're going to believe in each other. We're not going to criticize each other. We're not going to talk about each other. We're going to encourage each other. And when we play as a team when the whole season is over, you and I know, it's going to be Michigan again. Michigan."

The Michigan advantage of Schembechler's team play should be America's advantage as a nation. We were founded to function together as a nation of Biblical Theists, honoring the Lord and actualizing His guidance. Throughout our history our American experience found favor and progress when the M & M's of God's wisdom; i.e., His principles and practices were inserted into the very building blocks and mortar of our forming and developing society. The wisdom of the Lord was there for our well-being as Proverbs 3:13-26 states:

13 How blessed is the man who finds wisdom, and the man who gains understanding. 14 For its profit is better than the profit of silver, and its gain than fine gold. 15 She is more precious than jewels; and nothing you desire compares with her. 16 Long life is in her right hand; in her left hand are riches and honor. 17 Her ways are pleasant ways, and all her paths are peace. 18 She is a tree of life to those who take hold of her, and happy are all who hold her fast. 19 The Lord by wisdom founded the earth; by understanding He established the heavens. 20 By His knowledge the deeps were broken up, and the skies dip with dew. 21 My son, let them not depart from your sight; keep sound wisdom and discretion, 22 So they will be life to your soul, and adornment to your neck. 23 Then you will walk in your way securely, and your foot will not stumble. 24 When you lie down, you will not be afraid; when you lie down, your sleep will be sweet. 25 Do not be afraid of sudden fear, nor of the onslaught of the wicked when it comes; 26 For the Lord will be your confidence, and will keep your foot from being caught.

The hokmah of the Lord proved to be our American advantage. We possessed the coaching of the Biblical God to build our lives, raise our families, treat our neighbors, and lead our nation. Furthermore, the errors and iniquities of our country arose in violation and perversion of His wisdom and goodness.

Let us then unite as a team not under the banner of conservatism, liberalism, or moderation, but as Christian Actualists and let us turn our American experience away from destructive destinations and put ourselves and our nation on the roads that lead to personal and social improvement. Let us therefore engage a movement of actualizing proverbial wisdom.

Now, let's think for a moment. By the way most people don't think they just rearrange their prejudices.

In our nation's History who would stand against this movement?

Would our Founders?

Consider the following discourse given by Daniel Webster in 1820, honoring the Pilgrims arrival at Plymouth Rock in 1620. Webster, Senator from Massachusetts and writer of our America's original Dictionary, declared:

> "Finally, let us not forget the religious character of our origin. Our fathers were brought hither by their high veneration for the Christian religion. They journeyed by its light, and labored in its hope. They sought to incorporate its principles with the elements of their society and to diffuse its influence through all their institutions, civil, political, or literary....
>
> Our ancestors established their system of government on morality and religious sentiment. Moral habits, they believed, cannot safely be trusted on any other foundation than religious principle, nor any government be secure which is not supported by moral habits. Living under the heavenly light of revelation, they hoped to find all the social dispositions all the duties which men owe to each other and to society, enforced and performed. Whatever makes men good Christians, makes them good citizens...
>
> ...Let us cherish these sentiments, and extend this influence still more widely; in the full conviction, that that is the happiest society which partakes in the highest degree of the mild and peaceful spirit of Christianity."

> "A Discourse delivered at Plymouth, on the 22nd of December, 1820 by Daniel Webster, The Works of Daniel Webster" 1851, Vol I.
> Source: The Christian History of the Constitution of the United States of America, Compilation by Verna M. Hall, p. 248, 1966

Our Founders would not oppose engaging God's wisdom instead they would stand united to actualize the hokmah of the Lord.

Who would stand against this movement?

Would our early Congress?

Consider Benjamin Franklin. Franklin, the man most responsible for crafting, organizing, and disseminating the early American proverb, master of five foreign languages (French, Italian, Spanish, Latin, German), signer of both the Declaration of Independence and the Constitution, president of Pennsylvania's Anti-slavery Society is considered by many historians to be the member of Congress furthest removed from

Christianity. With that asserted consider the conviction of Franklin challenging Congress to daily morning prayer in 1787.

> "We have been assured, Sir, in the Sacred Writings, that 'except the Lord build the House, they labor in vain that build it.' I firmly believe this; and I also believe that without his concurring aid we shall succeed in this political building no better than the Builders of Babel. We shall be divided by our partial local interests; our projects will be confounded, and we ourselves shall become a reproach and bye word down to future ages. I therefore beg leave to move -- that henceforth prayers imploring the assistance of Heaven, and its blessing on our deliberations, be held in this Assembly every morning before we proceed to business, and that one or more of the clergy of this city be requested to officiate in that service."

> Franklin's Message Before The Constitutional, Convention, 1787;
> shalomjerusalem.com/heritage/heritage21.html;

To further tie Franklin's interaction with the dogma and deeds of Biblical Theism consider he penned his personal epitaph which appears on his grave site even today. The epitaph reads:

> "The body of B. Franklin, printer: Like the cover of an old book, its contents torn out, the script of its letter and gilding, lies here food for worms. But the work shall not be whlly lost, for it will, as he believed, appear once more, in a new and more perfect edition, corrected and amended by the Author."

Now, the acknowledgement of Biblical Theism among the founders, such as Franklin, does not necessarily equate each individual with possessing personal faith in Christ or what evangelicals and Christian Actualists call the 'born again' experience. However, with that stated, the overwhelming historical record evidences our original congressional leaders acknowledged dependency upon the Biblical God and His guidance both for personal and national well-being.

These men who set into motion our United States knew what they were doing in making the Lord God the Subject of our freedoms of life, liberty and the pursuit of happiness. Who among them would have opposed a modern Christian movement to actualize the wisdom of God to overcome the dysfunction and evils we face today as a people in order to engage a better nation?

> Our early Congress would not oppose the public engaging of the Lord's wisdom
> instead they would stand united to actualize His hokmah.

Who would stand against this movement?

Would our early Judiciary?

As established by our Supreme Court's 1892 ruling, documented earlier in this chapter, historically the third branch of our government, the Judiciary, defended and ruled in favor of the private and public practices of Biblical Theism. Take for instance,

The State Courts

The Supreme Court of Pennsylvania, ruled:

> "Christianity, general Christianity, is, and always has been, a part of the common law of Pennsylvania; not Christianity with an established church and tithes and spiritual courts, but Christianity with liberty of conscience to all men."

> Updegraph v. Comm., 11 Serg. & R. 394, 400 Holy Trinity v 1892

The Supreme Court of New York, asserted:

> "The people of this state, in common with the people of this country, profess the general doctrines of Christianity as the rule of their faith and practice..."

> People v. Ruggles, 8 Johns. 290, 294, 295, Holy Trinity, 1892

Our U.S. Supreme Court

In agreement with the State Courts and spanning a time of over one hundred and fifty years the highest court of our land defended the general principles and practices of Biblical Theism both in the private and public sector of American life and liberty. To understand such Theistic rulings from our Highest court one needs to remember the type of justice who sat behind our American bench. Here are a few examples:

Take for instance, the first Chief Justice of our United States Supreme Court, **John Jay** (1745-1829). Here are a few of Jay's testimonials concerning his faith in Christ.

> "I believe the fact to be, that except (for) the Bible there is not a true history in the world.... Uninspired commentators have dishonored the law, by ascribing to it, in certain cases, a sense and meaning which it did not authorize, and which our Savior rejected and reproved. The inspired prophets, on the contrary, expressed the most exalted ideas of the law. They declare that the law of the Lord is perfect; that the statutes of the Lord are right; and that the commandment of the Lord is pure; that God would magnify the law and make it honorable."

> 1797, John Jay's letter to Jededia Morse, February 28, 1797, quoted by
> Norman Cousins, In God We Trust, New York: Harper Brothers, 1958, p.362

> "Till America comes into this measure of [abolition] her prayers to Heaven will be impious. This is a strong expression, but it is just. I believe that God governs the world, and I believe it to be a maxim in His, as in our courts, that those who ask for equity ought to do it."

> 1780, Jay's Letter from Spain. Source: Acts of the Anti-Slavery Apostles by Rev. Parker Pillsbury (Concord, N.H., 1883)

> "While in France . . . I do not recollect to have had more than two conversations with atheists about their tenants. The first was this: I was at a large party, of which were several of that description. They spoke freely and contemptuously of religion. I took no part in the conversation. In the course of it, one of the men asked me if I believed in Christ? I answered that I did, and that I thanked God that I did."

> 1811, John Jay, in a letter to John Bristed, April 23, 1811, in CPPJJ, vol. 4, p. 359.

Please note: President George Washington nominated John Jay to be the first Chief Justice of the United States on September 24, 1789. The Senate confirmed the appointment on September 26, 1789. Two days later. What would happen if John Jay was a Supreme Court nominee today?

Consider the United States Supreme Court Justice, **Joseph Story**. Joseph Story served on the United States Supreme Court from 1812-1845. Story was appointed by President James Madison. He wrote nine commentaries on American law and was the founder of Harvard Law School at which he was a professor. He served on the Supreme Court for thirty-three years. Here are a few testimonials by Story:

"My own private judgment has long been…that Christianity is indispensable to the true interests and solid foundation of all governments….I know not…how any deep sense of moral obligation or accountableness can be expected to prevail in the community without a firm foundation of the great Christian truths."

> 1833, Joseph Story, in a letter to Jasper Adams, May 14, 1833, in JSAC, p. 139.

"One of the beautiful boasts of our municipal jurisprudence is that Christianity is part of the Common Law…. There never has been a period in which the Common Law did not recognize Christianity as lying at its foundations…. [I] verily believe Christianity necessary to the support of civil society."

> Life and Letters of Joseph Story, Wm.W. Story, ed., Boston:
> Charles C. Little and James Brown, 1851, II:8,92

"Christianity becomes not merely an auxiliary, but a guide, to the law of nature; establishing its conclusions, removing its doubts, and evaluating its precepts."

> 1829, Joseph Story, "The Value and Importance of Legal Studies," delivered
> August 25, 1829, Inauguration, Dane Professor of Law in Harvard University

Question: Would the founder of Harvard's Law School who fully advocated that Christianity was necessary for determining law in America be endorsed by the faculty and approved by our Congress today?

Consider the United States Supreme Court Chief Justice **John Marshall**. Marshall was appointed by John Adams to be Chief Justice. He had the longest tenure of any Chief Justice, expanding thirty four years from 1801-1835. Many historians consider Marshall, the greatest Chief Justice of the Supreme Court. Marshall asserted:

"The American population is entirely Christian, and with us Christianity and Religion are identified. It would be strange indeed, if with such a people, our institutions did not presuppose Christianity, and did not often refer to it, and exhibit relations with it."

> Marshall, letter to Jasper Adams, May 9, 1833

Consider David Brewer

David Brewer: nominated by President Benjamin Harrison on December 4, 1889, was confirmed by the Senate fourteen days later (December 18). Brewer served as Associate Justice for twenty years from 1889-1910. Brewer's conviction concerning the

American experience and Biblical Theism can be established by three assertions made in his book, <u>The United States, a Christian Nation</u>, published in 1905:

> "It is not exaggeration to say that Christianity in some of its creeds was the principal cause of the settlement of many of the colonies . . ."
>
> > David J. Brewer, The United States, a Christian Nation (Philadelphia: The John C. Winston Co., 1905), p. 19.

> "In the common schools the Bible has been as much a text-book as the New England primer. It is only within very late years that any objection has been raised to its daily use . . ."
>
> > David J. Brewer, United States a Christian Nation, 1905, p. 61.

> "In no other way can this republic become a world power in the noblest sense of the word than by putting into her life and the lives of her citizens the spirit and principles of the great founder of Christianity."
>
> > David J. Brewer, United States a Christian Nation, 1905, p. 70.

From our country's inception until the mid-nineteen hundreds our judiciary, populated by justices such as Jay, Story, Marshall, and Brewer, protected and propagated the private and public practice of Biblical Theism across our nation. In fact, one would be hard pressed to unveil a single court decision in the early life of American history when an atheist or anti-theist actually won their case against Biblical Theism in a court of law.

Our early courts did not oppose the public practice of the Lord's wisdom instead they stood as judicial allies to actualize the hokmah of God.

Who would stand against this movement?

Would our nation's two most iconic Presidents:
George Washington and Abraham Lincoln oppose this movement?

What about George Washington?

In Washington's First Inaugural Address in the City of New York, Thursday, April 30, 1789, he said: "...it would be peculiarly improper to omit in this first official act my fervent supplications to that Almighty Being who rules over the universe, who presides in the councils of nations, and whose providential aids can supply every human defect, that His benediction may consecrate to the liberties and happiness of the people of the United States a Government instituted by themselves for these essential purposes, and may enable every instrument employed in its administration to execute with success the functions allotted to his charge. No people can be bound to acknowledge and adore the Invisible Hand which conducts the affairs of men more than those of the United States. Every step by which they have advanced to the character of an independent nation seems to have been distinguished by some token of providential agency..."

> Washington's First Inaugural Address, April 30th, 1789

What about Abraham Lincoln?

Consider Lincoln's words at the beginning of the Civil War. "…whereas it is fit and becoming in all people at all times to acknowledge and revere the supreme government of God, to bow in humble submission to His chastisement, to confess and deplore their sins and transgression, in the full conviction that the fear of the Lord is the beginning of wisdom, and to pray with all fervency and contrition for the pardon of their offenses and for a blessing upon their present and prospective action.…

Therefore I, Abraham Lincoln, President of the United States, do appoint the last Thursday in September next as a day of humiliation, prayer, and fasting, for all the people of the nation.…to the end that the united prayer of the nation may ascend to the Throne of Grace, and bring down plentiful blessings upon our country."

Abraham Lincoln, National Fasting and Confession Proclamation, 1861

Washington and Lincoln would not oppose engaging the wisdom of the Lord throughout the entirety of our American experience; instead they would stand united to actualize the Lord's hokmah.

Who would stand against this movement?

Would the Christian Abolitionists?

Never forget in our national sins of American slavery it took Christ professing men and women black and white, slavey and free such as: Frederick Douglass, William Lloyd Garrison Rev. John Fee, Eli Lovejoy, Charles Sumner, Sojourner Truth, Harriet Tubman "Moses" who trusted in the Biblical God and called our American populace and institutions to repent of its evils, turn from the wrongs, and engage right. The abolitionist's were headed and populated by Biblical Theists calling our nation to justice.

The Christian Abolitionists grew to significant numbers after the Second Great Awakening. Abolitionists preached against slavery, entered into heroic acts of human rescue (The Freedom Train, otherwise known as the Underground Railroad), sought the passage of liberating Constitutional Amendments, initiated and passed Civil Rights legislation, and confronted judicial rulings that perpetuated iniquitous practices of African trafficking and inequality. The abolitionists determined to emancipate and equally empower blacks throughout our nation at the cost of their very lives. Consider Christian Abolitionist…

Sojourner Truth

"At the age of twenty-seven, Isabella (Sojourner) had a dramatic conversion to Christianity and attended John Street Methodist Church and the Black African Methodist Episcopal Zion Church in New York City."

Perryman, Unfounded Loyalty, p. 8

"'The Lord gave me the name Sojourner,' she declared, 'because I was to travel up and down the land, showing people their sins, and being a sign unto them.' At age eighty-eight, her dying words were, 'Follow the Lord Jesus.'"

Chuck Colsen: Radio Commentary:
The Christ-Inspired Heritage of Black History

"She was a staunch friend of Abraham Lincoln, and he gave her many words of encouragement and praise."

Sojourner Truth, Narrative and Book of Life, Entered, according to Act of Congress, in the year 1875, Reprinted 1970, Johnson Publishing Co., The Ebony Classics, p. 182

A Syracuse Newspaper extending an invitation for people to attend Sojourner's speaking at Fourth Presbyterian Church, Syracuse referred to her relationship with Lincoln stating:

"Sojourner Truth is too well known to need any endorsements, but I was greatly pleased yesterday to read that of the martyr president---so characteristic of Lincoln---'For Aunty.' "Sojourner Truth---let the Christian people hear her."

Sojourner Truth, Narrative and Book of Life, Entered, according to Act of Congress, in the year 1875, Reprinted 1970, Johnson Publishing Co., The Ebony Classics, p. 176

Concerning Sojourner Truth, Frederick Douglass stated: "I rejoice to find you strong in health, vigorous in mind, warm in heart, and, as usual, full of noble purposes, looking to the welfare of suffering men and women. May you long live to bless, cheer, and enlighten, and to lift up the oppressed, and smooth the pathway of the lowly..."

Sojourner Truth, Narrative and Book of Life, Entered, according to Act of Congress, in the year 1875, Reprinted 1970, Johnson Publishing Co., The Ebony Classics, p. 202

The Christian Abolitionists would not oppose engaging the wisdom of the Lord equally, rightly, justly, and fairly throughout our American way of living; instead they would stand united to actualize His hokmah.

Who would stand against this movement?

Would the early Christian Activists?

In the 1950's the Southern Christian Leadership Conference and the formation of the Christian Activist movement under Dr. Martin Luther King Jr. purposed to overcome the evils of American segregation. To evidence the degree by which Biblical principles directed this movement of human empowerment consider that every volunteer in the Birmingham Movement signed a Commitment Card that read:

"I hereby pledge myself—my person and body—to the nonviolent movement.
Therefore I will keep the following ten commandments:

1. Meditate daily on the teachings and life of Jesus
2. Remember always that the nonviolent movement in Birmingham seeks justice and reconciliation—not victory
3. Walk and Talk in the manner of love, for God is love.
4. Pray daily to be used by God in order that all men might be free
5. Sacrifice personal wishes in order that all men might be free
6. Observe with both friend and foe the ordinary rules of courtesy

7. Seek to perform regular service for others and for the world
8. Refrain from the violence of fist, tongue, or heart.
9. Strive to be in good spiritual and bodily health
10. Follow the directions of the movement and of the captain on a demonstration

Source: Martin Luther King, Jr. The Making of a Mind,
Orbis Books, Maryknoll, NY, 1982, p. 160-161

The Biblical convictions undergirding the early Activist movement can be further identified by recognizing the Christ centered ethics adhered to in the original Bus Boycott in Montgomery, Alabama as preached by Dr. King:

"Emphasizing the Christian doctrine of love, 'our actions must be guided by the deepest principles of our Christian faith. Love must be our regulating ideal. Once again we must hear the words of Jesus echoing across the centuries: 'Love your enemies, bless them that curse you, and pray for them that despitefully use you.'

If you will protest courageously, and yet with dignity and Christian love, when the history books are written in future generations, the historians will have to pause and say, 'There lived a great people—a black people– who injected new meaning and dignity into the veins of civilization.' This is our challenge and our overwhelming responsibility."

p. 61-62, Stride Toward Freedom, The Montgomery Story, Dr Martin Luther King, Jr. , Harper and Brothers, Publishers, New York., 1958, King Dedicated this work "To Coretta my beloved wife and co-worker"

To cement the establishment of Biblical Theism in the early Activist movement and how Dr. King called the American people to rightly, justly, and fairly apply the wisdom and goodness of God to overcome America's ills and evils read Dr. King's sermon "Rediscovering Lost Values" delivered on February 28, 1954 in Detroit, Michigan.

"We've left a lot of precious values behind; we've lost a lot of precious values. And if we are to go forward, if we are to make this a better world in which to live, we've got to go back. We've got to rediscover these precious values that we've left behind....

...we have adopted in the modern world a sort of a relativistic ethic....we have accepted the attitude that right and wrong are merely relative...But I'm here to say to you this morning that some things are right and some things are wrong. Eternally so, absolutely so...It was wrong in two thousand B.C., and it's wrong in nineteen fifty-four A.D.... It's wrong in every age, and it's wrong in every nation.

Some things are right and some things are wrong, no matter if everybody is doing the contrary. Some things in this universe are absolute. The God of the universe has made it so. And so long as we adopt this relative attitude toward right and wrong, we're revolting against the very laws of God himself....

...we have adopted a sort of pragmatic test for right and wrong---whatever works is right. If it works, it's all right. Nothing is wrong but that which does not work. If you don't get caught, its right. That's the attitude isn't it? It's all right to disobey the Ten Commandments, just don't disobey the Eleventh, 'Thou Shall not get caught.'

No matter what you do, just do it with a ...bit of finesse. You know....the survival of the slickest---who can be the slickest is...is the one who is right. It's all right to lie, but lie with dignity. It's all right to steal and to rob and extort, but do it with a bit of finesse. It's even all right to hate, but just dress your hate up in the garments of love and make it appear that you are loving when you are actually hating. Just get by! That's the thing that's right according to this new ethic...."

My friends, that attitude is destroying the soul of our culture! It's destroying our nation! The thing that we need in the world today, is a group of men and women who will stand up for right and be opposed to wrong, wherever it is....our world hinges on moral foundations. God has made it so! God has made the universe to be based on a moral law. So long as man disobeys it he is revolting against God....

The God that I'm talking about this morning is the God of the universe and the God that will last through the ages. If we are to go forward this morning, we've got to go back and find that God. That is the God that demands and commands our ultimate allegiance. If we are to go forward we must go back and rediscover these precious values—that all reality hinges on moral foundations and that all reality has spiritual control."

p. 251-255, The Papers of Martin Luther King, Jr., Vol. II, "Rediscovering Precious Values", July 1951-November 1955, Clayborne Carson, Senior Editor, UNIVERSITY OF California Press, 1997
Dr. King "Rediscovering Lost Values" February 28, 1954, Detroit, Michigan (Concerning Relativism and Moral Absolutes)

The early Christian Activists would not oppose engaging the wisdom of the Lord throughout our American way of living; instead they too would stand united to actualize His hokmah throughout the entirety of our populace.

Who would stand against this movement?

<blockquote>
Not our Founders
Not our early Congress
Not our early Judiciary
Not Washington or Lincoln
Not Christian Abolitionists
Not the early Christian Activists
</blockquote>

So, who would stand against the actualization of Biblical wisdom?
Answer - none of them - and neither should we.

As American Biblical Theists it is time we unite as a team and engage the wisdom of God.

The Biblical God is a God of hope

On May, 23rd, 1939 at approximately 8:45 A.M. the submarine USS SQUALUS (SS-192) sank on a test dive in the north Atlantic off the coast of New Hampshire. A catastrophic failure in one of its valves caused the sub to partially flood with water and it sunk killing 26 of their 59 men on board. The remaining thirty-three men came to rest in their sunken sub 243 feet at the bottom of the ocean. Completely entombed in the steel sub they immediately launched a buoy containing a device for the survivors to communicate with potential rescuers. Then they shot from the depths a rocket which penetrated through the ocean into the sky leaving a trail for ships in the location to discover their position. Soon another submarine the SCULPIN (SS-191) saw the rocket blast and discovered the buoy. They entered into communication with the thirty-three submariners. Now, other rescuers rushed to the scene. That afternoon, two additional ships arrived to join the SCULPIN in attempting to rescue the surviving crew of the buried SQUALIS, which had closed all the remaining water compartments in the sub. However, even by securing the hatches the water now had reached two feet deep. Then all communication lines between the rescuers and the entombed crew went dead. Throughout the long night there was no way of knowing whether the remaining thirty-three were still alive in that sub. Across America media the news spread of the dire need to rescue those sailors.

The next morning, May 24th, divers were sent down who walked upon the hull of the sunken ship. As they checked the condition of the vessel they listened intently for any sounds of life within the sub. Then they heard a sound coming from inside the steel vessel. There was a tapping noise coming from within the hull. The divers came to recognize the tappings as Morse code. The message tapped out by the thirty-three sailors still alive in that sunken sub was: "Is there any hope?"

"Is there any hope?" That was the question that filled the minds of those trapped helpless men. "Is there any hope?" That was the question blazing across the radio waves throughout our nation "Is there any hope?" It was a perfectly legitimate question for never before in the history of man had a person ever been rescued from a submarine that had sunk to that depth of level.

However, now there was one crucial difference from the deaths of all the other failed attempts of submarine rescue. The difference was that now the navy possessed a newly designed Diving Bell, "the McCann Rescue Chamber – a revised version of a diving bell invented by Commander Charles B. Momsen." The McCann Rescue Chamber was specifically invented for this type of catastrophe. It was created to be lowered to incredible depths and then connected by divers to the sub's escape hatch. "It would then equalize pressure between the two vessels and allow the sailors to be taken to the surface in small groups." But, would it actually work?

USS Squalus (SS-192): "The Sinking, Rescue of Survivors, and Subsequent Salvage, 1939."
http: ll www. history.navy.mil/faqs/faq99-1.htm,

When the navy vessel Falcon arrived at the scene they arrived with the McCann Rescue Chamber on deck. Now the process of rescue began in earnest and extended without stopping for thirteen straight hours. Up and down, up and down the McCann Rescue Chamber was used until all thirty-three men had been transported from their watery graves to safety on the deck of the Falcon.

"The Squalus Rescue", 1939, www. mevio. Com/episode/62320/mtih-343-the-squalus-rescue-1939/?mode=detail

Is there any hope? That question was gloriously answered in the saving of those men's lives who were entombed in that sunken sub. "Is there any hope?" That is the question so many people are crying out for today in their dire state of brokenness. I don't know what you are going through today. I don't know your circumstances or your heartbreaks. I don't know of your loss and suffering, but the Lord does, and Scripture tells us we have a Great Difference Maker who can reach down and bring you out of your darkness and into the light of life.

The Biblical God has always been a God of rescue for those who turn to Him. With respect to eternity He provided us with the Diving Bell, the rescue chamber of His Son. Through Christ we have the deliverance from our sins. This is the great eternal rescue of our God and Savior. He came down here to save man from his sin. The rescue chamber has been sent and His name is Jesus. He is there with His arms open to you. However, there is one requirement. Like the sailors in the sunken sub who had no way of survival but to get in that rescue vessel. So too you must get in the rescue chamber of Jesus Christ or die in your sins. However, if you embrace the deliverance of Christ, He will bring you safely into His presence in heaven. That is the great correction of eternal life. This is His rescue of salvation, but you must get in it for yourself. Then He will bring you safely to the top.

The rescue chamber of Proverbs

Likewise, the book of Proverbs also serves as a great rescue chamber; not in terms of eternity, but in terms of the temporal, practical areas of living right now. It is in the book of Proverbs we discover the necessary principles and practices to rescue us, to straighten out our paths, to give us the wisdom and moral coaching to overcome the dysfunction and evils that afflict us today as persons and as a people and bring us to a better place to be. As we need to get in the rescue chamber of the Savior so too we need to get in the rescue chamber of our Great Difference Maker's Scriptural wisdom. He has revealed this wisdom of straightening out our areas of practical living in the book of Proverbs.

Furthermore, we can get into this rescue chamber of Proverbs together. The wisdom and moral goodness of this Biblical book is there for human good. Proverbial knowledge is capable of uniting Bible honoring people throughout our nation whether African American, Arab, Asian, Caucasian, Hebrew, Hispanic, Native American, not only to walk hand in hand as brothers, but shoulder to shoulder as neighbors to overcome the challenges we face today as a people and bring us to a better place to be.

Yes, the hokmah of the Lord is there for our personal advancement and national well-being as Proverbs 3:13-26 states:

13 How blessed is the man who finds wisdom, and the man who gains understanding. 14 For its profit is better than the profit of silver, and its gain than fine gold. 15 She is more precious than jewels; and nothing you desire compares with her. 16 Long life is in her right hand; in her left hand are riches and honor. 17 Her ways are pleasant ways, and all her paths are peace. 18 She is a tree of life to those who take hold of her, and happy are all who hold her fast. 19 The Lord by wisdom founded the earth; by understanding He established the heavens. 20 By His knowledge the deeps were broken up, and the skies dip with dew. 21 My son, let them not depart from your sight; keep sound wisdom and discretion, 22 So they will be life to your soul, and adornment to your neck. 23 Then you will walk in your way securely, and your foot will not stumble. 24 When you lie down, you will not be afraid; when you lie down, your sleep will be sweet. 25 Do not be afraid of sudden fear, nor of the onslaught of the wicked when it comes; 26 For the Lord will be your confidence, and will keep your foot from being caught.

Through the books "Buyer Bewares" and "Buyer Buys" Proverbs communicates the Lord's guidance, revealing His performance skills and moral teachings to improve the human condition in areas including but not limited to…

Abortion	Abuse	Adultery
Anger	Animal Care	Animosity
Anxiety	Attitudes	Bad Company
Behaviors	Business Ethics	Character
Cheating	Child Rearing	Commendation
Contentment	Correction	Creation
Criticism	Cruelty	Death
Decision Making	Deception	Depression
Devotion	Diligence	Discipline
Dishonor	Drunkenness	Economics
Education	Equity	Encouragement
Entertainment	Environment	Envy
Ethics	Evil	Failure
Fairness	Faithfulness	Fathering
Fear	Foolishness	Friendship
Generosity	Gluttony	God
Good Company	Goodness	Governing
Greed	Hatred	Honesty
Honor	Hope	Humility
Husbands	Hypocrisy	Ignorance
Impurity	Injustice	Integrity
Joy	Justice	Kindness
Kings	Knowledge	Laziness
Leadership	Leisure	Listening
Love	Lying	Marriage
Mercy	Money	Mothering
Morals	Murder	Need
Neighborliness	Obedience	Order
Orphans	Peace	Pleasure
Poverty	Pregnancy	Prostitution
Rebellion	Rebuke	Rejection
Relationships	Righteousness	Ruling
Sadness	Self-control	Service
Sex	Shame	Slander
Soberness	Speech	Stealing
Strife	Success	Teachableness
Thinking	Trust	Truth
Unfaithfulness	Unfriendliness	Virtue
War	Wealth	Wickedness
Wisdom	Wives	Worry
Worship		

Portions of the above list came from The Bible Knowledge Commentary, Old Testament, Vol. 1. p. 905

What a book! If we would pull Proverbs out of our Biblical bag, learn to swing it properly and exercise its principles of recovery and refinement imagine what wonderful benefits would bless humanity! In so doing we would discover the fulfillment of the five purposes of the book as revealed in Proverbs 1:1-6:

1:1 "The proverbs of Solomon the son of David, king of Israel:
2 to know wisdom and instruction,
    to discern the sayings of understanding,
3 to receive instruction in wise behavior, righteousness, justice, and equity,
4 to give prudence to the naïve, to the youth knowledge and discretion
5 a wise man will hear and increase in learning and a man of understanding will acquire wise counsel,
6 to understand a proverb and a figure, the words of the wise and their riddles."

Once we grasp the reason for which God put Proverbs into His collection of sixty-six books then you as a person and we as a people need to learn to swing this Biblical book properly; i.e., we must successfully fulfill the three conditions of Proverbs 2:1-4:

1 "My son, **if you will** receive My sayings, and treasure My commandments within you, 2 make your ear attentive to wisdom, incline your heart to understanding, 3 for **if you** cry out for discernment, lift your voice for understanding, 4 **if you** seek her as silver and search for her as for hidden treasures…"

If you make a commitment to actualize the guidance of this book; pull out the club, get into its rescue chamber of guidance then according to Proverbs 2:5-22 the Lord will produce five crucial benefits in your course of living.

Benefit #1: You will know God (2:5-8)

5 **"Then you will discern the fear of the Lord, and discover the knowledge of God.** 6 For the Lord gives wisdom; from His mouth come knowledge and understanding. 7 He stores up sound wisdom for the upright; He is a shield to those who walk in integrity, 8 guarding the paths of justice, and He preserves the way of His godly ones."

Benefit #2: You will know His Goodness (2:9-11)

9**"Then you will discern righteousness and justice and equity and every good course.** 10 For wisdom will enter your heart, and knowledge will be pleasant to your soul; 11 discretion will guard you, understanding will watch over you."

Benefit #3: You will be delivered from Evil (2:12-15)

"To deliver you from the way of evil, from the man who speaks perverse things; 13 from those who leave the paths of uprightness, to walk in the ways of darkness; 14 who delight in doing evil, and rejoice in the perversity of evil; 15 whose paths are crooked, and who are devious in their ways;"

Benefit #4: You will be delivered from Sexual Harm (2:16-19)

"To deliver you from the strange woman, from the adulterous who flatters with her words; 17 that leaves the companion of her youth, and forgets the covenant of her God; 18 for her house sinks down to death, and her tracks lead to the dead; 19 none who go to her return again, nor do they reach the paths of life."

Benefit #5: Together we will produece a Good Land (2:20-22)

20 "So you will walk in the way of good men, and keep to the paths of the righteous. 21 For the upright will live in the land, and blameless will remain in it; 22 but the wicked will be cut off from the land, and the treacherous will be uprooted from it."

During the struggle to emancipate African Americans from the evils of American slavery the men and women of Christian Abolitionism kept calling people to trust in the Lord, fulfill the virtues of the Declaration of Independence justly and fairly, and apply the principles of Biblical goodness.   One of the most famous encounters dealt with abolitionist giants Frederick Douglass and Sojourner Truth. On this occasion Douglass had finished addressing a large audience of African American believers...

"Describing the wrongs [that had been perpetrated upon] the black race [during slavery]....[he] ended by saying that they had no hope of justice from the whites....they must fight for themselves and redeem themselves, or it would never be done." Douglass then took his seat despondent. Silence filled that auditorium. A sense of hopelessness fell upon the crowd, but then...

"Sojourner...on the very front seat...spoke out in her deep, peculiar voice, heard all over the house, 'Frederick, is God dead?'

The effect was perfectly electrical...not another word [was spoken]...it was enough."

Sojourner Truth, Narrative and Book of Life, Entered, according to Act of Congress, in the year 1875, Reprinted 1970, Johnson Publishing Co., The Ebony Classics, p. 130

In a nation founded to function as a unified team of Biblical Theists let us hear and heed the words of Sojourner Truth. God is not dead! He is still alive! He is fully capable of intervening on behalf of His people! He still answers prayer! Revival and social change is possible! However, for societal renewal we need to pull out the book He crafted for such a situation. We need to select the book of Proverbs, learn to swing it properly, actualize its wisdom, and watch God work!

End of Volume II

Where are we in this twelve volume series on
"Transforming America through Proverbial Coaching?"

In **Volume I** titled: **"The Paradigm of Christian Actualism and How to Run the Ground Game of the Faith"** this author established that our present paradigms of conservative, liberal, and moderate; whether spiritual or secular, whether Republican, Democrat, or Libertarian are failing our American way of living. However, the introduction of Christian Actualism offers a fresh, Biblical, historical alternative that can unite us to honor the Savior and engage Scripture for the glory of God and the good of man.

In this book; i.e., **Volume II** titled: **"Actualizing Biblical Wisdom"** this author analyzed what a Proverb is (1:1) and sought to apply the initial knowledge component of the first purpose of the book (1:2a) – "to know wisdom (hokmah)" to the personal and public life of our nation.

Next in **Volume III** titled: **"Actualizing God's Moral Coaching"** we will seek to understand and apply the second knowledge component of Proverbs "to know...instruction"; i.e., the moral coaching of God. In so doing we will target the proverbial knowledge of our Lord's ethical teachings to our lives, families, relationships, and in particular to address and aim to resolve America's most historically flawed and volatile failing – race relations.

Volume III